CW00429124

The Clinical Child Documentation Sourcebook

Practice *Planners*™ Series

The Clinical Child Documentation Sourcebook

A Comprehensive Collection of Forms and
Guidelines for Efficient Record-Keeping in
Child Mental Health Practice

Donald K. Freedheim
Jeremy P. Shapiro

John Wiley & Sons, Inc.

New York • Chichester • Weinheim • Brisbane • Singapore • Toronto

The forms on pages 62–71 and 97–108 are adapted from D. E. Wiger, *The Clinical Documentation Sourcebook* (Wiley, 1997).

The forms on pages 109–115 and 198–199 were adapted from the Boston Children's Hospital, Boston, MA.

The forms on pages 122–123, 165–171, 187–188, 200–204, and 205–212 were adapted from Children's Medical Center, Boston, MA.

The forms on pages 182–184 and 185 were adapted from Berea Children's Home and Family Services, Berea, OH.

The forms on pages 190–191 were adapted from Beech Brook, Pepper Pike, OH.

The forms on pages 195–196 were adapted from S. Kotsopoulos, S. Elwood, & L. Oke, *Canadian Journal of Psychiatry* (1989).

This book is printed on acid-free paper. ∞

Copyright © 1999 by John Wiley & Sons, Inc. All rights reserved.

Published simultaneously in Canada.

No part of this publication may be reproduced, stored in a retrieval system or transmitted in any form or by any means, electronic, mechanical, photocopying, recording, scanning or otherwise, except as permitted under Section 107 or 108 of the 1976 United States Copyright Act, without either the prior written permission of the Publisher, or authorization through payment of the appropriate per-copy fee to the Copyright Clearance Center, 222 Rosewood Drive, Danvers, MA 01923, (978) 750-8400, fax (978) 750-4744. Requests to the Publisher for permission should be addressed to the Permissions Department, John Wiley & Sons, Inc., 605 Third Avenue, New York, NY 10158-0012, (212) 850-6011, fax (212) 850-6008, E-Mail: PERMREQ@WILEY.COM.

This publication is designed to provide accurate and authoritative information in regard to the subject matter covered. It is sold with the understanding that the publisher is not engaged in rendering professional services. If professional advice or other expert assistance is required, the services of a competent professional person should be sought.

Designations used by companies to distinguish their products are often claimed as trademarks. In all instances where John Wiley & Sons, Inc. is aware of a claim, the product names appear in initial capital or all capital letters. Readers, however, should contact the appropriate companies for more complete information regarding trademarks and registration.

Note about Photocopy Rights

The publisher grants purchasers permission to reproduce handouts from this book for professional use with their clients.

Library of Congress Cataloging-in-Publication Data:

Freedheim, Donald K.
    The clinical child documentation sourcebook : a comprehensive collection of forms and guidelines for efficient record-keeping in child mental health practice / by Donald K. Freedheim and Jeremy P. Shapiro.
        p.   cm. — (Practice planners)
    Includes bibliographical references.
    ISBN 0-471-29111-0 (paper/disk : alk. paper)
    1. Child mental health services—Forms. 2. Psychiatric records.
I. Shapiro, Jeremy P. II. Title. III. Series.
RJ499.3.F74   1999
382.2′083—dc21   98-44173

Printed in the United States of America.

10 9 8 7 6 5 4 3

Practice Planner Series Preface

The practice of psychotherapy has a dimension that did not exist 30, 20, or even 15 years ago—accountability. Treatment programs, public agencies, clinics, and even group and solo practitioners must now justify the treatment of patients to outside review entities that control the payment of fees. This development has resulted in an explosion of paperwork.

Clinicians must now document what has been done in treatment, what is planned for the future, and what the anticipated outcomes of the interventions are. The books and software in this Practice Planner series are designed to help practitioners fulfill these documentation requirements efficiently and professionally.

The Practice Planner series is growing rapidly. It now includes not only the original *Complete Psychotherapy Treatment Planner* and the *Child and Adolescent Psychotherapy Treatment Planner,* but also *Treatment Planners* targeted to specialty areas of practice, including chemical dependency, the continuum of care, couples therapy, older adult treatment, employee assistance, behavioral medicine, pastoral counseling, and more.

In addition to the *Treatment Planners,* the series also includes *TheraScribe®: The Computerized Assistant to Psychotherapy Treatment Planning* and *TheraBiller™: The Computerized Mental Health Officer Manager,* as well as adjunctive books, such as the *Brief Therapy, Chemical Dependence, Couples,* and *Child Homework Planners, The Psychotherapy Documentation Primer,* and *Clinical, Forensic, Child, Couples and Family,* and *Chemical Dependence Documentation Sourcebooks*—containing forms and resources to aid in mental health practice management. The goal of the series is to provide practitioners with the resources they need to provide high-quality care in the era of accountability—or, to put it simply, we seek to help you spend more time on patients and less on paperwork.

ARTHUR E. JONGSMA, JR.

Grand Rapids, Michigan

Preface

We have written this book with two main sets of readers in mind: (1) clinicians in child mental health settings, who must document information about their work with clients; and (2) students preparing for a career in any of the mental health disciplines: psychology, social work, psychiatry, psychiatric nursing, counseling, and so forth. Mental health administrators and policy makers in mental health are another audience who are increasingly important in the determination of required documentation for clinicians.

Clinicians and students in any of these fields are faced with a daunting prospect in regard to record-keeping. The demands for accountability among all the professions are especially problematic in a field that is still young, still has many unknowns, and yet is increasingly complex.

Children's problems involve areas of much ambiguity. But the very nature of documentation is to reduce or eliminate ambiguity. We are not all in agreement as to the *meaning* of many of our terms, much less confident about the *effectiveness* of the procedures named in our terminology. So how—and what—does one record about the work, the interactions, the communications between clinician and client? Some may prefer not to record that data, but is that fair and appropriate to either clients or colleagues? How can the profession improve and continue to offer help to others without some accountability through documentation? These are questions that we pondered in writing this book.

We first consider issues around documentation and the ways in which current requirements increase paperwork for clinicians. Later, we present numerous examples of documents that may be useful to professionals in the mental health field who deal with children and their families.

The forms we present can be copied and used by purchasers of this book. In addition, this volume includes a disk containing the forms (WordPerfect 6.1). Purchasers are invited to print out the forms, modify them for placement on their letterhead and customize them for their specific settings and needs.

In presenting these materials, we must make two disclaimers. First, we could not begin to cover the entire field and the potential documents that are available or needed for recording important information about children with mental disabilities. Second, the usefulness and appropriateness of the forms we provide will depend on the specific needs of the setting and the clinician. There is no intrinsic value in any one form or another. The usefulness of a form depends on the user. No form can ensure careful note taking or wise interpretation.

Preface

We hope that this book can be a point of departure for teachers and students in addressing important issues about documentation. We also hope that the material will assist clinicians and administrators in coming to grips with the role of documentation in their professional lives and that the forms will prove helpful to children and families in mental health settings.

DONALD K. FREEDHEIM
JEREMY P. SHAPIRO

Cleveland, Ohio, 1998

Acknowledgments

We have many persons to thank for their contributions to this volume. First, we thank Florence W. Kaslow, Ph.D. for suggesting that we participate in the Wiley Practice Planners Series on documentation. We are most grateful to those who sent us samples of documents, many of which were influential in our development of the forms for the books. Thanks to Gerald P. Koocher, Ph.D. and Boston Children's Medical Center; to the following Cleveland agencies: Applewood Centers, Inc., Mark Lovinger & Associates, Berea Children's Home and Family Services, Beech Brook Children's Center, Laurelwood Hospital; and to Springfield, Ohio, Mental Health Services, Inc.; also to Thomas M. Krapu, Ph.D.; and Donald E. Wiger, who wrote the first book in the Wiley Practice Planners Series.

We discussed the issues of documentation with many professionals, who contributed important ideas and commentary. Thanks to Edward Carter, James Overholser, Kathy Spivak, Kyla Johnston, David Lloyd, Hugh Wirtz, and Thomas Wood. Also, we extend a special thanks to Nancy Winkelman, who coauthored the case example, and who read several drafts of the manuscript and contributed suggestions based on solid clinical judgment, practical understanding of everyday clinical practice, and a keen sense of what will and will not work in the real world.

The translating of ideas to diskette required the help of several persons. We are grateful for the time and skills of Helen White-Lenear from Applewood Centers, Nick Kost and Gail Gangidine from Case Western Reserve University, and especially for the tireless work of our chief assistant, Charlotte Gill-Grasz, who provided creative ideas along with many iterations of the documents. And, we thank Kelly A. Franklin from John Wiley & Sons for her help and assistance.

And last, thanks to our wives, Gerda Freedheim and Nancy Winkelman, for their constant support of our endeavors.

D.K.F.
J.P.S.

Contents

Contents

Contents

Chapter 1

A Conceptual Approach to Documentation: Cost/Benefit Analysis

Record-keeping has always been a part of clinical work in mental health (e.g., Freud took notes on his psychoanalytic sessions), but it is only recently that a significant amount of writing on the topic has appeared. It has taken approximately 100 years for clinical documentation to change from a routine chore to a bona fide topic warranting systematic attention. In the past, clinicians did not spend much time talking about documentation, but they do now, and sometimes with anxiety. The few published materials about documentation (Soreff & McDuffee, 1993; Wiger, 1997; Wilson, 1980; Zuckerman, 1997), including this book, were developed to provide guidance in this area of new concern.

THE NEED FOR DOCUMENTATION

The increased attention to records of clinical work derives from several sources. The growth of managed care, which has become a dominant influence on clinical practice, has brought new documentation requirements. State agencies funding the public mental health system have generally increased their recording requirements in recent years. Growing numbers of lawsuits have stimulated concern about the ability to produce clear evidence of appropriate practice. Finally, many clinics have sought and obtained some form of accreditation that involves documentation requirements.

Past writings on documentation have generally expressed a high degree of enthusiasm for this aspect of clinical work. For example, the dedication of Soreff and McDuffee's (1993) book states, *"Good documentation leads to great care"* (italics in original). There has been considerable discussion of the benefits of record-keeping, but there has been little discussion of its costs. Also, past discussions of the benefit side of the cost/benefit ratio have often been characterized by an across-the-board enthusiasm rather than by critical analysis. Recommendations for determining what information to record have often been made in a global fashion, without differentiation by purpose or type of case, leaving the reader with the impression that it is best to chart all the information for all clients.

Of course, past writers have not literally said "the more the better," and they recommend concise writing and omission of extraneous detail. But although the amount of recommended recording is not infinite or silly, it seems to be substantially greater than the amount of documentation clinicians have generally produced in the past.

Documentation quantity has not been treated as a controversial issue with two sides in need of balancing and integration. However, there may be disadvantages as well as advantages to performing highly detailed, extensive documentation. Because of the potential impact of record-keeping on everyday practice, we will examine this issue critically, with cost/benefit analysis.

Benefits

Clinical documentation can serve several functions that justify expending significant amounts of time and effort. These functions are important considerations not only to determine how much time is warranted for record-keeping but also to align recording procedures with the uses to which the records will be put and the audiences who will eventually read them.

Ethical Practice. Zuckerman (1997) notes that clinical record-keeping is now literally a requirement of professional practice, if for no other reason than that documentation is an ethical requirement of the major mental health professions and a legal requirement in many states. The American Psychological Association's Standard 1.23 (1992) states, "Psychologists appropriately document their professional and scientific work in order to facilitate provision of services later by them or other professionals, to ensure accountability and to meet the other requirements of institutions or the law." By holding ourselves out to the public as a practitioner of a profession, we agree to be held to our profession's standards. Therefore, in court or before an ethics committee, an absence of record-keeping will be considered malpractice in and of itself, even if the original challenge does not concern record-keeping. According to Weiner and Wettstein (1993), "An inadequate record will itself be seen as evidence of sub-standard care, no matter what care was actually provided" (p. 179).

Third-Party Payment. Insurance payers need some form of documentation indicating that the service for which reimbursement is requested did in fact occur. However, this level of documentation can vary widely depending on the type of insurance and the requirements of the insurer. Traditional, fee-for-service plans generally require only a date and a billing code indicating the length and type of service (e.g., diagnostic assessment or individual, family, or group therapy). Managed care organizations (MCOs) have a broad range of requirements. Some MCOs have no specific paperwork requirements and require only telephone calls for authorization of sessions. When documentation is required, the range extends from minimal, routine information to the completion of lengthy forms and the provision of detailed information about the clinical work.

The extent and detail of paperwork requirements derive from the particular MCO's definition of its role in treatment: Some MCOs limit their function to ensuring a generally appropriate type and quantity of care, whereas others take on an active watchdog role and attempt to oversee specific clinical procedures. The more an MCO seeks to micromanage care, the more information it will require from the mental health professional. MCOs use telephone conversations to varying degrees to learn about their clients' treatment, but usually their requests for information translate into paperwork requirements.

Competition for Managed Care Contracts. It is becoming common for MCOs to establish contractual relationships with group practices or clinics that then become exclusive or preferred recipients of referrals. Practices compete with one another to secure these contracts, and chart reviews may be an important element in the MCO's selection of a clinic. Groups desiring to secure and retain these contracts are strongly motivated to maintain records that would be impressive to an MCO review team. This motivation often translates into charting that is lengthier and more structured (with more use of forms) than was the case before MCO contracts became a goal, because practitioners often believe MCOs desire documentation that is lengthy, detailed, and highly structured.

Institutional Quality Control. Hospitals, clinics, and mental health centers typically have internal documentation standards, requirements, and/or specific forms for quality control purposes. Quality assurance/improvement or utilization review personnel may periodically review or spot-check clinician records and give corrective feedback when they deem it necessary.

Supervisory Review. Clinical supervisors may review records on a routine basis. These reviews may be limited to ensuring that the necessary information has been recorded, but usually the stated purpose also includes assuring the quality of the clinical work itself.

Documenting Fulfillment of Eligibility Requirements. There are situations in which information must be recorded to meet requirements for client eligibility for services or reimbursement. For example, diagnostic information may be needed to establish eligibility for services allocated to a specific client population, such as Seriously Emotionally Disturbed children. Reimbursement through Workers' Compensation requires documentation indicating that treatment addressed mental health problems originating at work.

Documentation Required by the Public Mental Health System. A significant portion of mental health services are paid for by the government through Medicaid, Medicare, Social Security, funds allocated for special populations, matching funds from local boards, and so forth. These funds are administered by the federal government, state departments of mental health, and local mental health boards. In keeping with the dictum "He who pays the piper calls the tune," these government entities exert substantial control over the services they make possible. As is the case in private managed care, the desire for control generally translates into documentation requirements, because one can control only what one can monitor; and paper, unlike the interactions constituting treatment itself, can be touched and seen.

Record-keeping standards of public mental health systems vary from state to state and locality to locality, but some generalizations do seem to characterize the country as a whole. There have been major increases in documentation requirements in the public mental health system. In Ohio, state standards for initial diagnostic sessions (the intake appointment) translate into approximately 15 pages of forms. Twenty years ago, there was less than half as much intake paperwork.

Legal Proceedings. When mental health professionals participate in court proceedings, records are generally subpoenaed as evidence. Records may be subjected to a high level of scrutiny in court, and their accuracy, completeness, and detail will never be at a higher premium. Documentation is especially important in malpractice cases, where the clinician's ability to demonstrate the appropriateness of treatment may depend on the description of this work contained in the chart.

Communication among Professionals. Diagnostic reports, chart notes, and treatment summaries are important means of information sharing among professionals working with the same client or family. This communication may take place contemporaneously, as when a multidisciplinary team shares information, or it may take place among individual therapists whose work is separated by intervals of time. Treatment summaries, in particular, can inform a future therapist about previous treatment and its results. Written records are particularly important when treatment episodes are widely spaced in time, because conversations between professionals may not be possible in these situations.

Clinical records are also an important means of communicating with professionals outside the mental health system. Clinical documents are sometimes shared with child-serving professionals in the medical, education, juvenile justice, and child protection systems to facilitate coordination of care. Again, verbal communication may be at least as effective as written records when services are provided at the same time, but when collaborating professionals cannot establish verbal contact, documentation will be the only available form of communication.

A Personal Aid for Therapists. Finally, record-keeping has been cited as a tool for helping clinicians organize their thoughts and plan their future work with the client. Documentation may enhance the quality of clinical work in two main ways, with one corresponding to the value of writing and one to the value of reading. First, the activity of writing may help clinicians organize and remember their thinking about a case; in addition, the design of a form may provide a useful structure for observations, inferences, and plans. Second, by reading records of past sessions, clinicians can recall information that might otherwise have been forgotten and can use this information for more effective treatment.

Clinical documentation can serve numerous valuable functions. When the possible uses of clinical documentation are arrayed together, they yield the impression of an important task warranting a major investment of effort. However, the benefits of record-keeping are only one side of the equation; the other side is costs.

Costs

Identifying the costs of record-keeping is both easier and more dull than identifying the benefits. The major cost of recording clinical material is obvious—it is simply time.

Wiger (1997) developed his form for psychotherapy notes on the basis of the criteria third-party payers use to determine eligibility for benefits. He proposed that the notes for each session should contain all the information needed for eligibility determination. Wiger reviewed the criteria used by Blue Cross/Blue Shield, and recommended that the following information be recorded for each session: (1) current client symptomatology, degree of impairment, and justification of the *DSM* Axis I diagnosis, (2) use of therapeutic procedures for which there is evidence of effectiveness in treating the client's diagnosis, (3) rationale for the intensity of treatment being provided in terms of length and frequency of sessions, (4) movement through the treatment plan, that is, documentation of the specific therapeutic procedures used in each session, (5) description of the client's progress or changes in functioning, and (6) general content of the session's discussion. In addition, Wiger recommends that each therapy note include a description of (7) client motivation, (8) any changes in treatment planning, (9) performance of past homework, (10) the next homework assignment, and (11) upcoming interventions. Wiger emphasizes that the preceding descriptions should be written in specific, measurable, behavioral terms, with citation of the evidence used to make inferences and plans.

Recording the information recommended by Wiger would take a great deal of clinician time. His example case notes are about 250–300 words in length. To write such a note in the 10 minutes between sessions, clinicians would need to write at a rate of about one word every two seconds. This rate would leave no time for organizing the session material, which would be problematic because Wiger's examples are efficiently packed with information, and most clinicians would need to do some thinking before producing such well-organized writing. Making time pressures still tighter, the 10-minute interstice is also the time when most clinicians prepare for their next session. Also, therapists sometimes run a bit over the 50-minute timepoint when it would be awkward or counterproductive to stop discussion of an issue on a dime.

Documenting initial diagnostic sessions involves problems that are similar to those for treatment sessions. Soreff (1993a) recommends a degree of detail for psychotherapy intake notes that exceeds common practice. His example is approximately 1,200 words long. To illustrate his level of detail, the sample note includes information such as that the patient ". . . once took an introductory psychology course, but found it too focused on 'physiology instead of Freud,'" and "lives with his wife and daughter in a suburban three-bedroom ranch house in a moderately expensive town with a 'great school system.'" There is nothing inherently wrong with recording this level of detail, except for the amount of time involved in doing so. While almost any type of information could potentially be relevant to some aspect of understanding and treating some patient, the practical constraint is that the billing code for initial diagnostic intake is meant to reimburse for approximately 50 minutes of time with the patient plus a little time afterward for documentation. Producing the recommended amount of text (about 5 double-spaced, typed pages) would take longer than seeing the patient and would not be reimbursed.

In-Session Record-Keeping

There is a simple, possible solution to the problem that extensive record-keeping takes a lot of time—clinicians could write notes during sessions, while working with clients. Then, the 10 minutes between sessions could be used to finish up the record and prepare for the next client. At first glance, this practice seems to offer a real advance in efficiency. Therefore, its pros and cons merit serious examination. There is no empirical evidence bearing directly on the issue of in-session note taking, and so decisions can be based only on indirectly relevant evidence and on theoretical and clinical considerations.

In Wiger's (1997) survey, 25% of the therapists indicated they write their progress notes at least mostly during the session. Wiger reported that some of these therapists stated that the "detail and accuracy" of their notes increased when they began performing this task in session. Some of the therapists also stated that in-therapy note-taking was difficult at first but became much easier with a few months of practice. Wiger's book provides an outline, that can be copied, for use as an aid in making this transition.

On the other hand, three-quarters of the therapists surveyed by Wiger indicated that they do not engage in significant charting during sessions with clients. Wiger described this choice as based on therapists' belief that taking detailed notes during sessions would keep them from attending fully to their clients. The amount of attention absorbed by charting is a function of both the quantity and the degree of organization of the records; it is more cognitively demanding to structure records under headings and subheadings than to take notes that simply follow the chronology of the session.

Absorption of clinician attention by documentation tasks might affect work with clients. Details, nuances, and nonobvious connections can be important in therapy, and thinking through client verbalizations and one's own intended responses can be cognitively demanding. Our own experience doing therapy is that, often, it is necessary to think as hard as we can. If so, withdrawing attention from the basic work of treatment might reduce the effectiveness of clinical work.

Wilson (1980) observed that in-session record-keeping reduces interpersonal connectedness between therapist and client. This is a potentially serious liability of the practice, because research on predictors of outcome has consistently indicated strong associations between the quality of the therapeutic alliance and treatment effectiveness (Blatt, Zuroff, Quinlan, & Pilkonis, 1996; Krupnick et al., 1996). Wiger suggested that in-session recording might increase rapport by communicating that the client's statements are important enough to write down, but he did not report this point being made by any of the therapists in his sample. Eye contact, which is a fundamental interpersonal behavior, is lost during note taking.

Wilson (1980) also observed that in-session writing often makes clients self-conscious and reduces emotional spontaneity and connection with the therapist; she recommends jotting down factual information in session but recommends against taking notes while a client is discussing emotional or difficult material. Given that discussion of emotional or difficult material is a major activity of psychotherapy, Wilson's recommendation is essentially that clinicians spend, at most, a small portion of the session taking notes.

Another form of relevant evidence comes from a set of videotapes produced by APA as a tool for training in psychotherapy. These videotapes present sessions conducted by 23 expert therapists who are considered leaders in their fields. None of these videotapes shows therapists writing notes during the session.

To the extent that treatment effectiveness receives highest priority (rather than, e.g., the needs of third-party payers or legal defense), it seems difficult to justify the practice of extensive in-session note taking during therapy sessions. (Somewhat more in-session recording seems appropriate to assessment, because there is more of a factual emphasis.) Breaking eye contact and producing extensive, well-organized written material while conducting psychotherapy may reduce the effectiveness of treatment. The value of the treatment alliance and of maximum attention to the client seem to outweigh the currently unknown value of highly detailed progress notes. It should be emphasized that this reasoning is based on the evidence currently at hand, which is of only indirect relevance; directly relevant empirical data would be of superordinate value and could potentially refute this reasoning.

CONCLUSION

The major potential benefit of extensive documentation is the recording of detailed information about clinical work. The potential costs depend on when the charting is performed. If extensive record-keeping is accomplished mostly after sessions, it will absorb a great deal of time, with consequences for the availability and cost of mental health services. If extensive record-keeping is performed mostly during sessions, there could be negative effects on the therapeutic alliance and the quality of the clinician's thinking and planning. The benefits of detailed record-keeping for clinical work seem indirect and uncertain. The costs of extensive documentation are linked to core aspects of clinical work and, therefore, seem liable to result in significant, adverse consequences to mental health services.

Generally, when the goals of documentation and treatment conflict, it seems best to resolve the conflict in the direction of service effectiveness, because that is the purpose of mental health work. Therefore, we recommend limiting the length and detail of clinical documentation. Documentation tasks should support clinical work, not the other way around. If carried too far, domination of treatment considerations by documentation priorities becomes an instance of the tail wagging the dog.

As a result of our dual concern with documentation costs and benefits, the forms we recommend for routine clinical use are shorter than most forms offered in previous books on the subject and promulgated by institutional sources of forms such as government regulators, agencies, and health care organizations. This difference in length may reflect an attitudinal difference characterizing our approach to the task of developing documentation forms. We approached this task with an attitude of caution (because of our concern about costs) and respect (because of our appreciation of benefits); in contrast, most past originators of forms seem to have approached their task with an attitude of wholehearted enthusiasm.

There may be a natural selection process in which forms come to be designed by people who are enthusiastic about record-keeping, because these are the individuals who gravitate to form development work. Also, when people find themselves in a position to influence an area of work, there seems to be a natural tendency for their appreciation of the importance and complexity of that area to grow. These factors would tend to result in the design of longer forms than practicing clinicians might prefer. Perspectives influence attitudes, and the amount of detail that seems important to include on a form is greater when one is engaged in discussion or thought about clinical documentation than when one is busily finishing up paperwork in order to see the next client. As practicing clinicians, we sought to balance the authorial perspective with the workaday one to produce forms that are lean and efficient.

Documentation is not a dichotomous issue. The question is not whether to keep records but, rather, how lengthy and detailed those records should be. If the potential benefits of documentation are focused on to the exclusion of considerations of cost, there will be no upper limit to the degree of detail and length that seems desirable. If potential benefits are ignored, documentation will be undervalued, an equally serious mistake. When costs and benefits are considered together, the goal becomes identification of a moderate, optimal level of documentation detail and quantity.

But we are going to try to do better than moderation and compromise. The relationship between documentation benefits and costs can be something more than a strict trade-off, with a zero sum, in which a given quantity of useful information-recording can be purchased only with an equivalent unit of time and effort. Documentation practices that allow clinicians to record relatively large amounts of information in relatively small amounts of time can be said to be *efficient*. Efficient practices would produce maximum benefits for minimum costs. Well-designed forms that facilitate quick and effective recording of information would serve this end. Clinician development of effective information-recording skills would be even more important. The goal of this book is to provide forms and contribute to the development of skills that, in combination, will result in efficient documentation.

Chapter 2

A Survey of Mental Health Professionals: The Work of Clinical Documentation

Although the general view in the mental health field is that practice should be guided, as much as possible, by research, empirical findings have been conspicuously absent as a source of increased emphasis on documentation. There is currently no research on the relationship between amount or quality of record-keeping and effectiveness of treatment. As a result, past discussions and recommendations concerning documentation have been based on professional judgment and opinion, which does not constitute as strong a foundation for practice as empirical evidence.

There are two feasible approaches to the collection of empirical information about effects of documentation practices on treatment effectiveness. In an experimental approach, the basic method would be to (1) randomly assign patients to two conditions, in one of which charting is extensive and in one of which it is minimal, (2) hold all other aspects of treatment constant, and then (3) assess outcome by measuring client functioning before and after treatment. Differences in treatment effectiveness could then be attributed to the variable of extensiveness of documentation. In a naturalistic approach, the independent variable would be measured rather than manipulated: documentation quantity could be measured either as amount of time spent on this activity or as number of words, and researchers could then examine associations between the documentation index and therapeutic outcome. It would be important to control statistically for possible confounding variables such as client diagnosis, problem severity, and clinician experience.

Both experimental and naturalistic research could test the hypothesis implicit in recommendations of extensive record-keeping, which is that quantity of documentation and treatment effectiveness will be positively related. Data analyses should investigate possible nonlinear as well as linear relationships. Research of this type could make a major contribution to current efforts to determine the optimal amount of time for clinical record-keeping.

In preparation for this book, we designed a brief questionnaire about clinical documentation issues and administered it to a sampling of mental health professionals. The questionnaire focused on the amount of time spent on documentation and the clinical utility of this time. In essence, the method was to aggregate reports and opinions of a group of practitioners.

As a form of information, clinician opinion does not have the validity of data on treatment effectiveness, and surveys are no substitute for outcome research as a source of guidance for clinical practice. However, compared with the current documentation literature, which is based only on the opinions of a few authors, survey data represents an advance, because it aggregates the judgments of a fairly large number of practitioners. Therefore, our survey contributes to the information base for documentation issues, and the results warrant serious consideration until the relevant clinical research is performed.

METHOD

Respondents for the survey were obtained in several ways. The majority were contacted through the mail. We randomly selected clinicians listed in the American Psychological Association (APA) Directory and the National Association of Social Workers Directory. Questionnaires were distributed at the 1997 midwinter meeting of APA Division 29 (Independent Practice) and a meeting of members of the Cleveland Psychological Association. Questionnaires were also distributed to mental health agencies in the greater Cleveland area, both through the mail and by special delivery.

Because of this mix of data collection methods, it was not possible to calculate a precise return rate. Our estimate is that approximately 25% of the questionnaires were returned, with a return rate of about 10% from the mailing and 40% from personal presentations of the survey.

The sample was not fully randomly selected, and there was no stratification by demographic variables, professional discipline, or work setting. Therapists in the Cleveland area were overrepresented. The sample does not constitute a proportional representation of the population of American psychotherapists. However, the sample is diverse, with adequate representation of work settings and the two largest psychotherapy disciplines, psychology and social work. Also, there is no apparent reason to suspect that sample composition was biased with respect to attitudes about documentation, in particular the issue of documentation burden versus usefulness. Therefore, the results obtained by the survey seem to provide meaningful information about current views toward documentation of practicing clinicians.

There were 131 respondents in the sample. Their job characteristics are described in the following list:

Professional Discipline	**Percent**
Psychologist	52%
Social worker	37
Clinical counselor	6
Psychiatrist	5

Primary Job Function	
Clinician	83%
Supervisor	9
Administrator	6
Other	2

Primary Work Setting	
Outpatient clinic	86%
Inpatient hospital	8
Residential treatment facility	6

Type of Outpatient Clinic	
Private practice	58%
Not-for-profit clinic	17
Public agency	11
Hospital-based	9
For-profit clinic	4
Health maintenance organization	1

RESULTS

Descriptive Data

The first set of items concerned the *source* of documentation requirements in the clinicians' work. In other words, these items asked where the documentation requirements came from. Respondents differentiated between primary and supplementary sources. Responses were as follows:

A Survey of Mental Health Professionals: The Work of Clinical Documentation

	Primary Source	Secondary Source
Managed care companies	35%	31%
Public mental health system	21	12
Hospital accreditation	8	10
Employer organization (in addition to above)	9	13
Self	26	33

The body of the questionnaire focused on the issues of amount of time spent on documentation and whether this activity facilitated or interfered with clinical work. There were separate items for intake assessment and ongoing therapy.

The first research question was simply, how many minutes do clinicians spend on documentation? Because we were also interested in the comparative amounts of time spent on documentation and client contact, we asked about time spent with the client at the intake/diagnostic appointment. We assumed therapy appointments are generally 50 minutes long. Results are presented below:

Intake Assessment	Mean	Standard Deviation
Minutes with client	64.62	27.01
Time documenting in session	18.22	24.40
Time documenting after session	24.40	24.66

Therapy	Mean	Standard Deviation
Time documenting in session	4.72	8.87
Time documenting after session	9.66	9.24

These data indicate that documentation time is concentrated during the assessment phase of treatment. Respondents reported spending an average of 43 minutes writing up intake assessments, which represents two-thirds of the amount of time spent in client contact. In contrast, respondents reported spending an average of only 14 minutes charting psychotherapy sessions, which is less than one-third the amount of time spent in session.

These data exhibit a high degree of variability, with standard deviations usually higher than means. Clinicians vary a great deal in the amount of time they spend on documentation.

Next, we asked for opinions about the proportionality and utility of time spent on documentation. These were the responses:

Intake Assessment	Frequency
Way too little	1%
Too little	5
About right	52
Too much	26
Way too much	16

Therapy Sessions

Way too little	0%
Too little	6
About right	67
Too much	22
Way too much	5

These results suggest that the much greater amount of time spent on documentation of intake, compared with therapy, does not reflect clinician beliefs about what is necessary and appropriate for completing these notes. Respondents were three times more likely to view time for charting assessments as greatly excessive, compared with time for charting therapy sessions.

The next questions inquired about the perceived value of documentation efforts in clinical work. These items asked, "Is this time useful for clinical conceptualization and planning, or does it interfere with efforts to do effective clinical work?"

Intake Assessments	**Frequency**
Very useful	5%
Mostly useful	24
Partly useful, partly interferes	49
Mostly interferes	13
Greatly interferes	9

Therapy Sessions	
Very useful	5%
Mostly useful	39
Partly useful, partly interferes	41
Mostly interferes	9
Greatly interferes	5

These results are consistent with the immediately preceding data in suggesting that clinicians find assessment documentation more burdensome than therapy charting. Twenty-two percent of the respondents said that assessment documentation mostly or greatly interferes with effective clinical work, compared with 14% for therapy documentation. Their responses express the view that the requirements for assessment should not be *as much* greater than therapy requirements as is the case.

Quotes from Respondents

The quotes on the next page were selected to be illustrative, not representative:

- "I do what is required for insurance payment and managed care—but not as a means of providing care or working on issues. I find it all rather intrusive and manipulative both for the therapist and client—it's too hard and inappropriate to standardize life experience."
- "Biggest concern for me: Having to veil what I say in progress notes or in other ways write what will pass audit."
- "I find progress notes as well as a psychosocial history extremely valuable in conceptualizing and evaluating a client's dynamics and issues to be addressed."
- "Number of forms seems to be increasing, details being asked for more, often forms have questions which don't really relate to the client's problem, particularly for children, adolescents, and family treatment."
- "I try to use the time spent satisfying managed care needs as an opportunity for the patient and I to discuss what we really think is happening—it can be helpful—Some of the time is wasted, however, since I also have to respond to managed care needs."
- "I write as I do therapy these days, to save myself from documentation overload outside of therapy."
- "I have begun taking notes during therapy sessions which I had not done in the past."
- "I keep records partly out of legal responsibility and to meet legal/ethical obligations to document my interventions, etc., and partly because writing helps me to formulate thoughts and then be able to focus on relevant themes, etc., in subsequent session."
- "Like most clinicians, I find managed care requirements more burdensome than helpful by far."
- "Managed care requirements of treatment plans after some predetermined number of sessions are useless. I do treatment planning for regular cases session by session as part of progress notes."
- "I often have repeat engagements with patients returning after a year or so. Documentation aids enormously in dealing with the new situation."
- "Most 'documentation' is irrelevant to quality of service and extremely burdensome to therapists and patients."
- "Some of the documentation required by managed care is a waste of time. To document routinely is useful in that it forces one to do some conceptualizing."
- "I provide two sheets, one representing non-managed-care record keeping—helpful—the other representing managed care requirements—obstructive, and mostly a defensive, meaningless time expenditure."
- "Managed care formats are obstructive, intrusive and waste clinicians' time."
- "After practicing for many years, I resent having to follow preset plans that may or may not be suitable for the situation or problems presented. I also strongly object to the loss of privacy for the patient."
- "Documentation seems to add little to services."
- "There is way too much paperwork in the mental health professions. I spend more time with paperwork than working with children and families."

Relationships between Variables

We conducted a set of analyses to examine variables possibly related to amount of documentation time and the clinical utility of charting activities. These analyses investigated whether the perceived helpfulness versus counterproductiveness of documentation varies as a function of different disciplines, work settings, and sources of documentation requirements.

We performed a t-test for dependent groups to compare documentation usefulness ratings for diagnostic intakes versus therapy sessions. The difference was significant, $t(127) = 3.65$, $p < .0005$, with higher ratings for progress notes than for intake record keeping.

We used t-tests for independent groups to investigate whether opinions about the clinical usefulness of documentation differed as a function of the type of work done by respondents. Psychologists and social workers did not differ in their assessment of the utility of documentation for diagnostic intakes, $t(113) = 1.65$, or therapy progress notes, $t(112) = .20$. Clinicians and respondents with other work roles ($n = 22$) did not vary in their opinions about intake documentation, $t(128) = .91$, or therapy record-keeping, $t(127) = 1.51$. Comparison of private practitioners ($n = 65$) and respondents from other work settings ($n = 66$) also yielded nonsignificant results for intake, $t(128) = 1.12$, and treatment sessions, $t(127) = .16$.

We performed t-tests for independent groups to examine whether different institutional sources of documentation requirements were related to amount of time spent on charting and to judgments of the clinical usefulness of this time. The tests compared respondents who stated that the system in question was the main source of their documentation requirements to respondents stating this system was either a secondary source or not a source of their record-keeping requirements. There were separate analyses for intake and therapy sessions, and for time quantity and clinical usefulness.

The variable of whether or not managed care was cited as the main source of documentation requirements showed no relationships with time spent on record-keeping; results were nonsignificant for charting time during intake sessions, $t(125) = 1.42$, after intake sessions, $t(125) = 1.08$, during therapy sessions, $t(125) = .75$, and after therapy sessions, $t(60) = .97$. The managed care variable was also unrelated to respondent judgments of the clinical utility of record-keeping time for intake sessions, $t(128) = 1.44$. However, for therapy, respondents citing managed care as their main source of documentation requirements judged record-keeping to be less useful and more of an interference than did other respondents, $t(127) = 2.43$, $p < .05$.

Respondents for whom the public mental health system was the primary source of record-keeping requirements reported spending more time on documentation during intake sessions, $t(125) = 2.31$, $p < .05$, and following intake sessions, $t(125) = 3.28$, $p < .005$, but not during therapy sessions, $t(81) = .22$, or after therapy sessions, $t(80) = .82$. The public mental health system as a source of documentation requirements was associated with judgments of low clinical usefulness for intake session documentation, $t(128) = 2.73$, $p < .01$. This variable was not related to judgments of the usefulness of therapy documentation, $t(128) = 1.58$.

Respondents citing hospital accreditation as their primary source of documentation requirements reported spending less time on record-keeping during intake sessions, $t(125) = 3.31$, $p < .005$, and during therapy sessions, $t(98) = 4.85$, $p < .0001$, compared with respondents not

15

citing this primary source. The hospital accreditation variable was not related to amount of record-keeping time following intake sessions, $t(125) = .11$, or after therapy sessions, $t(126) = .08$. Hospital accreditation as a requirement source was associated with a nonsignificant trend toward judgments of high usefulness for therapy record-keeping, $t(127) = 1.96$, $p < .06$, with a nonsignificant result for intake documentation, $t(125) = 1.08$.

The next variable was whether or not respondents cited their employer organization as the main source of their record-keeping requirements; the item specified employer requirements *beyond* those originating from the preceding sources and simply passed down to practitioners by the organization. This variable was unrelated to minutes spent on charting during intake sessions, $t(125) = 1.15$, after intake sessions, $t(125) = 1.04$, during therapy sessions, $t(125) = .13$, or following therapy sessions, $t(125) = .23$. Employer organization, as a source of these requirements, was also unrelated to judgments of the clinical usefulness of record-keeping for both intake, $t(128) = .84$, and therapy, $t(127) = .76$.

Approximately one-fourth of the respondents reported that they themselves were the primary source of their record-keeping practices. Respondents citing this internal source reported spending less time on charting after intake sessions, $t(125) = 5.13$, $p < .0001$, and following therapy sessions, $t(116) = 3.82$, $p < .0005$, than did respondents citing an external source of documentation requirements. This variable was unrelated to minutes spent on charting during both intake, $t(125) = 1.43$, and therapy sessions, $t(37) = 1.51$. Respondents who were their own primary source of record-keeping practices judged their documentation time as more clinically useful for both intake, $t(128) = 3.60$, $p < .0005$, and therapy, $t(127) = 2.44$, $p < .05$, compared with other respondents.

To examine the relationship between amount of record-keeping time and whether this activity is judged to facilitate or interfere with clinical work, we computed Pearson correlations between reported minutes of charting time and judgments of the usefulness of this activity. For intake, there was a significant negative correlation between record-keeping time during the session and the clinical usefulness of intake record-keeping, $r(127) = -.18$, $p < .05$. For time after the intake session, the correlation was nonsignificant, $r(126) = -.11$. For therapy, there were significant negative correlations between charting time and charting usefulness for record-keeping during sessions, $r(127) = -.22$, $p < .05$, and after sessions, $r(127) = -.41$, $p < .0001$. Thus, for three of the four tests, clinicians reported that the more time they spent on record-keeping, the less useful and the more interfering this activity was; this relationship was particularly strong for record-keeping after therapy sessions. These results suggest that, for clinical documentation, it is *not* the case that more is better.

DISCUSSION

These survey results have meaningful implications for documentation practices because they summarize the reports and judgments of a substantial sampling of mental health practitioners. The survey respondents, together, represent a great deal of experience with clinical documentation, and their opinions about record-keeping should be considered well informed.

A possible objection to the validity of these opinions would be that clinicians' have a personal stake in documentation requirements, and this might bias their judgments; perhaps clinicians are motivated to judge extensive documentation requirements negatively because they resent the work and time consumed by charting. However, this objection does not seem compelling, for several reasons. First, the results indicate that practitioners do see clinical value in record-keeping; most respondents judged their time spent on charting to be at least partly useful. Also, the survey questions did not ask whether documentation tasks were effortful but whether they were useful to clinical work. Assuming that practitioners' primary professional motivation is the desire to do effective clinical work, they are in a strong position to make meaningful judgments about the usefulness versus counterproductiveness of clinical procedures.

The results of this survey provide significant grounds for concern about current documentation requirements in the mental health field. Overall, the respondents made fairly negative judgments of these requirements regarding their effect on clinical work. Most respondents indicated that record-keeping activities were at least partially an interference in their efforts to provide effective services to clients, and a substantial minority stated that documentation was more of a hindrance than a help to clinical work.

These results seem to sound a cautionary note to the institutional sources of documentation requirements, the administrators who design record-keeping policies and procedures, and the mental health system as a whole. Although clinical utility is certainly not the only purpose of documentation (see Chapter 1), it seems appropriate for usefulness to be a primary consideration, since helping clients is the raison d'etre of mental health services. In addition, the other functions of record-keeping—monitoring of service quality by third parties, accreditation, protection against malpractice suits, and so forth—themselves derive from the goal of providing high-quality services. It would be ironic and unfortunate if efforts to monitor services, in order to ensure quality, themselves had a deleterious effect on service quality. The act of observation can affect the phenomenon observed (in both physics and psychology), and observors need to exert care that their influence does not interfere with the achievement of their own goals.

Perhaps the most important relationship between variables indicated by our results was that between amount of time spent on documentation and the perceived usefulness of record-keeping. Although, intuitively, one might expect that the value of an activity would increase with the extensiveness of that activity, the opposite was the case for clinical record-keeping; the more time was spent, the less useful this work was judged to be. Practitioners find that record-keeping exhibits the property of diminishing marginal utility, with each increment of work becoming less clinically useful as more time is spent. Perhaps clinicians record the most important information first and, if left to their own devices, stop there. When external guidelines require additional information, clinicians seem to find this record-keeping less valuable than alternative uses of their time would be.

Thus, our finding was not the more the better. Instead, the results suggest that less is more. Our results provide support for the value of efficiency in designing record-keeping procedures.

For the respondents as a group, documentation requirements appear to be more of a problem for intake than therapy sessions. Time for intake documentation was reportedly three times greater than time for treatment charting. Respondents considered this difference to be disproportionate to clinical utility; the group judged intake charting time to be less useful and more of an interference than therapy documentation time. These results suggest that documentation quantity for assessment is more driven by external requirements, and less intrinsically motivated by clinical considerations, than is documentation quantity for therapy sessions. There are obvious reasons why diagnostic sessions warrant more record-keeping than therapy sessions, and clinicians undoubtedly concur with external sources about this. However, respondents expressed the belief that the requirements for intake should not be *so much* greater than the requirements for therapy.

We examined relationships between judgments about documentation and a number of professional variables and job characteristics. Most of these analyses produced nonsignificant results; it seemed to make little difference whether respondents were social workers or psychologists, or what their work setting was. In contrast, the institutional source of documentation requirements did make a difference to reports and judgments concerning this work.

Procedures originating with managed care requirements were no more time-consuming than record-keeping based on other requirements. However, respondents judged managed care's record-keeping requirements for therapy as less useful than therapy documentation based on other requirements. Given the first result, respondents appeared to find managed care's requirements low in usefulness not because they were too time-consuming but, perhaps, because the information requested or the design of the forms was not helpful for clinical work.

The variable associated with the largest number of significant results was whether documentation practices were driven primarily by requirements of the public mental health system. These results had a consistent pattern. Requirements from the public mental health system were associated with more time spent charting intake sessions and lower judgments of the usefulness of this activity, but the public system variable was not related to either the amount of time spent charting therapy sessions or the perceived utility of therapy documentation. These results suggest that public mental health system requirements for intake documentation are burdensome for many clinicians and may interfere with their efforts to provide effective services. If so, these record-keeping requirements warrant critical reexamination and realignment with the goal of facilitating, rather than hindering, quality services to clients.

The clinicians themselves were the source of requirements most consistently associated with brief and useful charting practices. This result may be attributable to self-justification; clinicians may be biased toward making positive judgments of charting practices that they developed for their own use. However, the result can also be interpreted as suggesting that professionals chart most effectively when they are able to design their record-keeping practices in accordance with what they find most useful to their clinical work. If so, the finding would suggest that documentation policies should allow individual clinicians some latitude to tailor their charting procedures in accordance with what they find most effective.

Chapter 3

Efficient Documentation: Recording Maximum Information in Minimum Time

The practical challenge of clinical documentation is to record a maximum amount of information in a minimum amount of time. Information recording takes time, and time is a limited resource for clinicians. Because of this conflict, we must develop strategies for reconciling, or at least balancing, the goals of extensive documentation and quick documentation.

Theoretically, an almost limitless amount of writing could be done about any one clinical session. Mental health treatment is a profoundly important endeavor for the client, with nothing less than personal well-being at stake. Each session generates a great deal of information that could conceivably turn out to be significant either by itself, in combination with other statements, or in light of subsequent developments. Documentation should include the clinician's diagnostic and interpretive assessment of client statements, the writing of which may be lengthier than the client verbalizations themselves.

Records also need to include description of the therapist's interventions. Some authors (e.g., Wiger, 1997) recommend documentation of rationales for interventions and also reasons for not using alternative interventions. Because clinicians choose from among many possible therapeutic techniques, this record-keeping function seems intimidating.

Some authors (e.g., Zuckerman, 1997) also recommend writing concrete, behavioral descriptions, with "direct quotations whenever possible" (p. 269), rather than relying on conceptual or summary descriptions. This recommendation seems particularly dire in its implications for record length, because it would eliminate the efficiency of summary description.

Together, the preceding considerations suggest that each clinical session warrants extensive documentation. If these considerations and recommendations were followed uncritically, they would combine in a multiplicative fashion to result in an overwhelming amount of writing for each session. Perhaps, in the best of all possible worlds, clinicians would have the time to do this.

In this world, however, they do not: Not if the country's clients are to be served by the country's therapists, and not if clinical work is to receive appropriate reimbursement. Therefore, something has to give—the theoretical ideal of complete documentation must be intelligently adapted to the realities of practice. This can be accomplished without compromising the quality of clinical work.

THE NONEQUIVALENCE OF DOCUMENTATION AND TREATMENT

The first consideration is simply that *documentation is not the same thing as treatment.* This is an obvious and literal fact, and yet documentation enthusiasts sometimes talk as if it were not true, as in the dictum: "If it wasn't recorded, it didn't happen." (If meant literally, this dictum seems to be an instance of magical thinking.)

From the standpoint of clients, treatment and documentation are not identical events. Clients are generally unaware of what we record and what we do not (except when an institutional or state regulation requires clients or parents to see or sign their records). The majority of clients never see, ask to see, or show any interest in what is written in their records. Clients are concerned about what we do and what we say to help them with their problems. Writing things down in charts, in and of itself, does not help clients get better.

The dictum's validity pertains, not to the occurrence of events, but to *evidence for* the occurrence of events. It is true that, if it was not documented, it will be hard to *prove* it happened. Therefore, in situations in which we must not only practice competently but also prove that we practiced competently, documentation is of the utmost importance.

The dictum seems to apply, not to the general description of clinical sessions, but to important, specific events and actions. Situations involving a high degree of clinical risk or threat to client well-being require a competent therapist response; a record that fails to describe such situations and responses is incomplete and leaves the clinician unprotected against ethical or malpractice complaints.

The documentation dictum can reasonably be interpreted to mean that notes must always record information such as client statements suggesting child abuse and subsequent therapist notification of state child protection agencies, or client statements suggesting violent intent and subsequent therapist warning of the threatened individual. If we do not record such events, we will not be able to demonstrate that we practiced ethically and competently. However, such situations occur in only a small minority of sessions.

In the vast majority of clinical work, it is not necessary to provide detailed records of client and therapist statements. Routine clinical procedures, if effective, will help clients regardless of whether they are described at length. And future readers—whether courts, ethics committees, or other therapists—will generally be interested in major clinical events and interventions, not detailed accounts of routine clinical work.

BEHAVIORAL VERSUS CONCEPTUAL DESCRIPTIONS

Conceptual versus behavioral descriptions represent two opposite styles of communication. Another description of this dichotomy would be abstract versus concrete.

The issue of behavioral, concrete description versus conceptual, summary description seems particularly important in its implications for the length of clinical records. We propose that there is a fundamental trade-off in behavioral versus conceptual note-writing. If recording consists of the raw data of what clients and therapists say in sessions, notes will either be very lengthy or will describe only a small portion of what takes place. If recording consists only of formulaic, summary descriptions, notes can be short, but precision and specificity of information may be lost. Careful consideration of this trade-off can be helpful in developing an optimal balance between behavioral and conceptual description in clinical recording.

Conceptual description inherently involves summarization, and, for this reason, it can be much briefer than behavioral description. By conceptual description, we do not mean theoretical discussion, which can be lengthy. Conceptual terminology organizes raw behavioral data into higher-order constructs, and then identifies these data gestalts with single words or phrases. Diagnostic nomenclature is a perfect example: *DSM-IV* (*Diagnostic and Statistical Manual of Mental Disorders*, 4th ed.; APA, 1994) diagnoses, expressed in from one to several words, are shorthand summaries of all the information written in the manual's descriptions of these syndromes. The mental health field also has conceptual terms to describe, in an efficient fashion, many of the processes that occur in clinical work: interventions, client-therapist interactions, and so forth.

The conceptual style of communication has several advantages, the most important of which, for the present discussion, is speed. One can write: "John sat in a rigid posture, gripping the arms of his chair and tapping his foot. His jaw looked clenched, and his face was red. He said, 'I'm so worried about things, I feel like jumping out of my skin!'" Or, one can write, "John seemed very anxious." The brief conceptual statement contains most—although never all—of the information in the much longer behavioral description.

In principle, there is nothing expressible conceptually that could not also be expressed in concrete, behavioral terms, but the latter form of expression takes much more time. We are capable of stating behavioral definitions of terms like "suicidal ideation," "psychodynamic

21

therapy," "marital conflict," and "positive reinforcement," but, in communication with each other, professionals often prefer to use the technical terms by themselves.

Not only does conceptual terminology summarize raw, behavioral data, it also encapsulates theory-based knowledge acquired through professional education and experience. These words not only summarize what a lay observer would report if asked to describe a session, they also carry organizing and, sometimes, explanatory meanings based on research and theory. Diagnostic nomenclature may suggest information about common causative mechanisms, associated features, prognosis, and treatment implications. Terms for treatment techniques summarize therapist behaviors and also suggest etiological factors and intended mechanisms of change. A term like "cognitive therapy" carries implications about the relationship between beliefs and affect, the importance of rationality to adjustment, the role of preconscious self-statements, and so forth. Thus, conceptual terms represent brief syntheses of the clinician's reading, training, and experience.

Conceptual description also has disadvantages. For the most part, its weaknesses involve the same properties as its strengths; they are the other side of the coin. The advantages and disadvantages of conceptual description both derive from its capability to summarize and to carry implied meanings.

When applied to an individual case, conceptual language can convey an outline of what occurs, but some loss of information is inevitable. Abstract terms place the raw data of diagnosis and treatment into *categories,* and the names of these categories are used as the currency of communication. Because there is variation among individual instances within categories, the labels can never completely describe the individual instances. As a result, one man's "suicidal ideation" is never exactly the same as another man's, and one woman's "narrative therapy" is not the same as another woman's.

Conceptual statements are more vulnerable to misunderstanding and miscommunication than are behavioral statements, because conceptual words contain more implicit, implied meaning, whereas behavioral words denote a smaller, and more explicit, amount of information. The potential vulnerability to miscommunication of conceptual language is probably the reason past writers about clinical documentation have often recommended reliance on concrete, behavioral description. However, there is a basic characteristic of the clinical enterprise that provides substantial protection against miscommunication with conceptual terms.

Clinical work is conducted by the members of a small set of *professions* (psychology, social work, psychiatry, and counseling). These professions all have regulated training requirements, examinations that must be passed for licensure, and identifiable literatures. One of the defining features of a profession is the shared use of technical terms whose meanings are understood in the same way by all competent professionals. The law refers to these words as "terms of art." Terms of art are *inherently* conceptual, summarizing large amounts of concrete information with a few words. By definition, competent members of a profession share consensual understandings of their terms of art. Therefore, conceptual terminology can be legitimately used in documentation, and there need not be a complete reliance on behavioral, literal description of clinical material.

However, it cannot be assumed that all professionals correctly use all terms of art all the time. Each clinician may have this faith in himself or herself, but third parties are not often willing to make this assumption. As a result, government regulators and third-party payers have a reasonable concern about verifying that assessment findings and intervention techniques are accurately described by the conceptual terms used to identify them.

For example, charts must provide evidence that the client's "anxiety" included experiences that all competent professionals would identify with this term, and that "behavior therapy" did in fact involve the specific procedures identified with this treatment method. Without some behavioral description, regulators and care managers cannot be sure that a disorder was accurately diagnosed and treated. One function of documentation is to demonstrate that the clinician knew what he or she was doing and used conceptual language correctly.

Nevertheless, if pushed to an extreme, this function of documentation can become overwhelming. Also, the necessity of this type of credentialing function seems limited. Clinicians presumably demonstrate their competence by completing the requirements and passing the exams needed for licensure. They should not have to fully redemonstrate their competence and their correct understanding of terms of art every time they chart a session.

This array of issues constitutes a two-sided issue but not an insoluble dilemma. The idea that comes to the rescue is the notion of *diminishing marginal utility*. "Utility" means the value of outcomes accomplished by an effort. "Marginal" indicates the next increment of some succession or series (as, e.g., "marginal tax rate"). "Diminishing" means decreasing. Thus, "diminishing marginal utility" describes situations in which the next increment of effort produces less value than the previous increment. Such situations are extremely common; if they were not, we would be unable to believe that a piece of work is "good enough," and so is finished. We conclude projects—whether studying for an exam, planning a presentation, or dusting a room—when we believe we have reached the point of diminishing returns. The same should be true of clinical documentation. The challenge of efficient documentation is to identify the points at which work is characterized by diminishing marginal utility.

WHEN TO WRITE A LOT AND WHEN TO WRITE A LITTLE

In determining optimal proportioning of conceptual (summary) versus behavioral (detailed) writing, the following criteria can help determine how much writing needs to be done for particular sessions.

Clinical Atypicality and Complexity

Conceptual language refers to *prototypical* situations and processes. When we think of "oppositionality," we think of common forms of oppositionality, and when we think of "anger management training," we think of typical implementations of this technique. Conceptual, summative language is accurate when it describes prototypical instances of the phenomena it names. Such language is less accurate when it describes atypical or unusually complex clinical material. Therefore, the less neatly that clinical material fits into our conceptual categories, the more our record-keeping should utilize behavioral data. Exceptions need to be described concretely.

This is equally true for description of assessment and treatment. The more that a client's difficulties match a *DSM-IV* diagnosis—with those criteria fully present, and criteria of other diagnoses absent—the more we can rely on the diagnostic term to summarize the client's problems. When clients present atypical or complex clinical pictures—either because they exhibit no syndrome completely or because they exhibit criteria of more than one diagnosis—then we need to supplement diagnostic terminology with specific, behavioral description. This principle applies also to narrower constructs in psychopathology such as impulsivity, affective lability, low self-esteem, and so forth.

The same is true for documentation of treatment procedures. Some interventions are simple and prototypical in that they proceed from a single theoretical orientation, and they unfold in the manner and produce the effects predicted by that orientation. The ultimate example of this occurs when a treatment manual is followed, and no clinical events occur that are not effectively managed within the prescriptions of the manual. In these instances, citation of the manual provides fairly complete documentation of treatment.

In contrast, some treatment cases are complex in that they proceed from more than one theoretical orientation, involve use of several different techniques, unfold in unexpected ways, and do not always produce the expected effects. The ultimate example of this type of treatment occurs when therapists creatively combine and even improvise intervention techniques employing methods that, to their knowledge, have not been used before. Summative, conceptual terminology is not capable of adequately recording treatment of this type. In these situations, session notes should be specific, detailed and, accordingly, relatively long.

Clinical Severity and Dangerousness

Clinical issues differ in severity and dangerousness, and these factors, in turn, affect the amount of behavioral detail needed for satisfactory recording. The classic example here is suicidal ideation, for which adequate documentation needs to include precise detail and client quotation. In contrast, an argument between a parent and a child about room-cleaning can be recorded with little detail or elaboration, even if it was the focus of the session. When clinical material is routine, note writing reaches the point of diminishing marginal utility quickly, and records can be brief. When clinical phenomena are serious or emergent, documentation reaches the point of diminishing returns only after a considerable amount of writing, and records need to be relatively long.

Importance and Uncertainty of Outcomes Dependent on the Records

There is great variability in what is at stake in record-keeping, with variability in both the importance and the uncertainty of outcomes. In the following discussion, the issue is not the dependence of outcomes on clinical *work* (which is generally high), but the dependence of outcomes on clinical *records* (which varies widely).

The simplest situations occur when there is only one service provider, there will never be another treatment episode, only one child-serving system is involved, and the case will never be involved in a legal proceeding. In these common situations, there really are only two major documentation-dependent outcomes, or purposes, to be achieved by clinical notes—proof to payers that appropriate clinical work did occur and memory prompts for the clinician sufficient to ensure continuity of treatment across sessions. Compared with other possible outcomes, these are relatively low in importance. The worst case scenarios are that payment for the session might not be made and that the therapist might forget a bit of information relevant to ensuing treatment. These outcomes are also relatively low in uncertainty—payers generally reimburse clinicians for sessions, and therapists generally remember significant information from one session to the next whether or not they record it, particularly because later material will prompt memory for earlier information and plans. Therefore, routine session activities can be satisfactorily recorded in a succinct, conceptual manner, for instance, "Used cognitive techniques to reduce self-blame for parents' divorce."

At the other extreme of these continua, there are situations in which a great deal hinges on the records, with important outcomes likely to swing either way depending on the amount of information documented in the chart. These situations are usually associated with, and signaled by, possible court involvement.

Possible Legal System Involvement

A readily identifiable marker is often present when documentation-dependent outcomes are high in importance and uncertainty: a likelihood of court involvement. When clinical work is likely to be examined in court, record-keeping needs to be complete and detailed. Courts place much emphasis on written material, and clinical records are never scrutinized more closely than when they are examined in court, particularly by hostile attorneys.

Court involvement is usually a predictable occurrence. Overall, legal system involvement is rare in clinical work, and almost all cases that end up in court fall into one of a small number of categories. Examples include determinations of custody, parent visitation, competency, child maltreatment, involuntary commitment, possible malpractice by another professional working with the client, and any situation involving possible danger to self or others. Clinicians need to be knowledgeable about situations with potential legal implications and to be

25

alert to their occurrence as early in the treatment process as possible. A clinician who foresees possible court involvement can perform documentation accordingly. Records likely to end up in court should be written with a higher level of detail than is needed in routine clinical work, because courts will subject records to much more intensive scrutiny than one uses in refreshing one's memory about a previous session or than a colleague would use in picking up the case in the future.

Fortunate Covariation of the Situational Features

The situational features that signal a necessity for detailed documentation generally are not independent of each other but, instead, strongly tend to occur together. Courts rarely become involved in mental health issues; when they do, it is usually because it is unclear what should be done, the possible outcomes might have a major impact on the people involved, and/or the level of clinical seriousness is high.

Situations involving potential danger, either for the client (e.g., suicide risk), another individual (e.g., homicide risk), or the therapist (e.g., malpractice suit risk) are typically recognizable when they occur. Emergency treatment situations are associated with a large proportion of malpractice allegations (Gutheil & Applebaum, 1982). Potentially dangerous situations should call forth unusually extensive, detailed, and complete documentation. Such documentation constitutes evidence that the therapist recognized the seriousness of the situation and exercised due diligence in thinking it through and carefully planning responses. Extensive documentation, in itself, is evidence inconsistent with an allegation of negligence, which connotes thoughtlessness and carelessness.

Zuckerman (1997) recommends that, when confronting uncertain and serious situations, clinicians should document their decision-making process for possible future self-defense. Gutheil (1980, p. 482) suggests that, in such situations, one should "think out loud for the record" so that, if something disastrous does occur, it cannot be attributed to professional negligence. Cohen (1979) advises that clinicians obtain and document consultation in such situations. Gutheil and Applebaum (1982) recommend that, when forensically significant events or malpractice allegations seem possible, records should be written with the expectation that they will be read by critical, even unfriendly, readers.

It is prudent to make clear the potential limitations of any treatment efforts made by the clinician, so that the record acknowledges the difficult nature of the situation, and responsibility for negative outcomes does not fall on the professional as an individual. Statements to the client, parent, and the record about the probable efficacy of chosen interventions should not be overly optimistic, and there should be no guarantees of success (Gutheil & Applebaum, 1982). There should be documentation of difficulties encountered by the therapist in attempting to provide optimal treatment, such as failed appointments (Soisson, VandeCreek, & Knapp, 1987) and resistance by significant others (Cohen, 1979).

26

There can never be complete certainty about whether a case will take a serious turn. Even when cases seem entirely routine, and there are no red flags for serious outcomes or legal involvement, the probability that records will someday be scrutinized is never literally zero. One possible response to this reality is to chart all sessions with the highest level of detail, as if they will end up in court or before an ethics committee.

We recommend against this hypercautious approach, for three reasons. First, overall frequency of clinical records receiving strict scrutiny is not merely low, it is extremely low. Some clinicians go their entire career without any of their charts being examined by an adjudicative body. Second, constant efforts to prepare for extremely unlikely situations would exact a cost in the effectiveness of clinical work by decreasing time available for reading, discussion with colleagues, thinking through clinical material, and taking a moment to clear one's head between sessions.

Third, readers of records usually expect a high level of detail only when the situation warrants it, rather than at all times. Midcourse changes in level of documentation detail are feasible and appropriate. Thus, for example, sessions with a child referred for Oppositional-Defiant Disorder can be charted in a routine, brief manner unless and until information indicating a serious situation (e.g., abuse or self-injurious impulses) emerges; then, at the time, documentation can become highly detailed. Just as all cases do not require the same level of documentation detail, all sessions for a given client do not require the same type of record-keeping.

A factor that muddies the waters is that third-party payers or regulators might not look at things the way we do, or the way most practicing clinicians do. In particular, our survey results suggested that the public mental health system desires a level of documentation detail for assessments that many clinicians find to be a hindrance, rather than a help, to effective clinical work. Our results also suggested an interfering effect for managed care, although this did not seem attributable to the length of required records. The reasoning presented in this chapter is based on clinical and pragmatic considerations, but practitioners sometimes feel they are not free to function in accordance with purely clinical considerations because they have third parties with different priorities looking over their shoulders. These third parties are sometimes perceived as adhering to a "the-more-the-better" view of documentation, leaving the efficiency-oriented clinician in a quandary.

We have several responses to this problem. First, most third-party payers and regulators desire accuracy and substance, rather than detail and length, in the records they review. To the extent that they do not, influences such as this book, future research on documentation, and the input of practitioners may contribute to an improved situation in the future. Finally, although third parties can certainly narrow the range of workable flexibility, they do not negate the fact that different situations warrant different levels of documentation detail. Neither the public mental health system nor managed care desire the level of detail that is sometimes useful in court.

Therefore, clinicians need to be responsive to the demands of third parties, but they can still facilitate their work with clients by rationally varying their level of documentation detail in accordance with the nature of the case. A policy of writing all records as if they will eventually be scrutinized in court is unnecessary and counterproductive. Our treatment procedures vary widely as a function of the client, and our documentation procedures should too. Accurate assessment and rational planning can substitute for indiscriminately detailed and laborious record-keeping. Flexibility is critical to efficiency.

SITUATION-SPECIFIC LEVEL OF DETAIL

Level of detail can be operationally defined in a concrete manner as the ratio of words to minutes of clinical activity with the client. This ratio should be high in the following (frequently co-occurring) situations:

1. The clinical material suggests possible danger to self or others.
2. The clinical material is unusual or complex, so that it is not adequately described by conceptual language.
3. Important new information about the client is obtained (which always occurs in initial, diagnostic sessions and also occasionally occurs in the midst of treatment).
4. A marked change, especially a negative change, in client condition occurs.
5. Important new plans or decisions about treatment are made (which always occurs in initial treatment planning and also occasionally occurs when strategies are changed in the midst of treatment).
6. Examination of records by third parties is expected (particularly in the context of a legal proceeding).

Record-keeping is about *information* and *change* and, therefore, documentation should be more extensive when sessions reveal high levels of information and change. This is why documentation detail is generally greater for assessment than therapy; however, therapy sessions involving much new information or change are the exceptions that prove the rule, and should be documented in detail.

Level of documentation detail should be low when therapy sessions are *routine*. The word "routine," here, does not mean unimportant, uninteresting, or static but, rather, characterized by relatively low levels of new information or change from the ongoing direction of therapy. Therapy sessions are routine when the client's functioning has not changed qualitatively or radically since it was last described and when the therapist is continuing to use the interventions he or she said would be used in the treatment plan.

Routine sessions must be described clearly and accurately, but since these sessions represent continuations of what was previously described in detail, the ratio of words to session time can be low. Such record-keeping should focus on the specifics of treatment plan implementation and the client's responses to interventions, progress, or lack of progress.

Redundancy is the enemy of efficiency. The issue of redundancy, however, currently seems to be somewhat controversial, or at least unclear, in discussions of clinical documentation. Some insurance company guidelines (e.g., Blue Cross/Blue Shield; see Wiger, 1997) state that Axis I diagnoses should be rejustified, in terms of *DSM-IV* criteria, each session. A literal interpretation of this guideline implies that each therapy session should include a diagnostic interview.

Implementation of this recommendation would come at a considerable cost in time, both for writing and, much more so, for conducting reassessments during sessions. Insurance companies should not reimburse for medically unnecessary treatment, but weekly reevaluation seems unnecessary because disorders are fairly stable over time and generally do not appear and disappear on a weekly basis. Regimens of medication and physical therapy are not diagnostically rejustified every week or two, and this is similarly unnecessary for psychotherapy.

The approach we recommend emphasizes flexible response to clinical situations, rather than indiscriminate repetition of assessment procedures. If clients report or exhibit major changes in their functioning, this should be investigated, and the result might be a change in diagnosis. If the client describes or exhibits no major changes, reassessment would generally result in the diagnosis that has already been justified and documented.

Operationally, our recommendation is that therapists inquire about and document change in client functioning at every session. Whether or not this is followed by a diagnostic reassessment should depend on the information elicited; usually, no reassessment will be necessary. The goal of accurate monitoring of client functioning and medical necessity can be accomplished without constant repetition of diagnostic procedures and documentation. In practice, this is the way therapists generally operate and third-party payers generally evaluate treatment records.

Because clinicians must comply with the requirements of their sources of reimbursement, payers, as well as therapists, should adopt a pragmatic, discriminating, situationally flexible approach to documentation. Such an approach would minimize redundancy and allow clinicians to focus time and effort on effective treatment procedures.

Chapter 4

Current Documentation Formats and Structures

Although clinical documentation has not been an area of systematic inquiry or development, several documentation formats have evolved from clinical work. These methods and formats each offer a way of organizing clinical material, and these structures should be considered for what they could contribute to effective record-keeping. Therefore, before presenting our own forms, we offer a brief tour of documentation procedures that have been recommended and used in the past. First, we consider some basic issues relevant to evaluating record-keeping formats and structures.

PROGRESS VERSUS PROCESS NOTES

There have been two main types of session notes, namely, progress and process notes. Progress notes are part of the "official" chart. Generally, they are relatively structured, objective, and macroscopic. They comprise a description of the course of treatment, with identification of significant events and actions, and are more in accordance with the medical model, compared with process notes. Progress notes are potentially available to the client, and with proper release of information or exceptions to confidentiality, they are available to others. One purpose of progress notes is to provide a record of treatment for others.

In contrast (at least in theory), process notes are not part of the "official" record but, instead, are the therapist's personal notes. They are not kept in client charts, but typically are kept in folders in the therapist's desk. In writing style, process notes are generally more informal, associative, and colloquial than progress notes. Process notes are written by the therapist for the therapist, and are not intended to be read by others (but see later in this section). Their purpose is not to provide an official, potentially public record of treatment but, instead, to facilitate the therapist's conceptualization of the client and planning for ensuing sessions. A synonymous term is "working notes." Thus, while the primary purpose of progress notes is to *describe* therapy, the primary purpose of process notes is to *enhance* therapy.

The following list of functions and components borrows from Zuckerman (1997). Progress notes typically include the following forms of information:

- Objective data
- Symptoms assessed
- Problems addressed
- Basic session content
- Important life events
- Changes in functioning and movement toward goals
- Treatment techniques
- Recommendations for changes or interventions outside the sessions
- Homework assignments
- Referrals

Process notes can include the preceding forms of information, but this list does not capture their focus or spirit. Process notes differ from progress notes by emphasizing the following types of material (again borrowing from Zuckerman, 1997):

- Sensitive information
- The flow, process, and dynamics of sessions
- Style and form of client verbalizations and behavior
- Bits of material that may turn out to be significant
- Therapist connections between pieces of material
- Therapist analysis, hypothesizing, and theorizing
- Therapist intuitions and hunches
- Countertransference reactions
- Therapist plans for specific questions or statements
- Notes to the therapist by the therapist
- Notes that would be uninterpretable to anyone except the therapist

There is a major problem with the policy of writing process notes for personal use, with the expectation that they cannot be examined by others; in reality, process notes are not legally secure. Although the situation was different in the past, records can no longer be

31

considered securely personal or private. In settings covered by federal law, the Privacy Act of 1974 (Public Law 93-579) and the Freedom of Information Act of 1974 (Public Law 93-502) give clients the right to see any and all notes about them, with no distinction between official and personal notes (Zuckerman, 1997). In addition, state law, case law, or the act of filing a malpractice suit can provide clients with access to all notes about them (Fulero & Wilbert, 1988). Finally, courts can subpoena personal notes if the judge decides to do so. Therefore, the distinction between progress and process notes is not legally tenable.

An additional, important problem with the practice of writing these two sets of notes is that the practice is inefficient. Given that therapists generally have only about 10 minutes to write the record of a session, and given the numerous potential functions of progress notes and the amount of information they can include, multiplying the task of record-keeping by two seems impractical and time-consuming. Since progress notes are absolutely necessary, process notes are difficult to justify under most circumstances.

However, there are several exceptions. First, process notes can be useful in training and supervision, and so the preceding recommendation applies to work, but not education, in psychotherapy. Second, process notes may be helpful for cases that are unusually confusing, challenging, or difficult. Even for routine cases, it is occasionally useful to jot an informal question, hypothesis, or statement down on a scrap of paper or in one's appointment book, for easy access immediately before the next session with the client. These scraps of paper can be thrown away after their use.

ADVANTAGES AND DISADVANTAGES OF PREDETERMINED RECORDING STRUCTURES

A basic decision in formulating a record-keeping strategy is whether to use a predetermined structure, or simply to write on blank, lined paper. Records can be structured by either printed forms or by formats (e.g., SOAP) governing the writing of records. During most of the history of psychotherapy, clinicians wrote free-form notes on blank paper, but structured forms are increasing in popularity, as evidenced by the appearance of books (such as this one) offering sets of forms for clinicians' use. Generally, the same historical factors responsible for the increased emphasis on documentation have also contributed to an increasing interest in preprinted, structured forms.

Our position on this question is given away by the fact that we wrote this book, which consists largely of forms recommended for clinician use. Nonetheless, we recognize that adherence to a predetermined structure has both advantages and disadvantages. Also, record-keeping structure is not a dichotomous issue, because records can vary along a continuum of structure. At the structured extreme, there are lengthy, detailed forms, dense with subheadings and checklists, that provide a specific, predetermined template for record-keeping. At the other, unstructured extreme, there is simply a piece of blank, lined paper, with the title "Progress Notes" at the top, a heading for "Date" above the left margin, and no particular plan or habitual practice for the form of the note. In the middle, there are relatively simple forms, with just a few headings, lots of blank space, and substantial reliance on free narrative. Thus, the dichotomous question of whether or not to use forms should be refined into the more quantitative question of what *degree* of predetermined structure best facilitates effective documentation.

One advantage of predetermined structure is the provision of organization and focus. Forms and formats can facilitate both the writing and the reading of clinical records. With "a place for everything and everything in its place," writers need to spend no time deciding where to place various types of information, and readers immediately know where to find material of different kinds. Also, predetermined structures help ensure a basic level of quality control in record-keeping, because they remind writers to include the types of information that should be present in each note. Finally, forms and formats can aid in the conceptualization of clinical material.

The disadvantages of forms and formats are mirror images of their advantages; both derive from the fact that they are *predetermined*. Forms and formats are constraints, which are helpful when they push our efforts in directions they should go anyway, and are unhelpful when they push us in directions inappropriate to the task at hand. At their worst, predetermined structures are square pegs in round holes, Procrustean beds that do not fit the material to be described and so distort record-keeping. When unhelpful, predetermined structures feel like straitjackets and make us wish we could toss the form or format and just describe what happened in the session.

Part of the resolution is to use "good" forms or formats, but strong conceptual quality does not provide a complete resolution. The need is not for a structure that is perfect for most clinical situations; instead, we need structures suitable for virtually *all* material—including material that the designer of the form could not have foreseen.

Therefore, flexibility is a crucial characteristic of an effective form. Flexibility involves a moderation of constraint and provides writers with the freedom and space to gear record-keeping to the individuality of the client and session. If a form is excessively specific and detailed, it will fail to fit many clinical situations. Large proportions of such forms will be nonapplicable to many clients, redundancy will occur when the same basic information is repeated in response to many items, and information will be lost when it does not fit with the tight requirements of the items and headings.

Thus, to facilitate rather than hinder accurate description, forms and formats should have a moderate, optimal degree of structure. There is value in both open-endedness and structure, because all clinical material is unique and yet certain basic types of information need to be recorded about all clinical work. Lengthy, detailed forms may look impressive, but they are not the most effective tools for the performance of record-keeping. Sometimes, less is more. In designing the forms for this book, we attempted to strike a balance between simplicity, with freedom for the writer, and structure, with direction for the writer.

Several formats for structuring therapy notes have been in use for many years. Most of these formats were developed in medical settings, and this influence is apparent. We do not generally recommend these formats, but they are not without value and may be useful in some situations, so they warrant consideration.

DOCUMENTATION FORMATS DERIVED FROM THE MEDICAL MODEL

The SOAP Method

The *SOAP* format calls for writing four types of information about each unit of clinical material, as follows:

1. *S* stands for *subjective* data, as reported by the client, representing his or her perceptions and experiences. This section usually consists of client quotes, recorded verbatim.
2. *O* stands for *objective* data. This includes the clinician's observations of the client's behavior, the reported observations of other professionals, psychological test data, and functionally significant occurrences (e.g., suspension from school).
3. *A* stands for *assessment*—the clinician's inferences, interpretations, diagnostic impressions, and conceptual analyses of the subjective and objective data.
4. *P* stands for *plan,* that is, what the therapist intends to do in response to the assessment. This heading can include both immediate and long-term plans for treatment techniques, testing, referral and follow-up.

Zuckerman (1997) suggests the following three additions to this format, resulting in the acronym SOAPIER:

1. *I* stands for *intervention* or plan implementation. This section gives a more short-term and detailed description of the therapist's interventions than what is recorded under the Plan heading.
2. *E* is for the clinician's *evaluation* of the effectiveness of the intervention. In the plain SOAP format, intervention outcomes are described under S or O; here, they have their own heading.
3. *R* is for *revisions* of the plan. In the SOAP format, this would be described under P. In the SOAPIER format, the P section describes the implementation of the original plan, and the R section records midcourse changes in the plan.

Here is an example of a SOAP note:

S: "I hit my sister when she deserves it; she's always getting into my stuff."
O: Mother reports client continues being physically aggressive toward his sister.
A: Client continues externalizing responsibility for his aggression and is not showing improvement.
P: Continue confronting client's externalization of responsibility. Continue behavior reinforcement system. Homework: Client to make list of things he likes about his sister.

Current Documentation Formats and Structures

The following is an example of a note written in the SOAPIER format:

S: In dollhouse play, client depicted a child misbehaving, followed by an argument between the parents, and ending with the father walking out.

O: Client believes that child misbehavior causes marital conflict, resulting, in turn, in parental exits. Children's Depression Inventory score = 15.

A: Client feels her misbehavior contributes to discord between her parents, causes her father to spend time away from the family, and creates a danger of paternal abandonment.

P: Continue use of symbolic play as method of therapeutic communication. Continue psychodynamic techniques. Continue cognitive techniques. Homework: Father to play a game with client twice this week.

 I: Exploration of client's perceptions of and feelings about her family using symbolic play. Interpretation of this material to client. Correction of client's unrealistic beliefs about family functioning. Communication of this information to parents.

E: Client communication is increasing. Client seems cognitively able to process therapist's input. Slight reduction in depression level.

R: Have family session in which parents differentiate parent/child issues from marital issues.

The SOAP and SOAPIER formats certainly provide structures that prompt and organize clinical data and planning. However, they also have several liabilities.

When examined as abstract structures, these formats make sense, and it is easy to think up examples of clinical material that fit them nicely. However, when put into practice with day-to-day clinical material, difficulties of fit frequently arise. These formats often creak when they move. Fit between format and material can be poor in two ways: The format can force writing to be redundant, and there can be data or ideas that would be useful to record but which do not have a convenient place in the SOAP or SOAPIER structures.

When applied to clinical material, these formats often force writing to be repetitious. The S and O sections are redundant when the therapist finds the client's report to be credible and takes it at face value, particularly in the numerous situations when there is no external evidence against which to evaluate the objectivity of the client's statements. For example, if an adolescent says, "I've been feeling more secure with my boyfriend," the boyfriend is not participating in therapy, and the parents have no way of assessing this, then the S and O sections will usually be identical.

Redundancy also plagues the writing of the O and A sections. In principle, the difference between these sections is that the assessment is more macroscopic and conceptual, and the O section consists of raw, although objective, data. In practice, however, it can be difficult, pedantic, and not particularly useful to create different statements. For example, objective data such as, "Client's grades changed from C's and D's to B's and C's" would generate the assessment of "Improved school performance." In situations in which objective data can be usefully woven together into a conceptually meaningful assessment, the therapist can do so without regular use of this format.

The Plan section often involves another form of redundancy. Therapeutic plans often do not change much from week to week. As a result, the P sections of SOAP and SOAPIER notes often include many statements along the lines of, "Continue monitoring this," and "Continue doing that." Such statements have a low ratio of words to useful information. It is more efficient to assume continued implementation of the treatment plan and to use writing time for recording changes or additions to the plan.

The most glaring omission in the SOAP format is that it has no section for recording the therapist's activity in the session; the P section is for planning what the therapist will do in the future, not for recording what he or she said to the client in the session being documented. The Intervention section of the SOAPIER format fulfills this purpose precisely and so constitutes a major advantage over the SOAP format. However, records using the SOAPIER system tend to involve even more redundancy than those using the SOAP format, simply because there are seven, not four, sections. Slicing clinical material up into numerous sections can be laborious and cumbersome, and redundancy is almost impossible to avoid. Clinicians find themselves spending considerable time figuring out how to divide into the required sections a paragraph they could easily just write.

Although sometimes it can be helpful to separately record seven aspects of one unit of clinical work, in other situations this is not useful. The problem with commitment to a system is that the same categorizations must be followed whether or not the writer would create these separations if free simply to document the session as accurately and efficiently as possible.

In addition to creating redundancy, the SOAP and SOAPIER formats often exclude useful information, resulting in incomplete record-keeping from the perspective of clinical utility. Completing a number of record sections about one unit of clinical material takes considerable time and, as a consequence, it becomes difficult to write notes on more than one unit of material. In using the SOAP format, once the clinician records a piece of subjective data, he or she is obligated to complete the O, A, and P sections. The amount of work needed to complete the record is multiplied by four with the addition of each distinct piece of subjective data. This is not a major problem if the session had only one theme, but it is a significant problem if the session involved several issues, which is often the case. In practice, using a system of this type often results in a narrowly focused record, with a failure to document all but the primary theme of the session.

The Problem-Oriented Record

This system was developed by Weed (1971) for medical settings. It was slightly modified for use with psychotherapy by Sturm (1987). The Problem-Oriented Record (POR) is a system for organizing the chart around a numbered list of patient problems.

This procedure begins in the assessment phase with the identification, description, and numbering of the problems to be the focus of treatment. "Problems" are a smaller unit of analysis than diagnosis or level of functioning; they correspond to individual symptoms, diagnostic criteria, or specific functional impairments. The problem list is placed on top of the chart, providing a sort of table of contents or reference key.

All ensuing clinical documentation is cross-referenced to the problem numbers. One form of efficiency provided by this system is that problems need be described only once. For example, if poor school performance was identified as Problem 3, a referral to a tutor and all ensuing reports from the tutor would be marked with a "3." Notes on psychotherapy sessions are also organized and keyed in accordance with the problem list, which is revised whenever needed.

Customarily, the SOAP format is used with the POR system. Each session's work on a given problem is presented in this sequence of four sections. However, there is no necessity for adhering to this historical coupling: The POR system can be used without the SOAP format, and the SOAP format can be used without the POR system.

Zuckerman (1997) discusses several advantages of the POR method. Numerals are an efficient shorthand for problem descriptions. The cross-referencing system makes it possible to locate quickly the parts of the record pertaining to each of the client's difficulties. This system also focuses the record on the major problems that brought the client to treatment because there is no place for notes on ancillary or tangential issues.

Zuckerman (1997) also discusses the disadvantages of the POR system. These derive largely from the constraint of fitting all writing to the problem list; thus, the system's strengths and weaknesses seem to be mirror images of each other. One difficulty is that the format is ill-suited for documenting client strengths. The most basic difficulty is that the complexity of clients and clinical work often does not fit neatly into a list of discrete problems, so that this system can result in oversimplification and omission of significant information.

The POR map fails to match the clinical terrain when problem areas and the interventions addressing them are interwoven. For example, time-out may be used to treat physical aggression, homework refusal, and temper tantrums. When one intervention is used to treat multiple problems, which is often the case, treatment techniques must be redescribed under headings for several problems; specificity is lost, redundancy mushrooms, and the system becomes more trouble than it is worth.

The Genogram

The family diagram, or "genogram," can be an effective way of recording and organizing information about the client's family background. It is an unusual recording method in that it structures information with a visual/spatial format. Because there are rules for creating the spatial diagram, this visual record provides a type of conceptual organization for the information that is not present in records consisting of narrative or lists. When diagrammed in this way, patterns of family history can quickly become clear to the clinician and client. Thus, the genogram can be a therapeutic tool as well as a documentation format.

The genogram was developed by family systems therapists, and its use as an assessment method continues to be closely associated with this theoretical orientation. This diagrammatic structure provides a way of efficiently summarizing major life events of family members as well as patterns of family relationships over the generations.

Symbols such as circles, squares, and connecting lines are used to depict gender, relationships, and marital status across generations. One or two words can be placed by the symbol for the person to indicate salient characteristics (e.g., alcoholism, depression, career). Dates of births, deaths, marriages, divorces, serious illnesses, and other significant life events are included. Examination of these data can yield a quick assessment of the family history constituting the client's background.

The following symbols are conventionally used in genograms:

- Males: squares
- Females: circles
- Marriage: straight connecting line
- Cohabitation: wavy line
- Divorce: two slashes through line
- Marital separation: one slash through line
- Never married parents not living together: dashed line
- Custody after divorce: slash marks lean toward custodial parent
- Children: birth order left to right—
    Siblings connected by horizontal lines
    Connected to parents by vertical lines
- Death: X over the symbol
- Weak relationship: dotted line
- Conflictual relationship: jagged line

In work with cognitively advanced older children and adolescents (and with parents) when family functioning and history seem important, the genogram can be a truly useful documentation procedure. It is done in session, with the client, and has value for clinical work, as well as documentation, because it facilitates the identification of patterns by both therapist and client. However, genograms involve a form of information that is generally not emphasized by external sources of documentation requirements.

Computerized Case Management

There is a new, innovative documentation technology for case managers developed by Wallace Gingerich, PhD of Case Western Reserve University. MY ASSISTANT (Gingerich, 1995) is a computerized record-keeping system for case managers serving people with chronic mental illness. The software organizes recording of demographic information, goals, treatment plans, and tracking of client functioning. MY ASSISTANT has a structured format for developing and scaling client goals. There are search functions, a tickler system, and preprogrammed routine reports. The software performs caseload management functions such as maintaining lists of upcoming tasks, graphically depicting client progress, and conducting queries of the caseload. The system was designed to reduce time spent on paperwork and increase manager productivity and efficiency.

Chapter 5

Administrative Issues and Documents

INFORMED CONSENT

Informed consent is both a legal and a therapeutic issue, and one of the challenges in designing these forms is finding an optimal balance between these two considerations. Legal and therapeutic concerns can be in conflict, and the potential tension between the two is suggested by the types of form that would derive from each perspective. We suggest approaching this potential conflict in our usual way—by developing a document that maximizes the value of each side while minimizing the drawbacks of both, and also by discriminating between situations varying in the comparative importance of legal and therapeutic priorities.

The critical legal principle to understand is this: The concrete fact of a signature on a form entitled "Informed Consent" does not, by itself, constitute true informed consent. Legally, if one does not understand what one is consenting to, one cannot give *informed* consent. The legal necessities are for the text of the form to describe what treatment will be and for the client or parent to understand the text of the form.

From a legal perspective, a great deal of fairly technical information could be involved in making consent fully informed. From this perspective, it is not enough merely to inform the client or parent that "psychotherapy" or "psychological testing" is to be provided, because these terms cover a wide range of procedures that, furthermore, may not be well understood by the consenter. If a client thinks that "therapy" consists of talking about childhood memories but then finds that treatment consists of training in relaxation techniques, a signature on a form does not represent true informed consent. A possible solution to this problem would be to include blank space on the form in which the clinician can describe the specific procedures to be used. These would be treatment techniques in the case of therapy and assessment instruments in the case of testing.

A second, major issue is disclosure of possible risks and benefits. A promise to clients that psychotherapeutic interventions will solve the problems for which they seek treatment is tantamount to fraud, because mental health treatment is not always successful. Consenting to a treatment contract based on such a promise constitutes misinformed consent.

From a strict legal perspective, informed consent should include a written description of specific, possible risks and benefits. In the event of a negative outcome, the signed consent document would provide the practitioner with some protection against a malpractice claim, because there would be evidence that the consenter knew a negative outcome was possible when he or she signed the treatment contract.

Finally, legally oriented documents use words that make the basic facts being documented explicit and clearly specified. The first such fact is that the client or parent enters into the treatment contract voluntarily. This fact is sometimes documented by means of language along the lines of "I do hereby seek and consent." Legalistically written treatment contracts also include statements making it plain that the consenter can terminate services at any time.

Legal considerations seem to warrant informed consent forms that are lengthy, explicit, and fairly detailed in their description of procedures, risks, benefits, and contractual arrangements. However, therapeutic considerations suggest disadvantages to such forms. These therapeutic issues do not negate the preceding legal considerations, but they do qualify them, and these two sets of issues need to be integrated in designing informed consent forms.

First, most clients and parents are not interested in reading lengthy, legalistically worded forms. When clients complete these forms in waiting areas prior to appointments, they almost never ask questions about them, which is not what one would expect if clients were reading the forms with a true desire to understand them. When the forms are completed with the therapist, clients typically want a verbal statement of the gist of the form and then sign it following, at most, a cursory glance. Furthermore, the more dense, small print on the form, the less likely clients are to read it. To some extent, the more information is provided, the less information is taken in.

Written materials may be the basic currency of communication and agreement for attorneys, but clients often respond to legalistic language as if it were artificial, esoteric, and not really relevant to their personal situation. The fact that the form is preprinted may suggest that its words were chosen to address regulatory and legal issues, rather than to make a statement about what the client can expect personally from services. Clients are generally much more interested in hearing a personalized, spontaneous statement of what the therapist thinks about their situation and treatment prospects. As clients depart from their first appointment, their true sense of the treatment contract is probably much more a function of their interpersonal experience of the therapist—whether the professional seemed competent, trustworthy, and optimistic about helping them—than a function of the forms they have signed.

Consent would certainly be most informed if clients learned of the specific procedures to be used before they entered into their treatment contract. However, providing this information does not seem genuinely feasible. If preprinted, the information will be generic. Blank form sections provide an opportunity for individualization but, even with careful thought (which would take up session time), it would be practically impossible to find a few nontechnical words giving a meaningful description of the treatment plan. (Terms such as "psychody-namic," "response prevention," and "stress inoculation" are not informative for most clients.) Furthermore, psychotherapy usually involves a dialectic between assessment and treatment, and therapists generally revise their methods as they progress through the course of treatment (Persons, 1991). Thus, because of the complex, technical, and improvisatory nature of mental health services, informed consent on the level of specific procedures is not usually possible at the beginning of therapy.

Zuckerman's (1997) consent form for psychological testing includes technical statements about the procedures, such as that tests with established reliability and validity will be used. There are two difficulties with such statements. First, this vocabulary probably means nothing to most clients, and asking clients to sign forms they do not understand (or else divert session time to technical explanations) may not contribute to rapport and alliance-building. Generally, what clients or parents want to know is whether the psychologist believes the tests to be used are the most appropriate ones for obtaining information about the child's problems. If the answer is yes, parents generally do not desire technical explanations of reliability and validity, they want to move on with the assessment process.

A second issue is that psychologists sometimes use assessment tools whose reliability and validity have not been clearly established by past research (e.g., the TAT and Sentence Completion). These tools are used because some psychologists believe they provide clinically useful information. The question of whether unvalidated tests should be used to assess clients is beyond the scope of this discussion. However, it does not seem appropriate to settle the issue on a form.

Presentation of likely benefits and risks from treatment is also problematic. Clients vary widely in their response to treatment, and no statements can be made with certainty. Therapy involves risk, in that the condition of some clients worsens during treatment. Psychotherapy risks, however, are not analogous to the risks associated with surgical procedures and medicines. The risks and side effects of medical procedures can be specified on the basis of research, but research does not provide any specific statements about the likelihood and nature of unwanted effects from various psychotherapeutic procedures. Most clients improve over the course of treatment and many show no change; for the few who deteriorate, it is difficult to separate negative treatment effects from the effects of extratherapy factors such as life events. From a cost/benefit perspective, the value of vague and uncertain information about risks may not outweigh the alarm many clients might experience on reading such statements, particularly since positive expectations are important for the placebo-like effects that enhance response to mental health treatment.

Our main informed consent form represents an attempt to balance and, as much as possible, integrate legal and therapeutic considerations. There is a generically reasonable statement that the therapist will make his or her best professional effort to provide optimal treatment. There is also a statement that a positive outcome cannot be guaranteed. This statement is necessary because some clients might believe treatment always produces benefits, and any consent to treatment based on such a belief would represent an invalid contract. Our form does not, as some do, include a statement that treatment can be terminated at any time, because this seems so obvious that it is unnecessary to state (unless treatment is mandated, in which case the statement would be untrue).

The optimal balance of legal and therapeutic considerations in form design depends on the balance between legal and therapeutic factors in the situation in which the form will be used. The likelihood of a routine child therapy case eventuating in a legal dispute or suit is minuscule, particularly if the clinician practices competently and ethically. In these cases, language with no real purpose other than protecting the clinician against possible legal repercussions quickly reaches a point of diminishing benefits, especially if there are some associated therapeutic costs. *However,* if a case, from its outset, includes indicators of possible, eventual legal involvement, then the situation is entirely different, and this difference should be reflected in the form used to document informed consent.

The most common indicator of possible legal eventualities in child clinical work seems to be divorced parents. Divorce involves custody arrangements, and custody is itself a legal issue. Clinicians working with children of divorced parents need to be aware of legal considerations and adopt a more cautious, careful stance than is usually necessary, simply because this work is much more likely to become an issue in a court proceeding. Accordingly, we suggest a special form for use when divorce or child custody issues are present.

Many other situations can involve legal implications for clinical work. Examples include child abuse allegations, court-mandated treatment, assessments with a forensic purpose, dangers to self and others, and clients or parents who, for whatever reason, seem potentially interested in filing a malpractice suit. Clinicians should adapt our basic consent form, by increasing its detail and legal precision of language, if red flags are apparent.

An understandable, accurate, written treatment contract may have therapeutic value. Such a form can communicate basic features of the therapeutic relationship, such as that it is a contractual arrangement between adults, involving the purchase of professional services, with mutual obligations and expectations between the parties. Our informed consent form is intended to establish an honest understanding of mental health service contracts.

Consent for Mental Health
Treatment of a Minor

Therapist Qualifications

Psychotherapists have professional training in conducting mental health treatment. You have the right to inquire fully about the credentials, education, and experience of your child's therapist and to have your questions answered to your satisfaction. In this practice, treatment is provided either by a licensed member of a mental health profession (psychology, psychiatry, social work, or counseling) or else by an unlicensed professional with training enabling him or her to practice under the supervision of a licensed professional. If your child's therapist is an unlicensed professional, you should receive an explanation of the supervision arrangement and the name and phone number of the supervisor. You have the right to discuss your child's treatment with the supervisor.

What to Expect from Treatment

Your child's therapist will work to provide the most effective treatment possible. Studies of psychotherapy indicate that most clients benefit from treatment and experience improvement in the problem areas for which services were sought. However, treatment benefits, while likely, cannot be guaranteed. Response to therapy is different for each client and should be discussed on an ongoing basis with your child's therapist.

Psychotherapy can involve a variety of different activities, which vary from client to client. In general, your therapist will assess your child's problems and then will provide therapeutic services designed to resolve or reduce the problems. There may be individual work with your child, discussions with you possibly including ways to help your child outside of therapy, and/or family sessions. Therapy may focus on feelings, thoughts, relationships, and/or behaviors. With young children, therapy generally includes play activities used as a means of understanding and communicating with the child.

Confidentiality

Historically, psychotherapy was associated with complete confidentiality between the family and clinician. Currently, both law and professional ethics require therapists to maintain complete confidentiality in the vast majority of cases. In these cases, the therapist cannot release any information about your family without your expressed permission. However, as a result of legal developments, there are some exceptional circumstances in which therapists are required to communicate information about therapy to persons outside the family. These exceptions include the following situations:

- The client presents a clear and present danger to himself or herself and refuses to accept appropriate treatment.

- The client communicates to the therapist a threat of physical violence against a clearly identified or reasonably identifiable victim, or the therapist has a reasonable basis to believe there is a clear and present danger of physical violence against such a victim.

- The client introduces his or her mental condition as a defense in a legal proceeding.

- In child custody or adoption cases, the judge determines that the therapist has information bearing significantly on the client's ability to provide suitable care.

- The client initiates legal action against the therapist.

- The therapist has grounds to believe a child under the age of 18 or an elderly person (over age 60), or a handicapped adult, has been, or is at risk of being abused or neglected.

- The therapist has reason to believe that a child was prenatally exposed to a potentially addictive or harmful drug or controlled substance.

- The therapist has reason to believe a health care professional has engaged in professional misconduct.

- A judge orders the therapist to release client information.

It should also be noted that insurance companies reimbursing mental health services require information about these services. Therefore, if you are using insurance to pay for your child's treatment, information will be released to your insurer.

Financial Arrangements

- The initial appointment is a diagnostic intake session with a fee of $ _____. Subsequent therapy sessions are 50 minutes in length and have a fee of $ _____.

- We will follow your instructions to assist you in obtaining insurance reimbursement for our services. However, the final responsibility of paying for treatment is yours. This means that if insurance does not provide the reimbursement you expect or desire, the full balance is your responsibility.

I, _____, parent or legal guardian of _____, indicate by my signature on this form that I consent to the mental health treatment of this child, and that I understand and consent to the conditions described above.

Signature: _____   Date: _____

Consent for Psychological
Testing of a Minor

Clinician Qualifications

Psychologists have professional training in conducting psychological testing. You have the right to inquire fully about the credentials, education, and experience of your child's clinician and to have your questions answered to your satisfaction. In this practice, testing is provided either by a licensed psychologist or else by an unlicensed professional with training enabling him or her to perform testing under the supervision of a licensed psychologist. If your child's tester is not a licensed psychologist, you should receive an explanation of the supervision arrangement and the name and phone number of the supervisor. You have the right to discuss your child's testing with the supervisor.

What Is Psychological Testing?

Psychological testing consists of a number of procedures for learning about the mental functioning of the client. These functions include cognitive abilities, academic learning, emotions, thinking, and behavior. Your child's testing may examine some or all of these functions. You should be sure that you understand the purpose(s) of your child's testing by talking to your clinician.

Whenever possible, your clinician will use standardized tests, based on research, that are known to produce reliable and valid findings. Clinicians also sometimes use nonstandardized tests which are not research based, but which sometimes seem to produce useful information.

Confidentiality

Historically, mental health services were associated with complete confidentiality between the family and clinician. Currently, both law and professional ethics require therapists to maintain complete confidentiality of family information and communications in the vast majority of cases. In these cases, the therapist cannot release any information about your family without your expressed permission. However, as a result of legal developments, there are some exceptional circumstances in which clinicians are required to communicate information about mental health services to persons outside the family. These exceptions include the following situations:

- The client presents a clear and present danger to himself or herself and refuses to accept appropriate treatment.

- The client communicates to the clinician a threat of physical violence against a clearly identified or reasonably identifiable victim, or the clinician has a reasonable basis to believe there is a clear and present danger of physical violence against such a victim.

- The client introduces his or her mental condition as a defense in a legal proceeding.

- In child custody or adoption cases, the judge determines that the clinician has information bearing significantly on the client's ability to provide suitable care or custody and this information bears significantly on the welfare of the child.

- The client initiates legal action against the clinician, and client information is necessary or relevant to the clinician's defense.

- The clinician has grounds to believe a child under the age of 18 or an elderly person (over age 60), or a handicapped adult, has been or is at risk of being abused or neglected.

- The clinician has reason to believe that a child was prenatally exposed to a potentially addictive or harmful drug or controlled substance.

- The clinician has reason to believe a health care professional has engaged in professional misconduct.

- A judge orders a clinician to release client information.

It should also be noted that insurance companies reimbursing mental health services require information about these services. Therefore, if you are using insurance to pay for your child's testing, information will be released to your insurer.

Financial Arrangements

- Psychological testing is billed at the rate of $ _____ per hour, including test administration, scoring, interpretation, and report-writing. Additional fees may be charged for tests requiring computer scoring.

- We will follow your instructions to assist you in obtaining insurance reimbursement for our services. However, the final responsibility of paying for treatment is yours. This means that if insurance does not provide the reimbursement you expect or desire, the balance in full is your responsibility.

I, _____, parent or legal guardian of _____, indicate by my signature on this form that I consent to the psychological testing of this child by _____, and that I understand and consent to the conditions described above.

Signature: _____   Date: _____

CONSENT ISSUES FOR CHILDREN OF DIVORCED PARENTS

Obtaining consent to treat can be a complicated matter when the child's parents are divorced or separated. The basic fact is that consent must be obtained from the adult with legal custody of the child, and anything that complicates custody, or the agendas of the custodians, will complicate the consent process. Furthermore, complexity is not the only problem: The existence of conflict between the parents will make matters more difficult to handle, and the context of a legal dispute or proceeding will raise the stakes and magnify the consequences of any difficulties that occur or mistakes that are made.

The most simple and basic problem that can occur is that one parent wants the child to receive mental health treatment and one parent doesn't. When parents are married, the law assumes a general level of agreement between them regarding decisions for the child. It is sufficient to obtain written consent to treat from either parent, and it is acceptable to assume that the other parent does not oppose treatment.

When parents are divorced, the first question is who can provide legal consent. It is possible that the mother, the father, or both must sign a written consent form in order for treatment to proceed legally. The way to make this determination is to read the divorce decree. Parents should be asked to bring this document to the first session. A copy should be placed in the client's chart.

If legal custody is held by just one parent, the divorce decree will make that clear. Legally, parents with no custodial rights need not provide consent to treat. Custody, however, is not a dichotomous variable.

Currently, shared parenting (previously called joint custody) is the most common arrangement following divorce; for most judges, it is the presumptively optimal arrangement whenever both parents want custody and neither exhibits a personal problem likely to interfere substantially with child rearing. Therefore, providing services to children of divorced parents frequently requires clinicians to negotiate the legalities of shared parenting arrangements. These arrangements vary widely from case to case and must be ascertained by a careful reading of the divorce decree.

Several issues are common enough to deserve mention. First, it should not be assumed that only the parent with whom the child lives has legal custody. Sometimes, the nonresidential parent retains significant rights to influence decisions, such as obtaining treatment, made about the child. Shared parenting arrangements are often complex, assigning some rights and obligations to one parent, some to the other, and some to both. Divorce decrees are generally explicit about which parent(s) are to make decisions related to treatment, and this part of the document can usually be located easily. Failure to obtain written consent to treat from the parent or parents assigned this responsibility can have serious legal consequences (lawsuits) and professional consequences (ethical violations).

Although, legally, only the custodial parent needs to give consent, it may be clinically desirable for the noncustodial parent to be informed of and possibly also participate in the child's therapy. The main variable here is the extent of this parent's involvement in the child's life. If there is substantial involvement, it would usually be unfortunate for this parent to be unaware of the child's treatment. Such an exclusion typically results from an acrimonious relationship between the two parents. A withholding of this information by the custodial parent sometimes represents an acting out of anger toward the ex-spouse through the medium of child rearing; such situations can be emotionally harmful to children. If the child is told to keep the therapy secret from one parent, the result may be an uncomfortable, confusing situation for the child. Also, the noncustodial parent can sometimes make a significant contribution to the child's treatment, and this contribution will be lost if he or she is kept in the dark about the therapy.

Particularly when there is a custody dispute, the parent not informed about treatment may react angrily to the discovery of this information. There may be suspicion that therapy is part of an attempt to turn the child against this parent or to produce psychological evidence of problematic parenting. Secrecy tends to breed paranoia, and exclusion tends to produce anger. Furthermore, these suspicions are sometimes justified, if not in regard to the therapist's agenda then in regard to the parent obtaining child treatment without the knowledge of the ex-spouse. These suspicions can usually be ameliorated by providing the noncustodial parent an opportunity to give his or her side of the story and to participate in the child's therapy. Treatment is most likely to be effective if both parents are involved in efforts to help the child.

Clinical considerations interact with, but never negate, legal requirements. If custody is held by just one parent, the other parent can be informed about the therapy only with the permission of the custodial parent, and it is generally appropriate for the custodian, not the therapist, to do the informing. If the custodial parent does not want to do so, the clinician should find out why. Sometimes, the noncustodial parent has a history of inappropriate responses to sensitive information or of opposition to psychological interventions and, in such cases, it may indeed be best not to share information about the child's treatment.

If the parent's desire to withhold information seems based not on the preceding factors but on acrimony between the adults, the therapist should explain why communicating this information would be in the best interests of the child and of treatment. If the parent remains unwilling, the clinician's choice is between proceeding without the knowledge of the noncustodial parent and declining to take the case.

Authorization for Release of Information

I, _____, the parent or legal guardian of _____, hereby grant permission to _____, to:

___ receive from:_____

___ release to: _____

___ verbal   ___ written information concerning the past and present medical and mental health status and treatment of the above named child.

The purpose of this disclosure is:

___ Obtaining information for assessment

___ Obtaining information for treatment

___ Insurance or other third party reimbursement

___ Other: _____

Restrictions (if any):

_____

_____

_____

_____

_____

_____

_____

_____

_____

_____

_____

_____

I may revoke this consent at any time. Revocation does not pertain to previously made disclosures.

Signature: _____   Date: _____

Witness: _____   Date: _____

TREATMENT AUTHORIZATION FORM

Most third-party payers today (i.e., managed care companies, insurance providers, etc.) require some form of authorization to release funds for mental health treatment. Heretofore, telephone authorization has been commonly used, and it is not unlikely that direct computer communication will be used more in the future. Despite electronic transmission of data, it would be well for clinicians to have documentation of the sorts of information reported to third parties, both to protect themselves and ensure consistency in reporting information.

Many insurers have their own forms for such use, but the suggested document may be helpful to clinicians for their own records. The form provides for the basic information usually requested by third-party payers.

In reporting data on clients, there is always the issue of protecting confidentiality while offering minimal information that will be helpful in gaining appropriate benefits. Earlier we discussed this issue, but it is important to emphasize that confidentiality between therapist and client is the basis for doing productive work. This is a particularly sensitive area for children because they are the responsibility of their parents, who themselves have a legitimate claim to certain information about the child. During adolescence, in particular, trust in confidentiality is essential to the therapeutic relationship. At minimum, disclosure about what must be said to parents should be made to a child in treatment. Without such disclosure, later discovery of breaches in trust can be devastating to treatment, even after the treatment has been completed.

The controversy about what information is necessary to reveal to third parties will be an ongoing one for some time. Meanwhile, it is important to keep documentation so that data can be assessed and evaluated for its pertinence in making financial decisions.

In the following pages, we offer recommended authorization and recertification forms for managed care. Then, we provide an alternative, lengthier form.

Initial Managed Care Review

Patient: _____ Date: _____

ID #: _____ Gender: M F Age: _____

Provider: _____ ___ In network ___ Out of network

Address: _____

City: _____ State: _____ Zip code: _____

Phone: _____ Fax: _____ E-mail: _____

Presenting problems: _____
_____

History of present episode: _____
_____

Drug/alcohol problem? ___ No ___ Yes Prior behavioral treatment? ___ No ___ Yes

Risk to self: ___ None ___ Minimal ___ Moderate ___ High

Risk to others: ___ None ___ Minimal ___ Moderate ___ High

Dx: Axis I _____

Axis II _____

Axis III _____

Axis IV _____

Axis V _____

Receiving psychiatric medication? ___ No ___ Yes: _____

Goals	Interventions
1. _____	_____
2. _____	_____
3. _____	_____

Has primary care physician received information from you about this patient's care?

___ No ___ Yes

Other services needed (e.g., medication, psychological testing):   Referral

_____ _____

_____ _____

Authorization request:	No. of sessions	Period of time
Individual psychotherapy, 30 minutes	_____	_____
Individual psychotherapy, 60 minutes	_____	_____
Group therapy	_____	_____
Family therapy	_____	_____
Psychiatric medication evaluation	_____	_____

Subsequent Managed Care Review

Patient: _____   Date: _____

ID #: _____   Gender: M   F   Age: _____

Provider: _____   ___ In network   ___ Out of network

Address: _____

City: _____   State: _____   Zip code: _____

Phone: _____   Fax: _____   E-mail: _____

Progress/current symptoms/stressors: _____

_____

_____

_____

Risk to self: ___ None   ___ Minimal   ___ Moderate   ___ High

Risk to others: ___ None   ___ Minimal   ___ Moderate   ___ High

_____

_____

Dx: Axis I   _____

     Axis II   _____

     Axis III   _____

     Axis IV   _____

     Axis V   _____

Receiving psychiatric medication? ___ No   ___ Yes: _____

Goals	Interventions
1. _____	_____
2. _____	_____
3. _____	_____

Cumulative number of sessions since treatment began: _____   Year to date: _____

Authorization request:	No. of sessions	Period of time
Individual psychotherapy, 30 minutes	_____	_____
Individual psychotherapy, 60 minutes	_____	_____
Group therapy	_____	_____
Family therapy	_____	_____
Psychiatric medication evaluation	_____	_____

Is this likely to complete treatment? ___ No   ___ Yes

Treatment Authorization Form

Name: _____ Date: _____

ID #: _____ Gender: M F   Age: _____

Birth date: _____ Telephone number:

Address: _____

City: _____ State: _____ Zip code: _____

Provider ID #: _____ Subscriber ID #: _____

Provider name: _____ Subscriber: _____

Treating therapist: _____

Primary diagnosis: _____

Secondary diagnosis: _____

Initial history (to be completed with initial authorization only—include date of first session):

_____

_____

Precipitant of crisis (nature/date):

_____

_____

Suicidality/homicidality/psychosis (please include plan if stated):

_____

_____

Previous baseline functioning (brief description):

_____

_____

Previous mental health treatment (inpatient/outpatient and if available provide dates and intensity of services utilized):

_____

_____

Current medical problems:

_____

_____

Current GAF and supportive data:

_____

_____

Medication utilized (psychotropic and others):

Medication	Dose	Frequency
_____	_____	_____
_____	_____	_____
_____	_____	_____
_____	_____	_____

Treatment rationale: Please check appropriate item and provide details including type of psychotherapy implemented:

___ Crisis intervention: (brief intensive therapy to stabilize new or existing problems).

___ Remission maintenance: (longer term patients who continue to require therapy for acute symptoms).

Current mental status and plan of care (outline symptoms, goals, and interventions that will be utilized with this treatment plan and progress since initiation of treatment):

_____

_____

_____

Additional comments:

_____

_____

_____

Date of first session this year: _____

Number of sessions used since last authorization: _____

Frequency of visits (weekly, bimonthly, monthly, etc.): _____

Anticipated termination date (approximate): _____

Approved for _____ additional sessions through _____

Additional sessions approved through _____ to terminate treatment or arrange alternative financial plans.

Physician or case management comments:

_____

_____

_____

Signature: _____ Date: _____

CONFIDENTIALITY AND NOTE TAKING

The foundation of therapy is trust. Trust allows a client to feel that anything can be shared with the therapist without fear of negative consequences. For children, and especially for naturally suspicious adolescents, the trust issue is critical to the success of the therapeutic process. For example, much of the fear and unreality associated with fantasies can be alleviated by bringing them into "the light of day." To disclose fantasies and fears, children must feel secure that their disclosures will be kept within the walls of the therapy room.

However, it has become a legal fact that medical records are subject to subpoena, and anything written in the records of the psychotherapist is considered a medical record. What is communicated verbally between client and therapist is not subject to examination, although that privilege has been challenged in the courts from time to time. But any written notes are subject to scrutiny, even informal ones not necessarily meant for the official record.

Because of the possibility of subpoena, clinicians must use discretion and good judgment in deciding what to write down about therapeutic sessions. Particular care should be exercised around issues likely to be involved in some legal conflict, such as divorce or custody disputes. An excellent reference for those seeking guidance on confidentiality is D. N. Bersoff's *Ethical Conflicts in Psychology,* published by the American Psychological Association (1995).

PATIENT BILLING FORM

As a convenience to the agency, hospital, or other facility, as well as to the client being served, it is important to have a standard billing form that describes the services rendered and any codes necessary in billing third-party payers.

The sample form presented is not intended as a bill to the client, but as an internal document that provides the person in charge of billing with the information necessary to prepare an invoice.

Patient Billing Form

Name: _____   Date: _____

ID #: _____   Gender: M   F   Age: _____

Birth date: _____   Telephone number: _____

Address: _____

City: _____   State: _____   Zip code: _____

Date of appointment: _____   Time: _____ ____ A.M. ____ P.M.

Therapist name: _____   Provider number: _____

Supervisor's name: _____   Provider number: _____

Diagnosis: _____

Appointment: ____ Kept ____ Canceled ____ No show ____ Rescheduled (date) _____

Agency Code	Charge Code	Description	Unit Length	# of Units
Psychotherapy				
_____	_____	Initial evaluation	60–90 min.	_____
_____	_____	Psychotherapy	20–30 min.	_____
_____	_____	Psychotherapy	45 min.	_____
_____	_____	Psychotherapy	75–80 min.	_____
_____	_____	Family w/patient	45–50 min.	_____
_____	_____	Family w/out patient	45–50 min.	_____
_____	_____	Group	90 min.	_____
Psychopharmacology				
_____	_____	Psychopharmacology eval.	60–90 min.	_____
_____	_____	Pharmacology mgt.	15 min.	_____
_____	_____	Evaluation/mgt. established pt.	15 min.	_____
_____	_____	Evaluation/mgt. established pt.	40 min.	_____
Psychological testing and neuropsychology				
_____	_____	Psychological testing	60 min.	_____
_____	_____	Assessment of aphasia	60 min.	_____
_____	_____	Developmental test	60 min.	_____
_____	_____	Neurobehavioral status exam	60 min.	_____
Emergency services				
_____	_____	Psychiatric crisis eval.	60–90 min.	_____
_____	_____	Family w/out patient	45–50 min.	_____
Other				
_____	_____	Consultation (face-to-face)	60 min.	_____
Program director approval required				
_____	_____	Med. Interview with agency	15 min.	_____
_____	_____	Preparation of report	15 min.	_____

ALTERING RECORDS

Clinicians should rarely alter notes after they have been written and, if it is necessary to do so, this should be done carefully and properly. The key point is that alterations should involve only the addition of new writing and never the concealment of old writing. Any indication that a record has been altered with an intention to conceal represents, in and of itself, an instance of improper practice and, perhaps worse, will often suggest incompetent or unethical work with the client.

Any appearance of concealment should be strictly avoided. This impression is given when clinicians cross out their writing so heavily that it cannot be read. Therefore, therapists should never try to make it impossible for a reader to discern any writing in a chart, even if the writing was a mistake. The procedure for crossing out material is to draw a single line through the words and then to initial the change. In this way, the mistaken writing is identified as mistaken but is not removed from the record or concealed from the reader.

Generally, written material should be crossed out only at the time of its writing, and crossing out should occur only when the clinician momentarily fails to articulate his or her thoughts as intended. When this occurs, no date need be noted, since the date of the entry identifies when the crossing out occurred. On the rare occasions when changes need to be made after the time of writing, the later date should be indicated. When records appear to have been altered, if an examiner is unable to determine when this occurred, the worst case scenario will seem plausible; it may appear that the alteration occurred when the record was subpoenaed or otherwise requested.

Generally, material should not be crossed out if the revision involves a substantive change in the description or plan recorded in the chart. Substantive revisions should be accomplished not by deleting material but by adding a new entry that explains the new information, its conflict with what was recorded previously, and the new picture that has emerged. (E.g., "On 12/10/98, I recorded that Johnny's inattentiveness in school seemed attributable to ADHD. However, new information has emerged suggesting his inattentiveness is due to anxious rumination about his parents' divorce.") In this way, the record will accurately present the clinical situation as it unfolded, chronologically, to the writer.

Chapter 6

Intake and Assessment

TELEPHONE REQUEST FOR APPOINTMENT

Particularly in clinic settings, where telephone calls are taken by receptionists, requests for services need to be documented as accurately as possible. It is not unusual for someone calling for services to be anxious and concerned as to how much information needs to be given to obtain an appointment. Some callers attempt to give the entire history of a problem over the phone, and others may be afraid to impart any pertinent information. It is important to respect the privacy of a caller who prefers to give only minimal information. The fact of calling for an appointment may be enough information to at least have an intake interview. For those who wish to "spill their guts" over the phone, it may be best to discourage a long conversation and urge that they save the details for their visit.

Some callers may want to get the answer to their problem or their child's problem over the phone, without making an appointment. The skills of the receptionist are crucial in assuring the caller of the need for certain information and the importance of having an interview to provide other information and ask questions. If the caller is reluctant to go into the details of the complaint, it requires sensitivity on the part of the receptionist to take only the basic, minimal information necessary and assure the caller of privacy in making an appointment.

There are therapists and agencies that send out questionnaires to prospective clients before they come in for an interview. We discourage such practice, because it tends to force the potential client or parent of a client to reveal information before even meeting the personnel involved. An acquaintance who was referred to a therapist and asked to complete a fairly revealing questionnaire before he had his first interview commented, "I don't even know if I'll want to continue to see this guy, and he's asking all these personal questions." He canceled the appointment and saw someone who was willing to talk first.

Telephone Request for Appointment

Name: _____ Date: _____

ID #: _____ Gender: M F Age: _____

Birth date: _____ Telephone number: _____

Address: _____

City: _____ State: _____ Zip code: _____

Information recorded by: _____

Information supplied by (name and relationship to the client): _____

_____

Referring source: ___ Parent ___ Physician ___ Agency ___ Other _____

Address: _____ Telephone number: _____

City: _____ State: _____ Zip code: _____

Chief complaint:

_____

_____

_____

_____

Has the child been seen for this complaint? ___ Yes ___ No

If "yes," where: _____

_____

Medical history: ___ Yes ___ No   Approved by: _____

Program name: _____ No.: _____

Referral letter: ___ Yes ___ No Day: _____ Date: _____ Time: _____

Insurance carrier: _____ Policy number: _____

Group number: _____ Subscriber: _____

Referring MD/Auth no.: _____

Secondary insurance: _____ Policy number: _____

Group number: _____ Subscriber: _____

Referring MD/Auth no.: _____

PARENT QUESTIONNAIRES

Clinicians generally ask parents to complete some type of form prior to treatment, usually just before the initial intake appointment. These questionnaires vary widely in length, sometimes asking only for basic identifying and insurance information, and sometimes inquiring in detail about the child's development, medical and mental health history, current functioning, family environment, and goals for treatment. Decisions about the length of parent-completed forms should be based on an assessment of the costs and benefits of this information-gathering method, to be discussed.

Method, not content, is the key word here: The same questions can be asked orally, in an interview, or in writing, on a form. Therefore, clinicians should assess the advantages and disadvantages of receiving information in written versus oral form.

Having parents provide information in written form may have the advantage of efficiency. Because people can read faster than they can talk, parent questionnaires may save clinicians time. This method may also reduce the amount of writing clinicians have to do during intake interviews, since basic data has already been recorded by the parent. Thus, parent questionnaires enable therapists to accomplish some work without expending any of their time while the parent is in the waiting room.

Also, the task of providing biographical information about their child may help parents prepare for their imminent work with the therapist. Effective questions may help structure and organize the parent's thinking about their child's problems and goals for treatment. Because written answers are generally briefer than oral answers, questionnaires impose a certain discipline and may help parents focus on the most important points.

On the other hand, some considerations argue against use of lengthy parent questionnaires. First, because people talk faster than they can write, questionnaires may consume more time from parents than they save for clinicians. Parents expect to spend some time on forms when they begin child therapy, but if this extends beyond a certain point, the task will feel burdensome to many parents. Worse, the imposition of excessive paperwork on parents in this stressful, vulnerable position may communicate a lack of concern and empathy. Sitting in the waiting room of a therapist's office prior to their first appointment, most parents are looking forward, with anxiety and hope, to talking to an expert about their child's problems; under these emotional conditions, being required to complete a great deal of "paperwork" may put parents off.

Prior to the first meeting, parents may not be sure they will enter child treatment with the particular clinician about to be seen. Parents may want to ascertain whether the therapist has expertise in their child's specific problems, and they may want to see if they "click" with the clinician. Such parents may feel uncomfortable disclosing personal information, in writing, about their family.

Finally, use of parent questionnaires may involve a great deal of redundancy, since therapists will generally ask about presenting problems, past treatment efforts, family functioning, and so forth again in the interview. Asking the same question twice, once in writing and once in conversation, does not seem useful. The interview method, although more time-consuming for the therapist, is generally the more useful method because: (a) most parents are more accustomed to expressing themselves by talking than by writing; (b) the parent's manner of communicating information about the child, and the accompanying affect, can have informational value; (c) the interactivity of the interview process makes it possible to obtain much more relevant, specific and explanatory information than can be obtained by written responses to a form; and (d) the process of obtaining this information by interview can be part of alliance-building and initiating the treatment process.

Some parent questionnaires (e.g., Wiger, 1997) ask for frequency or severity ratings on a list of common childhood behavior problems. We do not recommend this practice, because such lists do not have a psychometric basis. If problem lists are desired, and these certainly can be useful, clinicians should use a standardized measure with norms (see Chapter 9 for examples).

For clinicians who want to obtain extensive information from parents in written form, we provide an example of a questionnaire that elicits a detailed history and other forms of information. Although we do not generally recommend use of this form, it might be useful in some clinical situations or for research purposes, although the instrument has unknown validity. The questionnaire can be filled out by the clinician or an assistant as part of an interview, or it can be completed by parents themselves.

Child and Family Information
Assessment Form

Name: _____ Date: _____

ID #: _____ Gender: M F Age: _____

Birth date: _____ Telephone number: _____

Address: _____

City: _____ State: _____ Zip code: _____

Information recorded by: _____

Information supplied by (name and relationship to the client): _____

_____

Presenting problem(s):

_____

_____

_____

_____

_____

_____

Child's Demographics

Child's full legal name: _____

Preferred nickname: _____ Ht: _____ Wt: _____

Hair color: _____ Eye color: _____ Birthplace: _____

Ethnic identification: _____ Year in school _____

Child's current residence: ___ With biological parents ___ Other: _____

If "other," please explain: _____

_____

Parents' Demographics

Father's name: _____ Birth date: _____

Biological parent? ___ No ___ Yes

Address: _____

City: _____ State: _____ Zip code: _____

Employer: _____

Address: _____ Telephone number: _____

City: _____ State: _____ Zip code: _____

Occupation: _____ Shift: _____

Mother's name: _____ Birth date: _____

Biological parent? ___ No ___ Yes

Address: _____

City: _____ State: _____ Zip code: _____

Employer: _____

Address: _____ Telephone number: _____

City: _____ State: ___ Zip code: _____

Occupation: _____ Shift: _____

Alternate Contacts

Emergency contact: _____

Telephone number: _____ Relationship: _____

Custody and Legal School District of Residence

Who has legal custody of the child? _____

___ Temporary ___ Permanent   Telephone number: _____

Address: _____ County: _____

City: _____ State: _____ Zip code: _____

If the Department of Human Service (Welfare) has custody (i.e., foster care placement), indicate the address of the parents at the time that the department took custody:

Parent's name: _____

Address: _____ County: _____

City: _____ State: _____ Zip code: _____

School district: _____

Parents' Marital History/Current History

Mother (Father)

Married: _____ To: _____

Separated: _____ From: _____

Divorced: _____ From: _____

Remarried: _____ To: _____

Other: _____

Family and Home Information

All persons currently living in the household:

Name	Birth date	Sex	Education level	Relationship
_____	_____	___	_____	_____
_____	_____	___	_____	_____
_____	_____	___	_____	_____
_____	_____	___	_____	_____

Natural parents of siblings who do not live in the household:

Name	Birth date	Sex	Education level	Relationship
_____	_____	___	_____	_____
_____	_____	___	_____	_____
_____	_____	___	_____	_____
_____	_____	___	_____	_____

Has the child lived with both parents since birth? ___ No ___ Yes
If "no," list changes chronologically (include residential placements).

From:	To:	Child lived with:

(Dates preferred, or child's ages).

_____	_____	_____
_____	_____	_____
_____	_____	_____
_____	_____	_____

If child is not living with both parents, please list reason:
___ Parents separated   ___ Parents divorced   ___ Parent deceased   ___ Other
If "other," please explain: _____
_____

If the child has a parent not living with the child, are there visitations?
___ No   How frequently: _____
___ Yes   Reason: _____

If there are any other children living in the family:
  A. Do any of them have physical or emotional problems?   ___ No ___ Yes
      If "yes," please explain: _____
      _____

  B. If "yes," have they received counseling or other forms of help? ___ No ___ Yes
      If "yes," please explain: _____
      _____

Is your house troubled by domestic violence?   ___ No ___ Yes
If "yes," please explain: _____
_____
_____

Does any family member have an alcohol or drug problem?   ___ No ___ Yes
If "yes," please explain: _____
_____
_____

Child's Developmental and Medical History

Were there any prenatal problems during pregnancy? ___ No ___ Yes

If "yes," please explain: _____

_____

Were there any problems during delivery? ___ No ___ Yes

If "yes," please explain: _____

_____

Birth weight: _____ lbs _____ oz.

Infancy:

  A. Were there any feeding problems? ___ No ___ Yes

      If "yes," please explain: _____

      _____

  B. Did your child sleep well? ___ No ___ Yes

      If "no," please explain: _____

      _____

  C. At what age was your child toilet trained? _____

      Were there any difficulties? _____

      _____

Milestones

At what age did your child:

_____ Wean   _____ Walk   _____ Sit up alone   _____ Talk

Were there any difficulties? _____

_____

Are there any problems with bedwetting/accidents? ___ No ___ Yes

      _____ Night   _____ Frequency

      _____ Daytime accidents   _____ Frequency

Please indicate age of child at the time of illness:

      _____ Chickenpox   _____ Mumps

      _____ Diphtheria   _____ German measles

      _____ Red measles   _____ Poliomyelitis

      _____ Rheumatic fever   _____ Scarlet fever

      _____ Tuberculosis   _____ Whooping cough

      _____ Pneumonia   _____ Other

      If "other," please explain: _____

      _____

Does or did your child ever have severe ear infections? ___ No ___ Yes

Does or did your child have allergies? ___ No ___ Yes

If "yes," to what does the child have allergies? _____

_____

How severe are the reactions? _____

Are there any special precautions that need to be taken? _____

_____

Does or did your child have lead poisoning? ___ No ___ Yes

If "yes," please explain: _____

_____

Please detail any of your child's hospitalizations:

Date	Age	Hospital	Reason	Length of stay
_____	_____	_____	_____	_____
_____	_____	_____	_____	_____
_____	_____	_____	_____	_____
_____	_____	_____	_____	_____

Please detail any medication history:

Date	Age	Drug	Reason	Physician
_____	_____	_____	_____	_____
_____	_____	_____	_____	_____
_____	_____	_____	_____	_____
_____	_____	_____	_____	_____

Family Medical History

Is there a history of any of the following in the family?

(Use "M" for mother's side; "F" for father's side.)

_____	TB	_____	Vision problems
_____	Birth defects	_____	Hearing problems
_____	Emotional problems	_____	Drugs
_____	Behavior problems	_____	Alcohol
_____	Mental retardation	_____	Diabetes
_____	Goiter (Thyroid)	_____	Convulsions/seizures
_____	Other		

If "other," please explain: _____

_____

Further comments: _____

_____

_____

_____

Agency Involvement/Service Treatment History

Please include (chronologically if possible) as complete a history as possible. Include agencies, physicians, counselors, institutions, therapists, etc.

Date	Age	Contact person	Services provided	Length of involvement
_____	_____	_____	_____	_____
_____	_____	_____	_____	_____
_____	_____	_____	_____	_____
_____	_____	_____	_____	_____

Has your child been court involved? ___ No ___ Yes

If "yes," please explain: _____

_____

Child's School History

School attendance:

	Date	Location	Problems (Y/N)	Reason for leaving
Preschool	_____	_____	_____	_____
Kindergarten	_____	_____	_____	_____
Grade 1	_____	_____	_____	_____
2	_____	_____	_____	_____
3	_____	_____	_____	_____
4	_____	_____	_____	_____
5	_____	_____	_____	_____
6	_____	_____	_____	_____
7	_____	_____	_____	_____
8	_____	_____	_____	_____
9	_____	_____	_____	_____
10	_____	_____	_____	_____
11	_____	_____	_____	_____
12	_____	_____	_____	_____

If answered "yes," to problems at any academic level, please detail here. Please give any information about treatment (if any) provided by the school at the time of occurrence:

_____

_____

_____

_____

_____

Typical Day Descriptions

A. On a school day, how does the child awaken? (by himself, by you, etc.)

_____

B. How does your child prepare himself for the day? (Who selects clothing, etc.?)

_____

C. Does the child ready himself quickly or require continual reminding?

_____

D. Does the child eat breakfast? ___ No ___ Yes   If so, who prepares it?

_____

E. Does the child watch the time and leave promptly or is frequent reminding necessary?

_____

F. Does the child come home for lunch? ___ No ___ Yes

If so, who prepares it? _____   Any problems? _____

Does the child watch the time and leave promptly or is frequent reminding necessary? ___ No ___ Yes

G. What does the child do after school?

_____

H. What occurs at dinnertime?

_____

   1. Does the family eat together? ___ No ___ Yes

   2. Is the child on time? ___ No ___ Yes

   3. Are there any problems during dinner? ___ No ___ Yes

   4. Does he/she participate in family conversations during meals? __ No __ Yes

If you answered "no," to any or these questions, or "yes," to question 3., please explain: _____

_____

I. What occurs after dinner?

_____

J. What happens at bedtime?

_____

K. What does the child do on weekends?

Friday night: _____

Saturday: _____

Sunday: _____

L. Does your family have much "family time" together (shopping, movies, etc.)?

_____

M. What activity do you enjoy most with your child?

_____

N. Does you child spend time with friends?

How much time on a weekly basis? _____

How many friends does you child have? _____

How do you feel about your child's friends? _____

O. Does your child belong to any clubs, groups, or organizations?

If so, which ones: _____

_____

P. Does you child have any interests or hobbies?

_____

Q. Does you child get an allowance? ___ No ___ Yes

If so, is it earned or given? _____

How does the child manage the money? _____

R. Does your child have specific chores? ___ No ___ Yes

If so, what are they? _____

Does you child try to avoid doing chores? ___ No ___ Yes

What does he do to try to avoid them (refuse, argue, etc.)? _____

_____

S. What methods do you use to discipline your child? _____

_____

How often is it necessary? _____

Does it work? _____

Behavior Checklist

Check the behaviors listed below that apply to your child within the past 6 months.

___ Makes no sounds.

___ Makes sounds but says no words.

___ Says a few words (specify: _____).

___ Speaks well but was slow in developing speech.

___ Repeats words over and over.

___ Was speaking but is no longer.

___ Is clumsy and awkward.

___ Is often drowsy.

___ Displays stereotypic behaviors (for example: wave hands in front of face, stares blankly, etc.) If so, which ones: _____

___ Engages in self-destructive behaviors:

    ___ hair pulling   ___ self-biting   ___ self-pinching   ___ head banging

    ___ other (please specify): _____

___ Has tantrums frequently.

___ Is hyperactive.

___ Seldom makes eye contact.

___ Demands too much attention.

___ Is often sluggish or slow moving.

___ Often has physical complaints (i.e., headaches, stomachaches, etc.).

___ Usually plays alone.

___ Disobedience, difficulty with disciplinary control.

___ Asks for help when it is not needed.

___ Gives up easily.

___ Does not interact appropriately with:

    ___ Parents   ___ Siblings   ___ Peers   ___ Others

___ Physically abuses:

    ___ Parents ___ Siblings ___ Peers ___ Pets ___ Toys ___ Furniture

___ Cries, whines, or pouts frequently.

___ Unreasonable noise, yelling.

___ Does not play with toys.

___ Rarely obeys requests, commands, etc.

___ Talks back to parents or other authority figures.

___ Reacts poorly when losing a game.

___ Unreasonable fears (heights, animals, the dark, etc.) Please specify: _____

_____

___ Does not recognize danger.

___ Runs away frequently.

___ Does not observe curfew.

___ Will not play alone.

___ Problems at mealtimes (disruptive, selective about foods).

___ Has a sleeping problem.

___ Cannot feed self.

___ Cannot dress self.

___ Is not toilet trained.

___ Is toilet trained but: ___ wet pants,   ___ soils pants,   ___ wets bed.

___ Frequent lying.

___ Sets fires.

___ Steals.

___ Seems to have a hearing problem.

___ Seems to have a vision problem.

___ Other physical handicap (specify: _____).

___ Negative comments to:

    ___ Parents   ___ Siblings   ___ Peers   ___ Others

___ Teasing of:

    ___ Parents   ___ Siblings   ___ Peers   ___ Others

___ Complaining.

___ Wanders off.

___ Sadness.

___ Complaints from neighbors.

___ Police contact.

___ School contact.

Please describe other problems: _____
_____
_____

What behavior distresses you the most? _____
_____
_____

What do you think are your child's greatest strengths? _____
_____
_____

Please describe the changes you hope to see in your child as a result of our work:
_____
_____
_____
_____
_____
_____
_____
_____

DEVELOPMENTAL HISTORY FORM

Recording developmental history can be as detailed as the interviewer chooses. In the vast majority of child assessments, a detailed history of all aspects of development is not necessary, although disruptions to the normal developmental process may be crucial in determining the etiology of emotional and behavioral problems.

Although there are many questions we could ask about every phase of a child's development, most parents do not have distinct, accurate memories of the developmental milestones children reach. Occasionally, parents keep a running record of events, usually for the first child. But with the realities of earlier and greater time away from home, children's histories are often lost in the myriad experiences of the past.

If a child has a difficult history, the details are more likely to be remembered. But for the average child, it may be difficult to pin down exact times and dates. Further, whether a child was born by natural or Cesarean delivery, whether walking began at 10 months or 15 months, or other developmental landmarks within normal limits, do not have important implications for later behavior.

It seems to us that the most important information to record is whether the developmental landmarks were reached within the normal limits and whether there were any separations, hospitalizations, or other potential traumas in a child's history. A form that could efficiently document any early problems would be valuable.

The form we recommend provides an opportunity for the parent to comment on the crucial times in the child's life—birth, walking, talking, and so forth—without necessarily giving exact ages, but simply stating whether the times were within normal limits. Also, by indicating the important preschool tasks that require parent-child interaction (e.g., eating, sleeping, toileting, and dressing), we give the parent an opportunity to recall whether there were any particular problems in mastering the tasks.

Notable events such as moves and hospitalizations should also be entered in any developmental history. The clinician needs to use good judgment in taking a developmental history by relating questions *to the presenting problem.* If a child is being evaluated for possible retardation or developmental delay, a careful history of ages at which developmental milestones were reached is important. For enuresis, a careful study of sleeping history is crucial in determining etiology. Histories should not be taken in a vacuum, but should be relevant to the problems under consideration.

Developmental History Form

Name: _____   Date: _____

ID #: _____   Gender: M   F   Age: _____

Birth date: _____   Telephone number: _____

Address: _____

City: _____   State: _____   Zip code: _____

Information recorded by: _____

Information supplied by (name and relationship to the client): _____

_____

Pregnancy: (circle)   Normal   Problem

If problematic, please explain: _____

_____

Delivery: (circle)   Normal   Problem   Weight: ___ lbs ___ oz.

If problematic, please explain: _____

_____

Early Developmental Milestones

Motor development (crawling, walking, etc.):   Accelerated   Normal   Problem

If problematic, please explain: _____

_____

Speech and language: Accelerated   Normal   Problem

If problematic, please explain: _____

_____

Toilet training: Accelerated   Normal   Problem

If problematic, please explain: _____

_____

Eating (weaning, using utensils, etc.):   Accelerated   Normal   Problem

If problematic, please explain: _____

_____

Dressing: Accelerated   Normal   Problem

If problematic, please explain: _____

_____

Sleeping (alone, thru the night, etc.):   Accelerated   Normal   Problem
If problematic, please explain: _____

_____

Peer and/or sibling socialization: Accelerated   Normal   Problem
If problematic, please explain: _____

_____

Hospitalizations: ___ No ___ Yes
If "yes," please explain (please include approximate dates and or age of the child at occurrence): _____

_____

Family losses (death, separation, etc.): ___ No ___ Yes
If "yes," please explain (please include approximate dates and or age of the child at occurrence): _____

_____

Relocations: ___ No ___ Yes

_____

_____

Family History

Maternal: Cognitive development   Emotional   Learning problems
If problematic, please explain: _____

_____

Paternal: Cognitive development   Emotional   Learning problems
If problematic, please explain: _____

_____

Siblings: ___ No ___ Yes
Please include ages and describe any problems with child/sibling interaction: _____

_____

_____

Notes:

_____

_____

_____

_____

_____

Substance Use History

Substance use and abuse is sometimes a major problem occurring in association with mental health difficulties. The relationship between drug use and mental health problems varies a great deal; for some clients, substance use is the central problem and mental health problems are minor and secondary; while, for other clients, emotional/behavioral problems are central and substance use is a minor and derivative problem. If drug and alcohol use is extensive and central to the client's maladjustment, treatment should be provided by a specialist in this area. However, many adolescents with mental health problems engage in some substance use, and these youth are most appropriately treated by a mental health professional with supplementary, but significant, expertise in drug and alcohol abuse.

Our substance use form can be administered either as a written questionnaire, completed privately by the client, or as an interview administered by the clinician. Use of a written format requires a fairly high level of reading ability from the client. A second important issue is client guardedness.

Client concealment of information is a major issue in substance abuse treatment, and the clinician's decision about whether to administer this form in writing or in person might influence the client's level of disclosure. Some clients may be more honest in writing, and some more open in an interview. We know of no reliable guidelines for deciding which of the two formats would be most likely to elicit honest recording. A possible tactic would be to ask the client which format would make it easier for him or her to be open. However, if the adolescent is manipulative (as many drug users are), he or she might respond by requesting the format he or she believes would make it easier to conceal information.

Another possible strategy would be to use both administration formats. The form could be administered first as a written questionnaire, and then there could be an interview following up on the client's response to each item. This strategy might result in the acquisition of the maximum amount of information obtainable through each format, which for clients as a whole is probably more information than would be obtained by either format alone. The interview could be an opportunity to use any externally supplied information to confront the client on any less than honest responses written on the form.

Regardless of administration format, because of the guardedness associated with substance use, clinicians should make maximum use of externally supplied information in conducting assessments. Client responses to the form should be compared with input supplied by parents and, if it is present, juvenile court and medical information (e.g., from drug testing). Evidence of discrepancies suggests that client disclosure was generally guarded, in which case the client's responses should be viewed as an underestimate of true substance use history.

This form is structured in two parts. First, there is a brief screening for substance abuse. If nothing problematic is in evidence, the assessment should stop there. If drug abuse is indicated, the full assessment should be administered.

The postscreening assessment is composed of several sections. The first four questions comprise the "CAGE" assessment, which is a set of questions commonly believed to differentiate casual substance use from serious abuse and addiction. The acronym inquires about past efforts to *C*ut down, *A*nnoyance when other people ask about the substance use, *G*uilt about the use, and taking substances in the morning, as an "*E*ye-opener."

The next sections inquire about several issues basic to substance abuse evaluation. Questions 7–10 are about withdrawal symptoms. Items 11 and 12 ask about loss of control. Numbers 13 and 14 inquire about attempts to control or end use. Questions 15 and 16 are about the solitary versus social contexts of use. Questions 17–23 inquire about the functional impact of substance abuse on the youth's life.

Substance Use History

Name: _____ ID #: _____ Date: _____

Screening

Please make a check mark by the drugs you have used during your life, and then explain when and how much you used the drug.

Substance	First used?	Last used?	Amount?
___ Alcohol	_____	_____	_____
___ Amphetamines ("speed")	_____	_____	_____
___ Barbiturates or sedatives ("downers")	_____	_____	_____
___ Cocaine (powder)	_____	_____	_____
___ Crack cocaine	_____	_____	_____
___ Hallucinogens (LSD or mescaline)	_____	_____	_____
___ Inhalants (glue or gasoline)	_____	_____	_____
___ Marijuana or hashish	_____	_____	_____
___ PCP	_____	_____	_____
___ Prescription anti-anxieties (Valium or Xanax)	_____	_____	_____
___ Prescription pain medicines	_____	_____	_____
___ Other: _____	_____	_____	_____

The following questions ask about a number of issues important in understanding alcohol and drug use. If you answer "yes" to a question, please explain your answer in the space provided. If your answer is "no," you can either give more information or not depending on whether there is something more that your therapist should know.

1. ___ No ___ Yes   Have you ever tried to cut down on your drinking or drug use?

_____

_____

2. ___ No ___ Yes   Are you annoyed when people ask you about your drinking or drug use?

_____

_____

3. ___ No ___ Yes   Do you ever feel guilty about your drinking or drug use?

_____

_____

77

4. ___ No ___ Yes   Do you ever have a morning "eye opener"?

_____

_____

If you reported no substance use, stop here. Otherwise, please answer the rest of the questions.

5. ___ No ___ Yes   Does it now take more alcohol or drugs than it used to for you to get the same feeling as in the past? How much more?

_____

_____

6. ___ No ___ Yes   Are you using more alcohol or drugs than 6 months ago?

_____

_____

7. ___ No ___ Yes   If you have ever tried to take less alcohol or drugs, did this make you feel sick?

_____

_____

8. ___ No ___ Yes   If you have ever tried to take less alcohol or drugs, did this make you feel nervous, angry, bored, or sad?

_____

_____

9. ___ No ___ Yes   If you have ever tried to take less alcohol or drugs, did this make it harder for you to go to school, do your work, or get along with people?

_____

_____

10. ___ No ___ Yes   Do you ever use alcohol or drugs to prevent these feelings or problems from happening?

_____

_____

11. ___ No ___ Yes   Have you ever used more alcohol or drugs than you intended or promised to?

_____

_____

12. ___ No ___ Yes   Have you ever taken a lot of drugs or alcohol in one night, day, or weekend?

_____

_____

13. ___ No ___ Yes   Have you ever wanted to quit using drugs or alcohol?

_____

_____

14. ___ No ___ Yes   Have you ever quit using for a while? If "yes," how long were you able to go before you started using again?

_____

_____

15. ___ No ___ Yes   How much of the time do you use drugs or alcohol alone?

_____

_____

16. ___ No ___ Yes   How many of your friends use alcohol or drugs?

_____

_____

17. ___ No ___ Yes   Does using drugs or alcohol take up a lot of your time, either because of what you need to do to get the alcohol or drugs, making sure no one finds out, being high, and/or recovering from the effects?

_____

_____

18. ___ No ___ Yes   Have you ever stayed away from school, activities, or other people because of alcohol or drug use?

_____

_____

19. ___ No ___ Yes   Have your grades gone down because of drugs or alcohol?

_____

_____

20. ___ No ___ Yes   Have you had problems with your family because of drugs or alcohol?

_____

_____

21. ___ No ___ Yes   Have you had problems with your friends because of using?

_____

_____

22. ___ No ___ Yes   Have you ever driven a car while high or drunk?

_____

_____

23. ___ No ___ Yes   Have you ever thought about hurting yourself or someone else while you were using or because of drugs and alcohol? Have you ever done something to hurt yourself or someone else?

_____

_____

Signature: _____   Date: _____

CULTURAL ASSESSMENT

Cultural (or "culturalogical") factors have received increasing attention in recent years, particularly in the public mental health system. The important insight has been that client difficulties and responses to treatment are influenced, not only by individual and family factors, but also by cultural factors such as ethnicity, country of origin, economic circumstances, and so forth.

By definition, cultural values, beliefs, and practices are shared by group members and transmitted intergenerationally. Cultural issues include religious beliefs, traditions, customs, views of mental health and illness, sex roles, desired level of family openness versus privacy, myths, taboos, beliefs about adult/child relationships, and attitudes toward receiving help. Factors such as these can be important to consider in both assessment and treatment. Clinician knowledge about the specific cultural features of clients' ethnic groups would undoubtedly enhance service quality.

Although these factors are sometimes important in clinical work, several problems are associated with assessing them in a formal way. First, the increasing emphasis on cultural assessment is not based on empirical findings indicating that treatment is more effective when there is explicit attention to cultural factors. This emphasis seems to derive largely from increased sensitivity to minority issues and a decrease in the ethnocentric assumption that the majority culture is normative in the United States. These values are certainly positive and reality based, but it is not yet clear how they would most effectively translate into improved clinical practice.

In some states, the public mental health system requires that diagnostic assessments include explicit interview questions about a list of cultural factors such as worldview, lifestyle patterns, and myths. Fulfilling these requirements is problematic, because cultural beliefs and values, by their nature, are usually so familiar, habitual, and assumed that they are difficult to articulate. This cognitive principle is illustrated by the saying, "If you ask a fish to describe his environment, the last thing he'll mention is water." As a result, it can be awkward to ask clients questions such as "What are some of the values in your culture?" These difficulties seem to be most pronounced for members of the majority culture, because these individuals usually have no self-conscious schema of their "culture," but the difficulties are similar for most minority clients. The strategy of dispensing with direct questions and collecting this information in the natural course of the interview will not work, because this information often does not reliably emerge explicitly in diagnostic interviews.

Another difficulty is that the issues examined in cultural assessments are not always functionally "cultural" in the strict sense of being determined by ethnic group membership rather than individual or family factors. Client worldviews, lifestyles, values, and spirituality are shared to varying extents by their respective ethnic groups and, thus, may be more or less "cultural" and more or less individual.

Questioning clients about their cultures has a cost in the interview time subtracted from discussion of the factors most reliably and directly related to assessment and treatment planning. These factors are numerous and often complex, so that covering them satisfactorily in a single interview is challenging under any circumstances.

Cultural issues seem to be among the plethora of psychological and contextual factors that emerge as important in the treatment of *some* clients. Effective treatment depends on clinician knowledge about and skill in addressing these factors. However, these issues are so numerous that it is inefficient to require their documentation on a form during intake, because then all clients must spend time talking about issues that are important only to some clients. A more pragmatic approach would probably combine alertness to these factors and readiness to address them as needed. This may be an occasion to remember that documentation is not identical with treatment, that forms are not capable of driving effective treatment in a comprehensive manner, and that clinician competence is better addressed by training than by forms.

Nonetheless, in many states, the public mental health system requires documentation of inquiry into cultural factors during intake, and there are certainly some clients within both the public and private systems for whom cultural factors are important to address at the outset. We offer a cultural assessment form to assist clinicians in fulfilling these purposes.

At intake appointments, parents are usually most interested in describing their child's functioning, discussing possible explanations, and exploring treatment options; these activities usually fill the time. Therefore, we do not suggest an explicit cultural assessment unless there is reason to suspect these factors need to be addressed immediately. One efficient strategy would be to give the parent or client control over whether session time is spent discussing cultural issues. Our form accomplishes this by presenting the cultural factors as a list of issues the parent or client may or may not feel need to be discussed as part of the assessment. The form asks the respondent to indicate which of these factors he or she thinks the clinician should know about. The clinician can then focus session time on just those factors. The form can be completed either by the parent, prior to the first appointment, or it can be completed by the clinician as part of the assessment interview.

Cultural Assessment

Name: _____ Date: _____

ID #: _____ Birth date: _____

Listed below are some questions that have to do with ethnic or cultural groups and that sometimes are important to take into consideration in child therapy. Please indicate which of these issues you think are important for your therapist to understand about your cultural or ethnic group. For the important issues, tell us some of the information you would like to discuss.

Lifestyle patterns (schedules, routines, way of life):

___ Want to discuss

___ Don't need to discuss

_____

_____

_____

_____

_____

Values and beliefs (right and wrong, what is considered important in life):

___ Want to discuss

___ Don't need to discuss

_____

_____

_____

_____

_____

Parent/child relationships (authority, respect, obedience):

___ Want to discuss

___ Don't need to discuss

_____

_____

_____

_____

_____

Ways to discipline children (rewards, punishment, discussion):

___ Want to discuss

___ Don't need to discuss

_____

_____

_____

_____

_____

_____

Religion and spirituality (church, synagogue, mosque, beliefs about God):

___ Want to discuss

___ Don't need to discuss

_____

_____

_____

_____

_____

Mental health and emotional/behavioral problems:

___ Want to discuss

___ Don't need to discuss

_____

_____

_____

_____

_____

Getting help from people outside the family:

___ Want to discuss

___ Don't need to discuss

_____

_____

_____

_____

_____

Views about the world (a good place, a bad place, a hard place):
___ Want to discuss
___ Don't need to discuss

_____
_____
_____
_____
_____

Thoughts about your cultural group:
___ Want to discuss
___ Don't need to discuss

_____
_____
_____
_____
_____

Clinician Notes

_____
_____
_____
_____
_____
_____
_____
_____
_____
_____
_____
_____
_____
_____
_____
_____

Signature: _____   Date: _____

Chapter 7

Diagnostic Evaluation

Once administrative functions have been completed, clinical work can begin in earnest, and this beginning typically consists of diagnostic evaluation, or intake assessment. This chapter presents forms for assessment purposes. In addition, we present guidelines for the content of diagnostic evaluations, including questions for assessment interviews of children, and an outline for psychodiagnostic report writing.

The interview questions correspond fairly closely to the sections of our recommended form and the headings of our recommended report outline. Thus, this chapter offers suggestions for obtaining as well as recording diagnostic information.

Even with proliferation of preprinted forms in the mental health field, narrative reports remain an important means of recording clinical information, particularly the detailed, extensive information generally involved in diagnostic assessment. Although full instruction in producing diagnostic reports is beyond the scope of this book, and is the province of professional education, we offer an organizational structure that may be useful for the narrative report genre of assessment documentation.

In many settings, diagnostic assessment and treatment planning are documented on one form. We present separate forms for these two purposes because the functions also sometimes occur separately. The two forms could easily be combined, if this is desired, simply by placing the treatment summary after the evaluation.

The interview questions and report outline cover most common issues and basic domains of child emotions, behavior, and symptomatology, but they are not exhaustive. Numerous specialized areas are not covered, and clinicians will need to fill in these outlines in response to the particular issues of each individual child.

Use of any predetermined structure—whether a set of interview questions, a report outline, or forms—if followed rigidly, will constrain clinician flexibility. These structures should be used as tools and not viewed as ends in themselves. The important goal is to record all important information, and doing so sometimes requires departure from a predetermined structure, either by adding headings or by writing more material than will fit into the space allotted by a form section. The forms we recommend were designed to fit most clients, but when fit is incomplete, the record-keeping practice should be accommodated to fit the clinical material, not the other way around. Information that does not fit into a form should be written on blank, lined paper and appended to the form.

The diagnostic interview questions are worded simply, and most of them can be used with children of average intelligence as young as 6 years old. With minor changes in wording, the questions can be extended up the age range into adolescence.

The questions are presented in their order of suggested use. Generally, the interview starts with questions about issues that are relatively easy to discuss and then works up to harder questions as rapport is developed and anxiety about the interview decreases. However, the emotional difficulty of topics varies greatly from child to child, and the interviewer should modify the order of the question accordingly.

Throughout this book, we present both recommended forms of our own design and alternative forms, usually adapted with permission from others. The recommended forms are briefer and may be more efficient for routine clinical work. The alternative forms may be preferable in some clinical situations or for research purposes, when more detailed, extensive information is needed.

Diagnostic Intake Interview Questions

1. Why did your mom/dad think you should come to see me?
   a. Do you agree or disagree with Mom/Dad about that?

2. Are there some problems in your life, or things you're unhappy about, or things you'd like to make better?

3. Help me get to know you a little bit: What kinds of things do you like to do for fun?
   a. Do you like sports? Which ones?
   b. What games do you like to play?
   c. What are your favorite toys?
   d. Do you have any favorite books?
   e. What TV programs do you like?

4. Tell me about your friends. (Perhaps get a description of one or two individuals.)
   a. What do you like to do with your friends?
   b. What kind of kids do you like?
   c. What kind of kids don't you like?
   d. Is it easy to get along with your friends, or is that a problem for you?
   e. Is it easy for you to make friends, or is that kind of hard?
   f. Do most kids seem to like you? Why or why not?
   g. Do you feel like you have enough friends, or do you wish you had more friends?

5. Do you like school?
   a. What do you like about school?
   b. Favorite subject?
   c. What don't you like about school?
   d. Least favorite subject?
   e. Is it easy to pay attention in school, or is it hard to pay attention? (Ask about mind wandering, sitting still, "ants in your pants," boredom.)
   f. Do you mind listening to the teacher and doing what he/she says, or is that a problem for you?
   g. Is it hard to do your homework, or is it no problem?

6. Tell me about your family (Mom, Dad, sibs, etc.).
   a. What does your mom do that you like?
   b. What does your mom do that you don't like?
   c. What does your dad do that you like?
   d. What does your dad do that you don't like?
   e. How do you get along with your brothers and sisters?

7. What are the rules in your house? Do you think they are fair, or do you think they're mostly stupid?
   a. Is it easy to do what your parents tell you, or is that hard sometimes?
   b. What do your parents do when you do what they want?
   c. What do your parents do when you don't do what they want? How do they punish you?
   d. What do you think of the rules at school? Are they mostly fair or mostly stupid?
   e. Is it easy to do what your teachers tell you, or does that aggravate you sometimes?
   f. Do you get in trouble sometimes? For what? Whose fault is it?
   g. Do you ever have problems controlling your temper?

8. What makes you happy?
   a. What makes you sad?
   b. What do you do when you feel sad?
   c. What do your parents do when you feel sad?
   d. What makes you mad?
   e. What do you do when you feel mad?
   f. What are you scared of?
   g. Are there things you worry about a lot?
   h. What do you do when you feel worried?
   i. All in all, how do you feel most of the time?

9. What do you think about yourself? How would you describe yourself? Do you like yourself?
   a. What do you like best about yourself?
   b. What don't you like about yourself?
   c. If you could change anything you wanted to about yourself, what would that be?
   d. Are there more things you like or more things you don't like about yourself?

10. (If evident depression or suicide risk) Have you ever felt so sad you kinda wished you were dead?
    a. (If yes) When? Why? What was going on? What were you thinking about?
    b. (If yes to 10) What happened? What did you do?
    c. (If appropriate) Have you ever thought about doing something to hurt yourself or to try to kill yourself? What?
    d. (If yes to c) Do you think you might do something like that? Do you have a plan to do something like that?
    e. (If appropriate) Have you ever done anything to hurt yourself or try to kill yourself? What?

11. Do you ever hear things that other people don't hear? What? When?
    a. Do you ever see things that other people don't see? What? When? (If in bed at night, seriousness may be lessened.) Have you ever seen a monster or a ghost?
    b. (If yes to item11) What do the voices say? Who are they?
    c. (If response to b) Do the voices ever tell you to do things? What? Have you ever done what they told you to do? Is it easy to keep from doing what they say, or is that hard?
    d. (If appropriate) Do you think the voices/things you see come from inside your head or from outside you?

12. Do your thoughts ever confuse you? Seem weird?

13. Do your thoughts ever go so fast that you can hardly keep track of them?

14. Do you ever do things fast, without thinking about it, and then afterward you wish you hadn't done it?

15. Are there certain little things that you feel you have to do over and over again?

16. Has anything really bad ever happened to you?

17. *Return to any aspects of the presenting problems that have not been adequately covered. Obtain information about problem:*
    a. *Onset.*
    b. *Frequency.*
    c. *Intensity.*
    d. *Duration.*
    e. What do you think causes these problems to happen?
    f. What do you think would help the problems get better? What could you do? What could your parents do?

18. Is there anything I haven't asked you about that you'd like to tell me?

Personality Evaluation Outline

A. Identifying information.

B. Reasons for referral.

C. Sources of information:
    1. Tests administered.
    2. Persons interviewed.
    3. Previous reports reviewed.

D. Behavioral observations:
    1. Description of child's appearance and behavioral style.
    2. Approach to the testing—
        a. Statement about validity of test results.
    3. Openness versus guardedness in interview.
    4. Mental status exam.
    5. Informative statements by child.

E. Test results (if reported test by test).

F. Evaluation results (if organized by content area):
    1. Ego/adaptive functioning—
        a. Reality-testing (accuracy: hallucinations and delusions).
        b. Thought process (e.g., disorganized, coherent, emotion-dominated, loose).
        c. Thinking style (e.g., impressionistic, constricted, abstract, elaborate, tangential).
        d. Impact of emotions/content on thinking.
        e. Congruence of affect and content.
        f. Coping/defense mechanisms and style.
    2. Mood and affect—
        a. Quality of mood (e.g., depressed, anxious, scared, angry, bored, excited, happy).
        b. Intensity of mood (mild, moderate, severe).
        c. Content: What the feelings are about.
        d. Affect (labile, wide or constricted range, flat).

3. Self-concept—
   a. Self-esteem level (high, average, low).
   b. Self-concept regulation (stability, range, fragility).
   c. Self-esteem issues (e.g., competence, goodness, lovability).
   d. Self-esteem content (specific areas of self-perceived strength and weakness).
   e. External influences on self-concept (parents, school experiences, life events).
   f. Self-concept strivings (achievement motivation, persistence, fear of failure, aspirations, confidence).

4. Interpersonal functioning—
   a. Generalized perceptions of other people (e.g., trustworthy, hostile, uncaring).
   b. Style of relating to other people (e.g., friendly, suspicious, manipulative, flirtatious).
   c. Differences based on characteristics of others (sex, age, role).
   d. Generalized expectations of relationships (optimism or pessimism, relationship quality).
   e. Object relations, underlying interpersonal scripts.

5. Family relationships—
   a. Parents.
   b. Siblings.
   c. Other relatives or important adult figures.
   d. General functioning of the family.
   e. Perceived marital relationship of parents.
   f. Divorce and custody issues, if present.

6. Important life events and circumstances not previously covered—
   a. Peer relationships.
   b. Romantic or sexual relationships or concerns.
   c. School.
   d. Medical conditions.
   e. Child abuse or neglect.
   f. Cultural factors.
   g. Economic stressors.
   h. Losses.

7. Mental health problems, symptoms, or issues not previously covered—
   a. Diagnostic issues.
   b. History.
   c. Frequency, duration, intensity of symptoms.
   d. Etiology and maintenance of symptoms.
   e. Environmental factors influencing symptoms.

8. Any relevant involvements in systems other than mental health—
   a. Special educational placement of services.
   b. Child protection.
   c. Mental retardation.
   d. Alcohol or drug.
   e. Juvenile justice.
   f. Other legal involvement.

G. Diagnostic formulation or summary.

H. Multiaxial *DSM-IV* diagnosis.

I. Recommendations:
   1. Needed level of intervention based on problem severity and client resources—
      a. Necessary intensity of services (outpatient, in-home, day treatment, partial hospitalization, residential, hospital).
   2. Psychotherapy—
      a. Modality (individual, family, group, parent training).
      b. Symptoms to focus on.
      c. Content issues.
      d. Specific approaches and techniques.
      e. Therapist style.
      f. Estimated duration and frequency.
   3. Any services needed in addition to psychotherapy—
      a. Psychiatric.
      b. Other medical.
      c. Neuropsychological.
      d. Mental retardation/developmental disabilities.
      e. Educational (including specific suggestions for teachers).
      f. Drug and alcohol.
      g. Speech and language.
   4. Any recommendations pertaining to life arrangements, circumstances, activities or routines—
      a. Custody or visitation issues.
      b. Recreational or social activities (e.g., Girl Scouts, art lessons, karate).
      c. Everyday routines (e.g., earlier bedtime, less TV, quiet place for homework).
      d. Increased or decreased contact with specific individuals.
      e. Basic recommendations for parents (e.g., stop triangulating, decrease alcohol use, reduce pressure for grades).

Child Diagnostic Evaluation

Name: _____ Date: _____

ID #: _____ Gender: M   F   Age: _____

Birth date: _____ Telephone number: _____

Address: _____

City: _____ State: _____ Zip code: _____

Information recorded by: _____

Information supplied by (name and relationship to the client): _____

_____

_____

Reasons for Referral

1. Chief complaint: _____

2. Any other presenting problems: _____

_____

3. Any additional referral purpose or context: _____

_____

Physical Description

_____

_____

_____

Current Functioning

1. Description of presenting problems and symptoms: _____

_____

_____

_____

_____

_____

_____

2. Functional impairment (impact of symptoms on life quality): _____

_____

_____

3. Strengths (areas of successful functioning): _____

_____

_____

4. Situational factors influencing presenting problems: _____

_____

_____

5. Child's view of his/her functioning if different from parents' view: _____

_____

_____

History

1. Onset of current episode (precipitating events if known): _____

_____

_____

2. Course of current episode: __ Improving __ Stable __ Deteriorating ___ Fluctuating

_____

_____

3. Functioning prior to current episode: _____

_____

_____

Previous Behavioral Health Treatment

1. __ No   __ Yes   If "yes," please include previous diagnoses, treatment, medications, and outcome: _____

_____

_____

_____

2. Special educational placement or services: __ No   __ Yes

_____

_____

3. Other services or systems (e.g., social service, legal, school counseling):
   __ No   __ Yes   _____

_____

4. Developmental delay or disorder: __ No   __ Yes

_____

_____

5. Past losses, trauma, and/or abuse: __ No __ Yes

_____

_____

6. Child's view of problem origin if different from parents' view: _____

_____

_____

Contextual Factors

1. Who lives in child's home: _____

_____

_____

   a. Child's relationship with mother: _____

_____

   b. Child's relationship with father: _____

_____

   c. Child's relationship with siblings: _____

_____

   d. With other family members: _____

2. Family mental health and substance abuse history: __ No __ Yes

_____

_____

3. Family history of trauma or abuse: __ No __ Yes

_____

_____

4. Cultural factors influencing problems or treatment: _____

_____

_____

5. School functioning (beyond problem description): _____

_____

_____

6. Peer relationships (beyond problem description): _____

_____

_____

7. Hobbies, interests, activities, tastes in music, books, and media: _____

_____

_____

Factors Related to Prognosis of Treatment

1. Child's motivation for change: _____
   _____

2. Any other prognostic factors: _____
   _____

Other Data

Data influencing case conceptualization (e.g., symbolic play, cognitive patterns, parenting practices, reinforcement contingencies, constructions of meaning, previously effective solutions, family and personal dynamics): _____
_____
_____
_____
_____
_____
_____

Diagnostic Summary and Formulation

_____
_____
_____
_____
_____
_____

Axis I   _____
Axis II   _____
Axis III   _____
Axis IV   _____
Axis V   _____

Recommendations

_____
_____
_____
_____

Signature: _____   Date: _____

Child Psychological Evaluation

Name: _____   Date: _____

ID #: _____   Gender: M   F   Age: _____

Birth date: _____   Telephone number: _____

Address: _____

City: _____   State: _____   Zip code: _____

Information recorded by: _____

Information supplied by (name and relationship to the client): _____

_____

Reason for referral: _____

_____

Physical Description

Identification given: _____   Ethnicity: _____

Ht. _____   Wt. _____   Eye color: _____   Hair color: _____

Other descriptors of appearance: _____

History

Current functioning. Symptoms and problems. Please include functional impairments (e.g., social, academic, affective, cognitive, memory, physical, etc.): _____

_____

Impairments as seem by professional: _____

_____

History of Presenting Problem

1. Onset: _____

   _____

2. Has there been any previous treatment? ___ No   ___ Yes   If "yes," please explain:

   _____

   _____

Course of illness: ___ Improving   ___ Stable   ___ Deteriorating

Please explain: _____

_____

Events affecting frequency and duration: _____

_____

Precipitating factors (e.g., emotional, environmental, social): _____

_____

Previous/current mental health treatment (and its effectiveness): _____

_____

Current/previous medications and dosages:

Medication	Dosage	Reason prescribed	Currently using?	Effective?
_____	_____	_____	___ No ___ Yes	___ No ___ Yes
_____	_____	_____	___ No ___ Yes	___ No ___ Yes
_____	_____	_____	___ No ___ Yes	___ No ___ Yes
_____	_____	_____	___ No ___ Yes	___ No ___ Yes

Hospitalizations/treatment (please include dates): _____

_____

Current special services (e.g., social, educational, legal): _____

_____

Note and resolve any discrepancies between information given and what records indicate:

_____

_____

Activities of Daily Living

1. Current level of daily functioning (hobbies, interests, and scope of interests):

Hobby/interest	Frequency	Duration
_____	_____	_____
_____	_____	_____
_____	_____	_____
_____	_____	_____

Realistic, appropriate, compare with previous functioning: _____

_____

2. Activities:

Do you live in a: ___ house   ___ apartment   ___ condo   ___ mobile home

Who else lives there? (Please include relationship and age of other household members): _____

_____

3. Living situation:

Describe living conditions (with family, alone, crowded, functional, group home, etc.): _____

4. Ability to relate to others:

(e.g., aggressive, deferent, shy, defiant, avoidant, oppositional, normal):

Adults: _____   Authority figures: _____

Teachers: _____   Police: _____

Peers: _____   Family: _____

Neighbors: _____   Younger children: _____

How did the client relate to examiner and/or office personnel during visit? _____

_____

5. Daily schedule:

Please list what child does in a typical day (i.e., chores, TV, play, yard work, hobbies, employment, school, etc.). Please list in time order:

Time	Activity
_____	_____
_____	_____
_____	_____
_____	_____

Notes: _____

_____

_____

6. Substance abuse:

Detailed history and current information regarding substance abuse patterns (if applicable).

Age of onset: _____   Substances used historically: _____

History of usage: _____

_____

7. Self-help skills:

(Describe child' ability and assistance needed).

Dressing: _____

Grooming: _____

Feeding self: _____

Avoiding dangers: _____

Independent activities outside the home: _____

Making change ($): _____

Taking the bus: _____

8. Concentration, persistence, and pace (ages 3–18):

(Describe ability to concentrate, attend, persist, and complete tasks in a timely manner.) _____

_____

_____

Developmental Milestones

Pregnancy: ___ normal   ___ problematic

If problematic, please explain: _____

_____

Behavior	Age	Comments
Walking	_____	_____
Talking	_____	_____
Toilet trained	_____	_____

Age Group of Child

___ A (0–3)   ___ B (3–6)   ___ C (6–16)   ___ D (16–18)

Please provide information on how the child's symptoms impact performance of age-appropriate developmental tasks and functional capacity: _____

_____

_____

1. Birth to 3 years:

Locomotion (e.g., crawling, walking, sitting up, pulling oneself into and upright position, etc.): _____

_____

Language (e.g., vocalization, imitative sounds, talking, receptive skills, ability to follow commands, etc.): _____

_____

Gross motor competence (e.g., reaching, throwing, jumping, grasping, pedaling a tricycle, etc.): _____

_____

Fine motor competence (e.g., pincer grip, grasp, colors, uses writing utensils, reaches for objects, etc.): _____

_____

Behavioral-social (e.g., excessive crying, hyperactivity, fear response to separation, aggressiveness, temper outbursts, lethargy, inability to bond, autistic features, efforts at toilet training, ability to relate to peers, siblings, parents, etc.): _____

_____

2. 3 to 6 years:

Locomotion (describe any abnormalities as listed above, describe development of competency): _____

_____

Communication (speech development, ability to form sentences, clarity of speech, expressive skills, receptive skills, ability to communicate needs, ability to respond to commands, ability to follow simple directions): _____

_____

Motor (describe any abnormalities in fine or gross motor activity, child's ability to use scissors, color within lines, copy simple designs such as a circle or square. Include observations of any impairments in coordination and/or balance): _____

_____

Social/emotional (toilet training, aggressiveness, hyperactivity, ability to play with others, to share with others, to separate from caregivers, competency in feeding, dressing, and grooming skills, temper outbursts, night terrors, manifestations of anxiety, phobias, fear response to separation, observations of bizarre of aberrant behavior): _____

_____

Ability to concentrate, attend, persist, and complete tasks in a timely manner: _____

_____

3. 6 to 16 years:

Locomotion (describe any abnormalities in walking, running, mobility): _____

_____

Communication (reading, writing, receptive and expressive language skills, speech): _____

_____

Social/emotional (relationships to peer group and to school authority figures). Any evidence of oppositional, rebellious, antisocial, aggressive behavior, withdrawal. Assess stress tolerance, potential employment, potential for substance abuse, impairment in reality testing. Comment on identity issues and development of body awareness: _____

_____

Ability to concentrate, attend, persist, and complete tasks in a timely manner: _____

_____

Other (comment on any volunteer or after-school work, vocational training, jobs associated with the school program in terms of work and ability to persist, complete tasks, and respond appropriately to supervision): _____

_____

_____

Parents or caregivers leave interview room at this time.

Mental Status Exam

Clinical Observations

1. Appearance:

   Posture: _____

   Clothing: _____

   Grooming: _____

   Hair: _____

   Nails: _____

   Health: _____

   Demeanor: _____

   Other: _____

2. Activity level:

   Mannerisms: _____

   Tics: _____

   Agitated: _____

   Hyperactivity: _____

   Picking: _____

   Limp: _____

   Rigid: _____

   Gestures: _____

   Combative: _____

   Gait: _____

   Other: _____

3. Speech:

   Slow: _____

   Rapid: _____

   Pressured: _____

   Hesitant: _____

   Monotonous: _____

   Slurred: _____

   Stuttering: _____

   Mumbled: _____

   Echolalia: _____

Neologisms: _____

Vocabulary: _____

Repetition: _____

Details: _____

Pitch: _____

Volume: _____

Reaction time: _____

Other: _____

  4. Attitude toward examiner:

Cooperative: _____

Ingratiating: _____

Attentive: _____

Interested: _____

Frank: _____

Defensive: _____

Hostile: _____

Playful: _____

Evasive: _____

Other: _____

Stream of Consciousness and Thought Processes

Number of ideas: _____

Flight of ideas: _____

Hesitancy: _____

Spontaneity: _____

Re: Questions answered:

Relevance: _____

Cause/effect: _____

Coherent: _____

Logical: _____

Rambling: _____

Evasive: _____

Language: _____

Speech: _____

Neologisms: _____

Associations: _____

Loose: _____

Clanging: _____

Thought Content

Obsessions: _____

Compulsions: _____

Phobias: _____

Suicide: _____

Homicide: _____

Antisocial: _____

Other: _____

Notes: _____

1. Thought disturbances:
    a. Delusions:
       Persecutory: _____
       Somatic: _____
       Grandeur: _____
    b. Ideas of reference:
       Controlled by others: _____
       Thought broadcasting: _____
       Antisocial: _____
       Validity: _____
       Content: _____
       Mood: _____
       Bizarre: _____
       Other: _____

2. Hallucinations/illusions:

    Example: Do you hear voices? Where? When do you recognize them? What do they say? Do you see things that other people do not? Do you experience particular tastes or smells? Are they agreeable or disagreeable? Are there strange sensations or feelings, such as electricity going through the body or odd sexual sensations?

    Voices: _____
    Visions: _____
    Content: _____
    Setting: _____
    Sensory system: _____
    Other: _____

3. Depersonalization:
    Detachment: _____
    Observations/evidence of thought disorder: _____

    _____

Affect/Mood

  A. Frequency/intensity in daily life (specific examples of impairments/strengths, frequency, duration).

Affection: _____

_____

Anger: Anger management issues, property destruction, explosive behaviors, assultive behaviors. How does the client act regarding anger expression? _____

_____

Panic attacks: 4 or more (abrupt development of palipitations, sweating, trembling, shortness of breath, feeling of choking, chest pain, nausea, dizziness light-headedness, derealization, fear of losing control, fear of dying, numbness, chills, or hot flashes): _____

_____

Anxiety: GAD: 3 or more, most of time, past 6 months (restlessness, easily fatigued, concentration difficulty, irritability, muscle tension, sleep disturbance): _____

_____

Depression: MDE: 5 or more (usual depressed mood, anhedonia, weight +/- 5% per month with daily appetite +/-, sleep +/-, psychomotor +/-, fatigue, worthlessness/guilt, concentration, death/suicidal ideation): _____

_____

Crying: _____

_____

Suicidal: _____

_____

Withdrawal: _____

_____

Irritability: _____

_____

Other: _____

_____

Mania: 3+ (Grandiosity, low sleep, talkativeness, flight of ideas, distractibility, goals/agitation, excessive pleasure.): _____

_____

Range of affect: ___ concordant ___ discordant ___ with speech/ideas

Predominant mood: _____

Fluctuations: _____

Affective expression: _____

B. Attention span during interview:

Fidgety	___ No	___ Yes
Remains seated	___ No	___ Yes
Distracted	___ No	___ Yes
Blurts answers	___ No	___ Yes
Follows directions	___ No	___ Yes
Shifts focus	___ No	___ Yes
Talks excessively	___ No	___ Yes
Interrupts	___ No	___ Yes
Listens	___ No	___ Yes
Impulsivity	___ No	___ Yes
Other	___ No	___ Yes

C. Rule out clinical syndromes:

Anxiety disorders, depression, autism, pervasive developmental disorders, ADHD, conduct/behavioral disorders, specific developmental disorders, learning disorders, incipient psychotic process, and substance abuse: _____

_____

_____

Sensorium/Cognition

1. Younger children (Provide a basic assessment of the following):

Consciousness (ability to concentrate, confusion, attending): _____

_____

Orientation (time, place, and person): _____

_____

Memory (recent, long-term, simple facts): _____

_____

Estimated intellectual functioning: _____

_____

Notes: _____

_____

2. Older children:

a. Reality contact (how in touch with reality is the client?): _____

_____

Is client able to hold normal conversations? ___ No ___ Yes

Notes: _____

_____

b. Orientation X3 (time, place, and person): _____

_____

c. Concentration:

Count to 40 by 3's. (1, 4, 7, 10, 13, 16, 19, 22, 25, 28, 31, 34, 37, 40)

Number of errors: ___   Time between digits: ___   Notes: _____

Count backward by 7's from 100. (100, 93, 86, 79, 72, 65, 58, 51, 44, 37, 30 . . .)

Number of errors: ___   Time between digits: ___   Notes: _____

2 + 3 = ___   3 − 2 = ___   4 + 8 = ___   9 + 12 = ___

4 x 3 = ___   7 x 4 = ___   12 x 6 = ___   65 − 5 = ___

Digits forward and backward:

Fwd: 42 ___   368 ___   6385 ___   96725 ___   864972 ___   5739481 ___

Bwd: 91 ___   582 ___   9147 ___   63892 ___   839427 ___   7392641 ___

Fwd. = _____   Bwd. = _____   Evaluation = _____

___ Below average   ___ Average   ___ Above average

d. Memory:

Remote memory (childhood data):

Schools attended: _____

Teachers' names/faces: _____

Street client grew up on: _____

Mother's maiden name: _____

Significant historical events relevant to child's lifetime: _____

Recent memory:

Activities past few months: _____

Past few days: _____

Yesterday (events, meals, etc.): _____

Today (events, meals, etc.): _____

e. Information (knowledge of current events):

Does the client: ___ read newspaper? How often? _____

                   ___ TV/radio news? How often? _____

Name current local/national news: _____

President's name: _____

List three large cities: _____

f. Judgment

"First one in theater to see smoke and fire": _____

"Find stamped envelope in street": _____

g. Abstractive capacity:

           Proverbs   Interpretation given

    "Rolling stone gathers no moss"   _____

    "Early bird catches the worm"   _____

    "Strike while the iron is hot"   _____

    Abstract versus concrete interpretations: _____

h. Insight (awareness of issues: what level?):

    ___ Complete denial   ___ Slight awareness   ___ Awareness, but blames others

    ___ Intellectual insight, but few changes likely

    ___ Emotional insight, understanding, changes can occur

    Notes on client's level of insight to problems: _____

    _____

i. Intellectual level/education/IQ estimate:

    Grade in school ___ Did client ever repeat a grade? ___ No ___ Yes GPA ___

    Special education classes: _____

    Intelligence: _____

    General knowledge: _____

    Selective nature of Sx: _____

    Observations (pain, fatigue, gait, dizziness): _____

    Comments: _____

j. Adverse factors affecting the child's ability to function (e.g., pain, side effects of medications, dysfunctional family, abuse, physical impairments, etc.): _____

    _____

6. Testing results:

    _____

7. Assessment:

Summary and diagnostic findings (tie together history and mental status findings and relate to diagnosis. Include onset of current Sx of the conditions and prognosis).

    _____

Axis I   _____

Axis II   _____

Axis III   _____

Axis IV   _____

Axis V   _____

Note: For Social Security do not make a statement as to whether the child is disabled.

Psychiatric Evaluation Form

Name: _____   Date: _____

ID #: _____   Gender: M F   Age: _____

Birth date: _____   Telephone number: _____

Address: _____

City: _____   State: _____   Zip code: _____

Information recorded by: _____

Information supplied by (name and relationship to the client): _____

_____

Telephone home: _____   Referred by: _____

Telephone work: _____   Primary MD: _____

Insurance carrier: _____

Address: _____

City: _____   State: _____   Zip code: _____

Policy number: _____   Account number: _____

1. Chief complaint: _____

   _____

   _____

   _____

   Onset of current symptoms: _____

   Parent request: _____

   Child request: _____

2. History of present illness: _____

   _____

   _____

   _____

   Current psychotropic medications:

   Medication: _____   Dose: _____

   Medication: _____   Dose: _____

   Medication: _____   Dose: _____

109

3. Current psychiatric review of symptoms:

___ Depressed mood	___ Increased goal-directed acts	___ Stealing
___ Anhedonia	___ Increased pleasurable acts	___ Lying
___ Appetite change	___ Elevated mood	___ Fire setting
___ Sleep change	___ Impatient	___ Truancy
___ Initial insomnia	___ Blurts out answers	___ Breaking in
___ Middle insomnia	___ Difficulty following instructions	___ Weapons
___ Early waking	___ Difficulty sustaining tasks	___ Separation anxiety
___ Hypersomnia	___ Fighting	___ Panic symptoms
___ Anergia	___ Loses things	___ Phobias
___ Worthlessness	___ Listens poorly	___ Encopresis
___ Distractibility	___ Interrupts	___ Enuresis
___ Pressured speech	___ Difficulty playing quietly	___ Unstable relationships
___ Racing thoughts	___ Fidgety	___ Self-mutilatory behaviors
___ Grandiose	___ Difficulty remaining seated	___ Concentration difficulty

Suicide: ___Ideation   ___Plan/intent   ___Attempt

Homicide: ___Ideation   ___Plan/intent   ___Attempt

If yes, please describe: _____

_____

Abuse history: ___ Physical   ___ Sexual   ___ Outside agency involvement

Substance abuse: ___ No ___ Yes

If yes, please describe: _____

_____

4. Past psychiatric history:

___ Depression	___ Antisocial	___ Meds
___ Suicide	___ Substance abuse	___ Inpatient hospital
___ Bipolar disorder	___ PTSD	___ Day hospital
___ Psychosis	___ Sexual/physical abuse	___ Residential
___ Anxiety disorder	___ Seizure	___ Other
___ ADHD	___ Tics	___ Number of hospitalizations: _____
___ OCD	___ Dev/LD	___ Other: _____
___ Eating disorder	___ Therapy	

If yes, please describe: _____

_____

5. Medical history:

   ___ Active medical problems   ___ Allergies

   ___ Major medical illness   ___ Other medical problems

   ___ Medications

   If yes, please describe: _____

   _____

6. Family history:

   Family demographics:

   Father's full name: _____ Age: _____

   Years of education: _____ General health: _____

   Occupation: _____

   Mother's full name: _____ Age: _____

   Years of education: _____ General health: _____

   Occupation: _____

   Significant other's name: _____ Age: _____

   Years of education: _____ General health: _____

   Occupation: _____

   Brother(s): _____ Age(s): _____

   Sister(s): _____ Age(s): _____

   Race: ___ White ___ Black ___ Hispanic ___ Oriental ___ Portuguese ___ Other

   Primary language: ___ English ___ Spanish ___ French ___ Other

   Patient's living situation:

   ___ Biological intact family   ___ Group home

   ___ Biological single parent   ___ Shelter

   ___ Adoptive family   ___ Residential

   ___ Foster home   ___ Homeless

   ___ Lives alone   ___ Other: _____

   Family illness history:

___ Depression	___ Eating disorder	___ Bipolar disorder
___ Suicide	___ PTSD	___ OCD
___ Anxiety disorder	___ Seizure	___ Substance abuse
___ ADHD	___ Tics	___ Psychosis
___ Antisocial	___ Meds	___ Dev/LD
___ Sex/phys abuse	___ Therapy	___ Other

   If yes, please describe: _____

   _____

Environmental stressors:

___ Marital stressors   ___ Illness   ___ Financial stressors

___ Div/sep   ___ Foster care   ___ Other stressors

___ Death   ___ DSS

If divorced, separated, foster care, or DSS, please complete:

Onset: _____   Living situation: _____

Legal custody: _____   Visitation: _____

7. School/work/social problems:

___ School attendance problems   ___ Repeated grades   ___ Peer problems

___ Appropriate grade level   ___ Academic problems   ___ Other

___ Behavior problems   ___ Special help

If yes, please describe: _____

_____

8. Developmental problems:

___ Prenatal   ___ Perinatal   ___ Infancy   ___ Milestones

If yes, please describe: _____

_____

9. Mental status examination (Appearance/description):

Brief Psychiatric Rating Scale: Check Rating

1 = Not present   2 = Very mild   3 = Mild   4 = Moderate
5 = Moderately severe   6 = Severe   7 = Extremely severe

1. Uncooperative—negative, resistant, difficult to manage.

___ 1 ___ 2 ___ 3 ___ 4 ___ 5 ___ 6 ___ 7

2. Manipulative—lying, cheating, exploitive of others.

___ 1 ___ 2 ___ 3 ___ 4 ___ 5 ___ 6 ___ 7

3. Disoriented—confusion over people, places, or things.

___ 1 ___ 2 ___ 3 ___ 4 ___ 5 ___ 6 ___ 7

4. Distractible—poor concentration, short attention span, reactible to peripheral stimuli.

___ 1 ___ 2 ___ 3 ___ 4 ___ 5 ___ 6 ___ 7

13. Anxiety—clinging behavior, separation anxiety, occupation with anxiety topics, fears or phobias.

___ 1 ___ 2 ___ 3 ___ 4 ___ 5 ___ 6 ___ 7

14. Tension—nervousness, fidgetiness, nervous movements of hands and feet.

___ 1 ___ 2 ___ 3 ___ 4 ___ 5 ___ 6 ___ 7

15. Depressive mood—sad, tearful, depressive demeanor.

___ 1 ___ 2 ___ 3 ___ 4 ___ 5 ___ 6 ___ 7

16. Sleep difficulties—inability to fall asleep, intermittent awakenings, shortened or lengthened sleep time.

___ 1 ___ 2 ___ 3 ___ 4 ___ 5 ___ 6 ___ 7

5. Hyperactive—excessive energy expenditure, frequent changes in posture, perpetual motion.

___ 1 ___ 2 ___ 3 ___ 4 ___ 5 ___ 6 ___ 7

6. Stereotype—rhythmic, repetitive, manneristic movements or posture.

___ 1 ___ 2 ___ 3 ___ 4 ___ 5 ___ 6 ___ 7

7. Speech—loud, excessive, or pressured speech.

___ 1 ___ 2 ___ 3 ___ 4 ___ 5 ___ 6 ___ 7

8. Underproductive speech—minimal, sparse, inhibited verbal response pattern or weak low voice.

___ 1 ___ 2 ___ 3 ___ 4 ___ 5 ___ 6 ___ 7

9. Speech deviance—inferior level of speech development, underdeveloped vocabulary, mispronunciations.

___ 1 ___ 2 ___ 3 ___ 4 ___ 5 ___ 6 ___ 7

10. Emotional withdrawal—unspontaneous relations to examiner, lack or peer interaction, hypoactivity.

___ 1 ___ 2 ___ 3 ___ 4 ___ 5 ___ 6 ___ 7

11. Blunted affect—deficient emotional expressionism, blankness, flatness of affect.

___ 1 ___ 2 ___ 3 ___ 4 ___ 5 ___ 6 ___ 7

12. Hostility—angry or suspicious affect, belligerence, accusations, and verbal condemmations of others.

___ 1 ___ 2 ___ 3 ___ 4 ___ 5 ___ 6 ___ 7

17. Appetite/weight—significant appetite/weight gains or losses.

___ 1 ___ 2 ___ 3 ___ 4 ___ 5 ___ 6 ___ 7

18. Feelings of inferiority—lacking self-confidence, feelings of personal inadequacy.

___ 1 ___ 2 ___ 3 ___ 4 ___ 5 ___ 6 ___ 7

19. Suicidal ideation—thoughts, threats, or action.

___ 1 ___ 2 ___ 3 ___ 4 ___ 5 ___ 6 ___ 7

20. Peculiar fantasies—recurrent, odd, unusual, or autistic ideations.

___ 1 ___ 2 ___ 3 ___ 4 ___ 5 ___ 6 ___ 7

21. Delusions—ideas of reference, persecutory, grandiose ideation.

___ 1 ___ 2 ___ 3 ___ 4 ___ 5 ___ 6 ___ 7

22. Hallucinations—visual, auditory, or other hallucinatory experiences or perceptions.

___ 1 ___ 2 ___ 3 ___ 4 ___ 5 ___ 6 ___ 7

23. Thought processes—looseness of associations, ideas of reference, flight of ideas, tangentiality, circumstantiality, thought intersection, blocking.

___ 1 ___ 2 ___ 3 ___ 4 ___ 5 ___ 6 ___ 7

Mental status exam comments: _____

10. Formulation:

_____

11. *DSM-III-R/IV* diagnosis:

Axis I codes	Axis I disorder(s)
1. _____	_____
2. _____	_____
3. _____	_____
4. _____	_____
5. _____	_____

Axis II: _____

_____

Axis III: _____

_____

Axis IV:

___ None = no acute events or enduring circumstances that may be relevant to the disorder.

___ Mild = broke up with girlfriend or boyfriend; change in school; overcrowded living quarters; family arguments.

___ Moderate = expelled form school; birth of sibling; chronic disabling illness of parent; chronic parental discord.

___ Severe = divorce of parents; unwanted pregnancy; arrest; harsh or rejecting parent; chronic life-threatening illness in patient; multiple foster home placements.

___ Extreme = sexual or physical abuse; death of parent; recurrent abuse.

___ Catastrophic = death of both parents; chronic life-threatening illness.

___ Inadequate information.

Axis V:

___ 81–90 Absence of or minimal symptoms, good functioning.

___ 71–80 Transient, no more than slight impairment of functioning.

___ 61–70 Mild difficulties, some meaningful relationships.

___ 51–60 Moderate symptoms or impairment of function.

___ 41–50 Serious symptoms including suicidal ideation.

___ 31–40 Major impairment in many areas.

___ 21–30 Delusions, hallucinations, suicidal preoccupation.

___ 11–20 Danger to self or others, minimal hygiene, incoherent.

___ 01–10 Persistent danger to self or others.

Plan

___ No further treatment recommended

___ Contacted outside caregivers:

Name: _____ Phone: _____

___ Contacted health carriers:

Name: _____ Phone: _____

___ Contacted school: _____

Referred outpatient psychiatric service: ___ Children's OPD ___ Other

If other, please specify: _____

_____

Type of recommended therapy:

___ Individual   ___ Family   ___ Behavioral/Cognitive   ___ Other

If other, please specify: _____

_____

Recommended duration of therapy:

___ Brief (1–10 visits)   ___ Intermediate (10–25 visits)   ___ Long-term (>25 visits)

Pharmacotherapy: ___

	Medication	Dosage
1.	_____	_____
2.	_____	_____
3.	_____	_____
4.	_____	_____
5.	_____	_____

Medical hospitalization: ___   Medical unit: _____

___ Suicide precautions   ___ Consultant called

Day treatment: ___   Day treatment facility: _____

Residential placement: ___   Residential facility: _____

Consultations: ___

___ Social service   ___ Medicine   ___ Legal services   ___ Neurology
___ SATT/CPT   ___ Other

Psychology testing referral: _____

Reviewed with attending psychiatrist: ___

Attending psychiatrist: _____

Other comments: _____

_____

_____

_____

_____

_____

_____

_____

Signature: _____   Date: _____

Have the parameters of confidentiality been reviewed with the patient and/or the patient's parents or legal guardians?

Mental Status Exam

The purpose of a mental status exam is to obtain a basic evaluation of the client on the major domains of psychological functioning. It can be accomplished in a single, 50-minute interview.

Mental status exams were originally the province of psychiatry, and they retain a medical character, which is evident in the structure of reports and the forms of language used. Reports of both physical and mental status exams essentially list the major domains of functioning and give brief statements of where the patient stands on these dimensions. Physical exams go through the cardiac, respiratory, digestive systems, and so forth. Mental status evaluations examine speech, thought process, mood, and so forth.

Mental status evaluations are briefer than full diagnostic evaluations, of which they are often a part. The main source of this difference in length is that, while full assessments include much attention to content, and describe the client's conflicts, relationships, and so forth, mental status evaluations do not. These exams briefly mention specific issues but mostly focus on the *form* or basic characteristics of the client's functioning, with an emphasis on documenting symptomatology. Another difference is that full diagnostic evaluations attempt to conceptualize and explain the client's difficulties, whereas mental status evaluations have the narrower purpose of identifying symptoms and schematically describing the client's functioning. Comprehensive evaluations attempt to provide something analogous to a rich portrait of the client. Mental status exams provide something more akin to a drawing.

Mental status reports generally provide very brief, formulaic descriptions of the dimensions of functioning that were not found to be problematic (e.g., "Speech was articulate," "Thought process was organized and coherent"). These reports provide more detail on those aspects of functioning found to be impaired or symptomatic.

Our form takes this type of efficiency one step further, by providing a box that can be checked to indicate the client's functioning on that dimension appeared to be within normal limits. There are many different words to designate unremarkable functioning, with different terms for each domain, but the important information is simply that no notable finding was made. Therefore, a check mark efficiently indicates that the domain was assessed and found to be within normal limits. Writing time can then be used to provide more detailed description of the areas of functioning in which the client exhibited difficulties or unusual features.

Mental Status Exam

Name: _____   Date: _____

ID #: _____   Gender: M F   Age: _____

1. Appearance: ___ Unremarkable (If not, explain)

_____

_____

_____

_____

2. Physical movements: ___ Unremarkable (If not, explain)

_____

_____

_____

_____

3. Orientation (person, place, time):   ___ Unremarkable (If not, explain)

_____

_____

_____

_____

4. Speech: ___ Unremarkable (If not, explain)

_____

_____

_____

_____

5. Level of openness: ___ Unremarkable (If not, explain)

_____

_____

_____

_____

6. Interpersonal stance toward examiner: ___ Unremarkable (If not, explain)

_____

_____

_____

_____

7. Thought process: ___ Unremarkable (If not, explain)

_____

_____

_____

_____

8. Reality testing: ___ Unremarkable (If not, explain)

_____

_____

_____

_____

9. Affect (mood):   ___ Unremarkable (If not, explain)

_____

_____

_____

_____

10. Potential harm to self: ___ Unremarkable (If not, explain)

_____

_____

_____

_____

11. Potential harm to others: ___ Unremarkable (If not, explain)

_____

_____

_____

_____

12. Insight: ___ Unremarkable (If not, explain)

_____

_____

_____

_____

_____

Diagnostic formulation: Hypothesized factors causing or maintaining child's mental health problems.

_____

_____

_____

_____

_____

_____

_____

_____

_____

Diagnosis

Axis I _____

Axis II _____

Axis III _____

Axis IV _____

Axis V _____

Recommendations

_____

_____

_____

_____

_____

_____

_____

_____

_____

Signature: _____ Date: _____

Chapter 8

Consultation and Referral

CONSULTATION REQUEST/REPORT

Requests for consultation are a routine matter in most medical and human service facilities. It can be safely said that most mental health problems are multidetermined, often involving both psychological and physical aspects of an individual. Even if the causes are solely determined by one or the other, there are often psychological consequences to an overwhelmingly physical problem and vice versa.

In the vast majority of assessments involving mental retardation, for example, issues of speech communication, general health care, and adjustments to the community are best approached by professional specialists. No one profession has complete expertise in all aspects of brain development, damage, or disability. The patient will be best served when the relevant professionals consult in treatment planning.

Having a standard form for requesting evaluations and inputs from several sources may save time and effort. The consultant could use the same form to complete his or her report for the requesting party. However, carbons or copies of the original request are important to keep for safeguards against losses, as well as a record of the original request.

The following example of a one-page Consultation Request/Report form has relatively little space for details about the case at hand or reasons for the request. Some clinics may choose to add space for background information and specifics about the request. In any case, it is helpful to pair up the request with the response to ensure that the pertinent questions have been answered.

Consultation Request/Report

Name: _____   Date: _____

ID #: _____   Gender: M   F   Age: _____

Birth date: _____

Consultation requested: _____

_____

_____

Diagnosis: _____

_____

_____

State specific points on which consultant's opinion is desired: _____

_____

_____

_____

_____

_____

Name of person requesting consultation: _____

Consultant's report (to be signed by consultant): _____

_____

_____

_____

_____

_____

_____

_____

_____

_____

_____

Signature of attending consultant: _____ Date: _____

Clinical Neurophysiology Request Form

Name: _____   Date: _____

ID #: _____   Gender: M   F   Age: _____

Birth date: _____   Telephone number: _____

Address: _____

City: _____   State: _____   Zip code: _____

Requested by: _____

Current medications:

Medication	Dose	Frequency
_____	_____	_____
_____	_____	_____
_____	_____	_____
_____	_____	_____

Type of study requested:

EEG	Special EEG	Evoked Potentials
___ Routine	___ BEAM I (Brain electrical mapping)	___ BAEP (Brainstem auditory EP)
___ Nasopharyngeal electrode	___ BEAM II (With special activation procedures)	___ BAEP with intensity latency study for peripheral auditory acuity
___ Portable EEG	___ Long-term monitoring with video	
___ Video EEG	___ Sleep lab	
___ Ocular compression		___ BSEP (Brainstem somata-sensory EP)
___ Prolonged EEG		___ PREP (Pattern-reversal visual EP)
___ Sphenoidal electrodes		
___ Valium injection		___ Cortical auditory
___ Pentothal injection		___ Cortical somatasensory EP
___ Brevital injection		___ Strobe flash visual EP
___ Wada test		___ Lower extremity sensorimotor EP
___ Intraoperative corticography		___ Intraoperative EP monitoring
		___ Other: _____

May patient be sedated with chloral hydrate? ___ No ___ Yes

Brief description of problem, clinical findings, and questions to be addressed: _____

_____

_____

_____

_____

_____

_____

_____

_____

_____

_____

_____

_____

_____

_____

_____

_____

_____

_____

_____

_____

Signature of requester: _____ Date: _____

Technologist's technical impression: _____

_____

_____

_____

_____

_____

_____

_____

_____

REQUEST FOR SCHOOL INFORMATION

Information from the child's school can be a crucial source of data for making a diagnosis as well as making a treatment plan. However, school information may be difficult to obtain due to regulations. Further, getting the appropriate information from the appropriate school personnel is not always easy. The clinician needs to know what information to ask for and from whom.

It is probably best to speak directly with the school personnel, usually over the phone, instead of waiting for a written report from the school. By speaking to the provider of the information, one can judge how well he or she knows the child and can ask pertinent questions concerning such information.

If a document from the school is needed, the following form may be helpful in obtaining information on a child.

It is also important to consider what information a clinician feeds back to the school, following an assessment or period of treatment. The challenge here is to convey information to the school that will be most helpful to the child, and not misinterpreted by the school. Because one never knows the ultimate destination of a report to a school (i.e., will it stay in the principal's office, or follow the child from teacher to teacher?), the clinician must be careful in providing information.

The clinician must also be aware of the consequence of any data or test results provided, as school placements are sometimes made on the basis of this information. For example, a child's IQ may be a sole determinant to a class placement. If a psychologist reports a certain score, the child's entire school tracking may begin by the report of that number. If there are contingencies that require a more comprehensive evaluation of the child, and not solely the IQ figure, the psychologist must be able to bring the appropriate information to bear on the tracking decision.

Just as it is important to know the parents before interpreting test results to them, it is important to know how the school will deal with information given to them.

Because school information is not simple to receive, it is best for the clinician to become familiar with the school personnel from whom information might be requested or conveyed, before requesting any specific consultation from or to the school. It is a tremendous aid to a clinician who works with a number of children from a particular school to have a good working relationship with the school personnel. With an established relationship, schools are often pleased to provide information that will be helpful to them as well as to the child. Offering to be a consultant to the school is a good entry, or offering to speak at a PTA meeting can help solidify a relationship that could prove beneficial when evaluating a child from that institution.

Request for School Information

Name: _____ Date: _____

ID #: _____ Gender: M   F   Age: _____

Birth date: _____ Telephone number: _____

Address: _____

City: _____ State: _____ Zip code: _____

Grade or year in school: _____ Previous schools attended: _____

_____

Parent(s) name: _____

Information requested from: _____

Address: _____

City: _____ State: _____ Zip code: _____

Telephone number: _____ Fax: _____

Signature: _____

____ Consent form attached

Permission has been obtained from the following to receive information on the above-named child: _____

Specific information requested: _____

_____

_____

_____

Additional information requested: _____

_____

_____

_____

Response (please use additional pages if necessary): _____

_____

_____

_____

Name of person providing information: _____

Signature/Title: _____ Date: _____

Psychopharmacology Progress Note

Traditionally, psychiatrists were the only mental health professionals providing information on psychopharmacology. As the only prescribers of psychotropic medication, they were charged with that aspect of a patient's treatment. As other professionals (nurses, social workers, psychologists) have become more educated in psychopharmacology, they are increasingly called on to advise nonpsychiatric physicians on the efficacy of medications for mental health patients.

There are settings today (e.g., military installations) in which trained psychologists are responsible for prescribing to and tracking mental health patients. Nurses also have prescription privileges for many types of medication.

Keeping accurate records on medication is extremely important. Because there are so many physiological changes in children as they grow, it is urgent to know the status of any drug regime when assessments are made of a child's behavior. It is not unusual to have multiple prescriptions given to children (as is even more true with the elderly), and interactive effects of medications must be carefully evaluated.

As children enter adolescence, the effects of some drugs may reverse in their effect. Some drugs prescribed for hyperactivity in children (e.g., Dexedrine) are prescribed for inducing activity in adults.

Psychopharmacology Progress Note

Name: _____ ID #: _____ Date: _____

Information recorded by: _____

Information supplied by (name and relationship to the client): _____

_____

Clinical course/target symptoms (include evidence of symptoms change)

Taking meds as previously prescribed: ___ No ___ Yes

If "no," please describe: _____

_____

Changes in mental status: ___ No ___ Yes

If "yes," please describe: _____

_____

Suicidal ___ No ___ Yes   Homicidal ___ No ___ Yes   Psychosis ___ No ___ Yes

Side effects of current medications: ___ No ___ Yes

If "yes," please describe: _____

_____

Clinical status:

   ___ Reduction of target symptoms   ___ No change in baseline status

   ___ Global functional improvement   ___ Increase of target symptoms

   ___ Continued improvement   ___ New symptom development

Vital signs:

   BP sitting: _____   BP standing: _____   Height: _____

   HR sitting: _____   HR standing: _____   Weight: _____

Lab results since last visit: _____

Plan (include medication changes, labs ordered, next appointment): _____

_____

_____

Changes in medication: ___ No ___ Yes

If "yes," please describe and indicate completion of informed consent process: _____

_____

Current medications (medications recommended at end of current intervention):

Medication	Dose	Frequency
_____	_____	_____
_____	_____	_____
_____	_____	_____

Axis I diagnosis:

Axis I codes	Axis I disorder(s)
1. _____	_____
2. _____	_____
3. _____	_____

Axis II diagnosis: _____

_____

Axis III diagnosis: _____

_____

Axis IV diagnosis:

____ Problems with primary support

____ Problems related to social environment

____ Educational problems

____ Occupational problems

____ Housing problems

____ Economic problems

____ Problems with access to health care services

____ Problems related to interaction with legal system/crime

____ Other psychosocial and environment problems

Axis V diagnosis:

____ 81–90 Absence of minimal symptoms, good functioning

____ 71–80 Transient no more than slight impairment of functioning

____ 61–70 Mild difficulties, some meaningful relationships

____ 51–60 Moderate symptoms or impairment of functioning

____ Serious symptoms include suicidal ideation

____ Major impairment in many areas

____ Delusions, hallucinations, suicidal preoccupation

____ Danger to self or others, minimal hygiene, incoherent

____ Persistent danger to self or others

Clinician: _____ Degree: _____

Psychopharmacology Telephone Note

Name: _____ ID #: _____ Date: _____

Information recorded by: _____

Information supplied by (name and relationship to the client): _____

_____

Contact person: ___ Parent ___ Patient ___ Therapist ___ School personnel ___ Other

Reason for telephone contact: ___ Routine/schedule check ___ Response report
___ New symptom ___ New side effect ___ Other _____

Outcome of phone contact:
___ Change in medications   ___ Continued observation   ___ Consultation
___ No change medications   ___ Planned follow-up   ___ Referral
___ Other: _____

Fill in appropriate sections:

Clinical course/target symptoms (include evidence of symptom change): _____

_____

_____

_____

_____

_____

Changes in mental status: ___ No ___ Yes
If "yes," please describe: _____

_____

_____

Suicidal ___ No ___ Yes   Homicidal ___ No ___ Yes   Psychosis ___ No ___ Yes

Side effects of current medications: ___ No ___ Yes
If "yes," please describe: _____

_____

_____

Clinical status:

    ___ Reduction of target symptoms   ___ No change in baseline status

    ___ Global functional improvement   ___ Increase of target symptoms

    ___ No change with continued improvement   ___ New symptom development

Lab results since last visit: _____

_____

_____

_____

Plan (include medication changes, labs ordered, next appointment): _____

_____

_____

_____

_____

_____

_____

_____

_____

Changes in medication: ___ No   ___ Yes

If "yes," please describe and indicate completion of informed consent process: _____

_____

_____

___ Risks and potential benefits discussed

___ Informed consent of parent/legal guardian obtained

Current medications (medications recommended at end of current intervention):

Medication	Dose	Frequency

Prescription given: ___ In person   ___ Mail   ___ Phone   ___ Other _____

Clinician: _____   Degree: _____

OUTPATIENT REFERRAL

Referrals for outpatient services are an essential aspect of any clinical work. Few clinics or agencies, and certainly fewer individuals have all the background and experience to provide comprehensive evaluations, especially with special problem children (e.g., children with developmental disabilities). It is the wise clinician who knows when to turn to others for advice and consultation.

Forms for outside services need not be lengthy or formal. The clinician needs to provide basic information to the consultant or referral agency, with clearly stated questions or precisely put issues to be considered. With this information, the specialist can deal with the issue at hand and provide useful information for the benefit of the child under question.

Outpatient Referral

Name: _____   Date: _____

ID #: _____   Gender: M F   Age: _____

Birth date: _____   Telephone number: _____

Address: _____

City: _____   State: _____   Zip code: _____

Referring provider: _____   Daytime phone: _____

Referring program: _____   Evening phone: _____

Referred to: _____   Referred to program: _____

Primary care provider: _____

Insurance Information

Health plan: _____

Policy #: _____   Authorization #: _____

Expiration date: _____   Date: _____

Appointment Information

Appointment date(s): _____   Time: _____

Staff coordinating appointment (referring): _____

_____

Staff coordinating appointment (specialty): _____

_____

Scheduling comments: _____

_____

Select one of the following:

    ___ Consultative opinion (one visit only)

    ___ Consultative opinion with diagnostic services. Indicate number of visits: _____

    ___ Offsite provider or home care services

    ___ Team visit (specify): _____

Diagnosis/Comments

_____
_____
_____
_____
_____
_____
_____
_____
_____
_____
_____
_____
_____

Referring provider's signature: _____ Date: _____

Date of onset: _____

Follow-up information: ___ Appointment kept   ___ Appointment not kept

      ___ Appointment rescheduled (specify date): _____

Specialist's Comments

_____
_____
_____
_____
_____
_____
_____
_____
_____
_____
_____

Chapter 9

Treatment Plans, Notes, and Summaries

As Zuckerman (1997) notes, there is little consensus about treatment planning in the mental health field. There is no set of components generally viewed as needed in a plan, nor any widely accepted format.

ADVANTAGES AND LIMITATIONS OF PLANNING IN ADVANCE

In addition to the omnipresent issue of record length, treatment planning involves the conceptual question of just how much a priori planning is useful at the beginning of treatment. Hare-Mustin, Maracek, Kaplan, and Liss-Levinson (1979) point out a number of clinical situations that make initial goal-setting difficult, such as when clients have trouble being specific and when clients' initial goals derive from an inadequate understanding of their problems.

Intake sessions often focus on the child's one or two most serious problems. These problems may eclipse other difficulties that, although less severe, are clinically significant and legitimate targets of treatment. When the most serious problems are ameliorated, secondary difficulties often emerge.

As causal understandings of client problems develop, new goals may emerge both as keys to resolving initially identified problems and as ends in themselves. A child's depressive symptoms might emerge as due to social isolation, which might, in turn, be attributable to weak social skills. The result would be two new goals for the treatment plan.

Treatment plans are typically written after one assessment session, but there is a common view that psychotherapy often unfolds in unpredictable ways. Despite the clear distinctions of billing codes, assessment and treatment do not seem to occur as separate activities but instead alternate in a reciprocal fashion (Persons, 1991). Therapists often change their techniques as they learn about the dynamics of client difficulties and observe client responses to techniques that are tried. In these situations, plans require ongoing revision to stay current with the evolution of treatment.

Although treatment planning is sometimes difficult, it has potential value in clinical work. Treatment planning fulfills several core functions. Third-party payers, whether governmental or private, have a legitimate interest in knowing the specific procedures for which reimbursement is sought. Mental health interventions, like any goal-oriented activity, are generally less than optimally effective if conducted in a purely spontaneous and improvisatory fashion, and treatment undoubtedly benefits from planning. For clients as well as clinicians, therapeutic work may be better organized and more focused if it is structured around a well-thought-out plan. Finally, documentation of such plans provides a fundamental record of treatment.

Treatment plans should be tools, not straitjackets, for therapy. Because recorded plans for treatment are both desirable and attended by difficulties, the challenge is to develop an approach that achieves the value of planning while also acknowledging and resolving, or at least circumventing and minimizing, the potential difficulties. Our forms were designed to maximize the advantages of both planning and improvising in conducting and documenting treatment.

Because treatment goals evolve, therapy cannot always limit its work to the goals identified in the initial diagnostic section. Clients should not be penalized for failing to identify all their needs in their first session with the clinician. Obviously, therapists should not eschew interventions they believe would be effective because these interventions were not part of the original plan. Therefore, our form includes provision for both ending and adding interventions (without rewriting the whole plan). By including dates of these changes, a single, evolving record can provide full documentation of the interventions used throughout treatment.

CURRENT SYSTEMS FOR TREATMENT PLANNING

Treatment planning generally involves the following four, broad components:

1. Assessment and diagnosis.
2. Definition of goals of treatment.
3. Interventions designed to achieve the goals.
4. Measurement of progress toward the goals.

We provide separate forms for assessment and treatment planning because, in some settings, these are separate tasks. Therefore, our treatment plan form includes only the last three of the preceding four components. However, there are also many settings in which assessment and treatment planning are performed together. For such settings, our assessment and treatment planning forms could easily be combined.

The literature describes several proposed systems for treatment planning that warrant consideration, including the PIC Model and the Expanded Problem-Oriented Record.

The PIC Model

Levenstein (1994a) suggests a simple system described by the acronym "PIC":

- *P* stands for problem; it includes assessment, diagnosis, and goal definition.
- *I* stands for intervention; it includes planned therapeutic strategies.
- *C* stands for change; it includes operational definitions of progress.

Levenstein (1994b) adds a section, with the initial *R,* for resistance or obstacles to the success of the interventions. This system can be used as a format for progress notes as well as treatment plans.

The Expanded Problem-Oriented Record

Zuckerman (1997) recommends this system as simple, flexible, and comprehensive. Treatment plans in this format would include the following six sections, in the order shown:

1. The presenting problems.
2. Treatment goals and objectives, with measurable criteria for levels of progress.
3. Client strengths and resources to be utilized in treatment.
4. Client liabilities and internal or external barriers to the achievement of the goals.
5. Treatment methods to be used and expected frequency and duration of treatment.
6. Methods and dates of evaluation of progress.

Other systems have been developed by Kennedy (1992) and Sperry, Gudeman, Blackwell, and Faulkner (1992). These systems involve levels of complexity, elaboration, and specificity that would make them cumbersome in everyday practice, and so they are not reviewed here.

CONSTRUCTING MEASURABLE GOALS

Formulating treatment goals in measurable terms can be the most difficult aspect of writing treatment plans. It is important to meet this challenge because, without measurement of progress, it is impossible to know whether therapy is effective. Assessment of treatment effectiveness is necessary for decision making about when to terminate services and for determining whether to continue ongoing interventions or to make midcourse corrections.

The source of difficulty in defining goals in measurable terms is that human functioning is highly complex, and measurement inherently requires an element of simplification. Complex phenomena are difficult to define, and clear definition is necessary for measurement. To measure behavior, it is necessary to *accept* that simplification, if done skillfully, does not cause a full loss of the reality of the phenomenon being measured. The challenge is to find behavioral components that are simple enough to measure *and* that are closely related to the clinical realities of concern. In this way, the behavioral component can be used to track the complex syndrome it represents. For example, minutes of insomnia per night can be used to track depression.

Internal, emotional problems are usually more difficult to define in measurable terms than externally visible, overt acting out. In addition to complexity, measuring feelings requires clinicians to deal with the problem of subjectivity. Temper tantrums can easily be counted, but anxiety may not be visible to an observer.

This problem is not as formidable as it seems at first, because client verbalizations of their internal states *are* observable behaviors. If a client is not highly guarded or defensive, his or her verbal statements constitute measurable behaviors that can be used to track treatment progress. This is the rationale of the numerous self-report measures of diagnostic entities. As a practical reality, differences in subjectivity between internal and overt behaviors are not as great as they may seem, because clinicians usually do not directly observe overt client problems but instead rely on self-reports and parent reports, which are themselves subjective. Fortunately, however, subjectivity does not necessarily mean inaccuracy.

Quantification

Quantification is not literally essential to measurement, but it is generally a practical necessity for assessing change over time. Change usually occurs gradually so that, without quantification, we can say whether a goal has been reached or not, but we cannot say whether progress is occurring toward a goal. Therefore, goal definition needs to include some type of quantification.

A practical issue with quantitative measurement is that it is difficult for children and parents to make behavioral reports in precise numbers. If the reporting task is presented to clients in this way, they may find it intimidating and frustrating, and they might even make up numbers for the therapist in their struggle to comply. The clinician should make sure clients feel able to perform the reporting tasks they are assigned, even if this requires reducing the level of quantitative precision.

Fortunately, quantification does not have to be precise or fine-grained to be useful for tracking client progress. People sometimes think that "quantitative" equals "precise," but this is not the case. Rough, approximate estimations constitute elementary, but nonetheless useful, quantitative measurement. Approximate estimates are usually all that is necessary in clinical situations because our primary interest is not in slight, subtle changes but in large, functionally significant ones.

When explaining reporting tasks to clients, clinicians should emphasize that the need is to communicate a sense of the direction and approximate magnitude of change, not to obsess about numbers. The important task for the reporter is to make fair, unbiased observations. As Alan Greenspan, chairman of the Federal Reserve Board, said about the Consumer Price Index, "It is better to be roughly right than exactly wrong."

Clinicians should emphasize words like "approximately" and "about" when explaining reporting tasks to clients. When percentages are used, they should be rounded to fives or tens, if not more. The same is true for counts of high-frequency behaviors and estimates of behavioral durations. For some clients, simple fractions are more useful than percentages. If necessary, numbers can be replaced with words. Terms like "a little," "a lot," "somewhat," and "very" contain rough quantitative information, and they are much better than nothing.

Quantification of behavior generally takes four forms: frequency, proportion, duration, and intensity. These four dimensions of behavior vary in their ease of measurement.

Frequency is usually the easiest behavioral dimension to use in clinical situations, because it is a simple matter of counting. Typical examples of treatment goals involving frequency would be, "Reduce crying to once per week," "Reduce verbalization of fears to once every two days," and "Increase positive statements about personal competencies to once per day."

Inconveniently, some client problems do not lend themselves to frequency-based measurement. At base, frequencies involve only a dichotomous scale of measurement; the behavior either happened or it did not. But even if they pertain to the same symptom, all behavioral instances are not equal. For example, an argument between siblings can last two minutes or two hours, so that merely tabulating the frequency of arguments loses a great deal of information. Sometimes it is useful also to set goals for behavioral *duration*. Examples would be: "Reduce average length of fidgeting episodes from 45 minutes to 15 minutes," "Reduce average duration of resistance to parental directives from 5 minutes to 1 minute," and "Increase time spent on individual play activities from an average of 10 minutes to 30 minutes."

When the important aspect of behavior is not how often or how protractedly it occurs but, instead, how reliably it happens when it needs to occur, then the important behavioral dimension is proportion. Generally, frequency and duration are behavioral dimensions associated with free operant situations; discrimination learning is a matter of the proportion of desired responses to a stimulus or situation. The most common example is child compliance with parental directives. Parents issue directives to young children so many times per day that it is impossible to measure compliance by counting. In addition, more directives occur on some days than others, and it would not make sense to treat a day with fewer directives as if it involved a lowered level of compliance. Duration is not a salient dimension of obedient behavior. The salient question regarding compliance is, what proportion of parental directives are obeyed? Thus, a goal of treatment might be to increase compliance from a one-fourth rate to a two-thirds rate.

There is an additional type of behavior that is most effectively measured in terms of proportion. Frequency and duration are usable dimensions only when the behavior in question occurs in distinct episodes, with an identifiable beginning and end. These dimensions do not fit behaviors or qualities of behavior that are interwoven seamlessly into everyday life. Because parents cannot function like research assistants with clipboards and stopwatches, behaviors such as cooperative play with siblings, surly behavior with parents, on-task behavior, and sad affect do not lend themselves to measurement in terms of duration and frequency. These behaviors, which often do not occur in discrete episodes, are usually best described in terms of proportions or percentages that capture the quality of the child's functioning in everyday life.

Intensity is the most difficult-to-define of our four behavioral dimensions, but it cannot always be left out of the picture. A depressive statement such as "I'm no good at sports" has a different intensity than a depressive statement such as "I'm no good at anything." Therefore, describing the frequency, proportion, and duration of such statements does not capture all the clinically important information.

Intensity information can be difficult to quantify, especially in advance, when the treatment plan is being developed. The task is worth doing if the information is important to capture and, particularly, if the clinician judges that intensity may not vary along with the other dimensions and so needs to be tracked independently. Examples of goals for changing behavioral intensities might include, "Physical aggression will change from hitting and kicking to pushing," "Verbal expressions of anger will change from screaming to arguing," and "Disobedience will occur not for major parental directives (e.g., drug use) but at most for minor directives (e.g., style of dress)."

CONSTRUCTING USEFUL GOALS

Clinicians operating from psychodynamic or humanistic theoretical orientations sometimes feel that quantified monitoring of treatment progress fails to capture the full complexity, nuance, and depth of both human problems and human growth. They are right—goal definitions such as the previous examples certainly do not portray the richness of individual journeys through therapy. This does not mean such goal definitions are useless, however, because portraying the depth and richness of change is not the only clinical function that needs to be served. Goal definitions have the purpose of making possible quick, efficient monitoring of progress in a form that is both easily summarized and understandable to third parties. In addition, the simplifying focus of goal definition can sometimes structure the efforts of both therapist and client in a way that facilitates treatment.

Nonetheless, it *is* important to the development of useful treatment goals that clinicians not lose sight of therapy's subtlety and complexity. Simple, measurable goals are useful only if they adequately represent, albeit in a partial fashion, complex, difficult-to-measure goals. For example, frequency of shared pleasant activities is closely related to the quality of the parent-child relationship. Because shared activities are a reasonable operational definition of relationships, they provide a proxy measure or index that is convenient to use in tracking progress of the much broader construct. If constructs are operationalized correctly, then the simple behavior and the complex issue will progress or regress together, and it is both convenient and valid to document change only in the simple behavior. The key to defining goals is to develop operational definitions of complex issues that are like the tips of icebergs; we can see them easily, and they represent much more than what can be seen.

Identification of treatment goals is a complex clinical activity requiring both thought and collaborative work with the parent and, usually, the child. As with documentation tasks in general, there is a danger of this work deteriorating into a mere "paperwork requirement" that distracts from the real therapeutic process. However, if performed skillfully, goal formulation can organize and focus the thinking of both the therapist and the client. Tasks are generally easier to accomplish when they are clearly defined. Also, goal formulation and tracking can make a vital contribution to regulating treatment duration.

Who Defines the Goals?

The question of who, among the therapist, parent(s), and child, defines the goals is not a simple one. In many cases, there will be consensus among the therapy participants, in which case this issue will not emerge as a problem. However, clinicians need to be prepared for the common situation in which participants do not agree about the desired outcome of treatment. In these cases, arriving at some type of resolution about goals (which need not always mean a consensus) is necessary to establishing the treatment contract, without which clinical work cannot proceed.

Potential disagreements can be organized in terms of the dyads involved. These disagreements involve different issues.

Parent(s) versus Child. From a legal perspective, this is the simplest situation—parent goals trump child goals. Particularly for disorders involving maladaptive acting out, it is common for children and adolescents to view their behavior as acceptable and to resist both treatment itself and specific goals of treatment. In these cases, the ego-syntonic nature of the symptoms is part of the problem requiring amelioration, and the child's agreement with the goals of treatment may itself be a therapeutic subgoal that will take some work to accomplish. Parent/child disagreement about treatment goals presents problems for therapeutic strategy but not for the treatment contract or for documenting the treatment plan. As a clinical problem, parent/child disagreement about therapy goals is generally both more common and more serious for adolescents than for younger children.

Parent versus Parent. Disagreements about treatment goals between parents who share responsibility for the child represents a serious problem that must be resolved if treatment is to begin. If the parents are divorced or unmarried, and the parental rights of one parent have been terminated, then only the wishes of the custodial parent need be considered. If the parents are divorced, the divorce decree should be carefully examined for information about distribution of decision-making responsibilities. If these are shared between divorced parents, or if the parents are married, then the two parents and clinician must work out an area of consensus, or treatment cannot proceed without a danger of both clinical and legal problems. Consensus need not be total for any services to be provided, but only those services for which there is full agreement should be conducted. It may be necessary for the clinician to do significant work with the parents to establish a shared foundation for therapy.

Therapist versus Parent(s). As is the case for parents sharing custody of the child, the therapist and parent(s) must agree about any services to be provided; the assent of each party is necessary but insufficient. Therapists and parents have different, but equal, roles in child treatment. Legally, clinicians are agents of the parents, providing services at the parents' behest. However, it would be unethical for a clinician to provide treatment that he or she does not believe to be in the best interests of the child. Therefore, the foundation of the treatment contract is agreement between therapist and parent. Discussing and resolving any initial disagreements constitute important clinical tasks. Disagreements about therapeutic strategies can often be resolved by straightforward education of the parent. Disagreements about treatment goals may require addressing some personal issues of the parent as well as providing information. On rare occasions, these disagreements cannot be resolved, and the ethical necessity is to decline to treat the child.

Useful formulations of treatment goals have several core characteristics, each of which is sometimes associated with distinctive difficulties. Treatment goals should be (1) linked with the diagnosis, (2) realistically achievable, and (3) measurable.

The Relationship between Diagnosis and Goals

Particularly given managed care's emphasis on establishing the medical necessity of treatment, treatment goals should clearly represent the elimination or amelioration of the diagnosis on the basis of which services are reimbursed. Achieving a correspondence between diagnosis and goals requires a shared understanding between the therapist and parent concerning the purpose of treatment.

While the two should be clearly linked, it is not useful to write goals simply as the absence of a diagnostic feature; for example, "reduce anxiety," or "increase compliance." Goal definitions of this type are redundant because it goes without saying that treatment purports to ameliorate diagnosed disorders. For their construction to be useful, goals should consist of more than the absence of diagnoses and should involve additional information.

Goals should be narrower and more specific than full diagnostic syndromes and should consist of the specific objectives together constituting syndrome resolution for the particular client. Also, goals can be positive statements about how the client wants to feel and behave at the conclusion of services, whereas diagnoses focus on behaviors and emotions to be reduced or eliminated. Third, goals should include some type of quantitative identification of the level of functioning considered "good enough" for treatment to be considered successful; diagnoses are either present or absent, and so they involve a form of information less quantitative and specific than that provided by goals.

Setting Realistic Goals

Treatment goals need to be realistic and achievable. If goals are set too high, clients will be unable to gain a sense of accomplishment and satisfaction from their progress. Also, unrealistically ambitious or perfectionistic treatment goals can result in excessive treatment duration, which contributes to escalating health care costs and reduces availability of services to clients in serious need.

For clients, one key to developing realistic treatment goals is to distinguish between mental health problems and the normal disappointments of human life; therapy can do a lot about the former but very little about the latter. Parents need to have realistic expectations for child behavior, which inevitably includes some noncompliance, aggressiveness, moodiness, and so forth. Children and adolescents need to understand that life inevitably includes some disappointments, conflict, and sadness. The continued existence of some life difficulties does not mean that treatment has failed or is incomplete.

To help clients and parents verbalize realistic goals for child functioning, clinicians can frame their questions using words like "good enough," "okay," "satisfactory," and "regular kid problems." The important distinction is between a "serious problem that needs therapy" and "just life."

Goals should be set at levels of functioning sufficient for children and parents to feel they can manage any problems that arise on their own, that the behaviors involved in the presenting problem no longer dominate their experience, and that they have a basically good life. Sometimes these levels of functioning will be above the boundary of diagnosable psychopathology, but care should be taken to distinguish goals from fantasies.

Therapy goals can be too low as well as too high. Sometimes parents expect too little of their children, and youth sometimes expect too little of themselves and their lives. Treatment aspirations can be unrealistically low for behavioral control, school performance, family relationships, level of emotional pain, or any area that is the target of intervention. In such situations, the therapeutic task is to support realistic hopes for appropriately positive behavior and emotional experience by communicating that the client's level of dysfunction or unhappiness is not okay and needs to be addressed.

Most parents and children seem to arrive with appropriate levels of aspiration for treatment, and this aspect of planning is usually accomplished quickly and easily. When levels of aspiration are unrealistically high or pessimistically low, then establishing shared, realistic treatment goals can be an instance of documentation work facilitating effective clinical work.

STANDARDIZED INSTRUMENTS

Research-based, validated measures can be a valuable tool for measuring client progress. Achenbach has developed broad measures of child behavioral and emotional problems that provide both summary scores and narrower factor scores. These are instruments with parallel content that are completed from three informant perspectives; the Child Behavior Checklist (Achenbach, 1991a) is completed by parents, the Youth Self-Report (Achenbach, 1991b) is completed by children ages 11–17 years, and the Teacher Report Form (Achenbach, 1991c) is for teachers. The Child and Adolescent Functional Assessment Scale (Hodges & Wong, 1997) is a broad measure of functional impairment completed by therapists based on information from parents, children, and, sometimes, other professionals who have worked with the child. Briefer measures, focusing on specific symptomatic areas and utilizing child self-report, include the Children's Depression Inventory (Kovacs, 1985), the Children's Manifest Anxiety Scale (Reynolds & Richmond, 1985), the Trauma Symptom Checklist for Children (Briere, 1996), and the Attention Deficit Disorders Evaluation Scale (McCarney, 1989). Sederer and Dickey (1996) provide an extensive review of tests for measuring treatment progress and outcome.

Tests by themselves do not provide a complete solution to the problem of assessing progress toward goals, for several reasons. First, the content of standardized instruments often does not precisely match the presenting problems and therapy goals of individual clients. Children sometimes have problems not described by the items and, more commonly, parent weightings or levels of concern sometimes do not match the item weightings of the test. In such cases, test scores will not accurately represent the family's perception of the child's problems.

Tests can conveniently assess client functioning at the beginning and end of treatment, but clinicians need more frequent, ongoing measurement of progress. The longer, broader measures are too time-consuming to be completed at each session. Time is less of a difficulty for the shorter measures, but there is still the serious problem of the effects of repeated testing on score validity. Thus, we need a methodology in addition to standardized tests for tracking therapeutic progress from session to session.

GOAL ATTAINMENT SCALING

The Goal Attainment Scaling (GAS) procedure was originated by Kiresuk and Sherman (1968) and is discussed and applied in a book edited by Kiresuk, Smith, and Cardillo (1994). We present an adaptation of this procedure as part of our forms for treatment planning, tracking, and termination summary. The GAS takes little time to complete, and the activity it does require would generally occur anyway as a natural part of clinical work.

The GAS is not a measure with predetermined content but rather a method of structuring individual client material within a pre-determined format. There is no one goal attainment scale; each client has his or her own scale, because they are custom-designed for each case. Because there is a set procedure for defining points on the scale, scores have fairly comparable meanings across clients. The GAS method represents an attempt to achieve the advantages

143

of an individualized approach without sacrificing all of the advantages of standardized instruments.

The therapist and family collaborate in constructing the scale as part of the treatment planning process, usually performed during the initial diagnostic session. One scale is developed for each presenting problem or, sometimes, for each major component of a single presenting problem. The format provides a clear correspondence between presenting problems, treatment goals, and measurement scales. Most clients should have between 2 and 4 individual scales.

Once the treatment issues have been identified, the task is to define the scale-points in measurable terms. We recommend the following 5-point scale:

1. *Worse*   Functioning below the level of presenting problem
2. *No progress*   Functioning = presenting problem
3. *Some progress*   Any improvement of presenting problem
4. *Major progress*   Functioning about halfway between the presenting problem and the treatment goal
5. *Goal attainment* Achievement of the goal defined at intake

The parent usually supplies most of the input for scale-point definition. The child's role depends on his or her age, self-awareness, understanding of the purpose of treatment, and verbal ability. The therapist's role is primarily to help the family fit their concerns and goals into the structure of the GAS. As discussed earlier, it is sometimes necessary for the clinician to help the family develop realistic levels of aspiration for treatment. It should be emphasized that Scale-point 5 does not correspond to fantasies of a perfect child or an idylically happy life. From the professional's perspective, Scale-point 5 denotes resolution of mental health problems. Goal attainment can be defined for families as the degree of improvement at which it would no longer be necessary to continue treatment.

The scale is not as complicated as it looks. Significant thinking is necessary only for Scale-point 2 (presenting problem) and 5 (goal attainment). These two points anchor the scale, and the other three points derive automatically from them. Scale-point 1 (worse) indicates any noticeable deterioration from the level of functioning defined as the presenting problem. Scale-point 3 (some progress) denotes any noticeable improvement from this level. Defining Scale-point 4 is a matter of interpolation—identifying the level of functioning halfway between the presenting problem and the treatment goal.

The scale-points should not be developed in their order. The presenting problem (2) should be described first. Then, the treatment goal (5) should be defined. Once this is accomplished, the work is essentially finished. Scale-points 1 and 3 (worse and some progress) do not even require any writing. Scale-point 4 (major progress) should be defined last.

For the procedure to work, the two anchoring scale-points (2 and 5) must be carefully defined in terms that are at least roughly quantitative; otherwise they cannot be used as points of reference. Because the procedure's purpose is to document *progress,* problems and goals cannot be described simply as present or absent but must include some metric for capturing information about severity. Problems and goals should be described in terms of frequency, duration, proportion, and/or intensity. (One of these dimensions is usually enough.)

The GAS format we recommend does not have optimal statistical properties in that intervals between the scale-points are not equal. Instead, the GAS represents an ordinal scale of measurement; quantitative information is limited to the set order of the scale-points. From a purely statistical perspective, interval scales are preferable to ordinal scales. In constructing the scale, we sacrificed some statistical quality to practical, clinical considerations.

For a measurement technique to be clinically useful, it is of paramount importance that clients can respond to the task in a natural fashion. We chose our scale-points to match, as closely as possible, the language used by clients and parents to describe changes in functioning. From a statistical standpoint, the natural language of change does not seem to correspond to equal intervals of improvement (e.g., zero, 33%, 66%, 100%). Instead, one hears reports of behavior being "worse," "about the same," "a little better," "much better," and "good." These five terms correspond just about exactly to the five points of the scale included in our forms. This correspondence should maximize the procedure's convenience and ease of use.

One other clinical consideration was included in our development of Scale-point 3 (some progress), specifically, our desire to have a point representing any noticeable progress toward the treatment goal. Clinically, clients often find it encouraging to receive attention for any positive change, even if slight. This scale-point was included partly to provide a format for this type of reinforcement. In addition, clinically, there seems to be an important difference between being a little bit better and being no better at all, and this difference seems useful to document.

Constructing these scales with clients requires some work and time. However, the GAS procedure achieves efficiency in that time for documentation is not taken away from time for true clinical work; most of the work involved in developing the client's scale would happen as a natural part of the intake even if the GAS were not being used. Presenting problems must always be defined as part of the diagnostic process, goals must be defined if therapy is to have clear direction, and the other three scale-points do not require any significant time. Thus, several tasks are accomplished simultaneously. If done effectively, this collaborative task can attain the highest goal of documentation: facilitation of clinical work.

SPECIFYING PLANNED TREATMENT METHODS

In broad terms, one half of the business of treatment planning is to define the goals of services, and the second half is to specify the therapeutic procedures for achieving the goals. The defining of goals is aided by the conceptual foundation and vocabulary of psychopathology, assessment, and diagnosis. The defining of therapeutic procedures is potentially intimidating because treatment is complex and varies from client to client. However, this task is made manageable by our knowledge of the major theoretical orientations and psychotherapeutic techniques, which furnish a useful shorthand for recording maximum information in minimum words.

Complete reliance on concrete behavioral description would result in much more writing than practicing clinicians have the time to do. It is not necessary to reiterate definitions of methods like "behavior therapy," and "disputing irrational beliefs" every time they are used, because these are terms of art with fairly consensual meanings learned by therapists in the course of graduate education and professional training. Some potential for confusion and miscommunication exists because of variation in what these terms are understood to mean and because of gaps in professional training. To address this problem, this chapter provides a list of definitions of current major therapeutic approaches (adapted from Shapiro, Welker, & Jacobson, 1997b). Clinicians can check their use of terms against this list to ensure they are using conventional definitions of the treatment methods being documented. With the list as a preprinted anchor, the therapist can indicate treatment methods by naming them, without providing description. The list could be useful if a third party needs information about the therapist's work, because it provides a public, standard definition of terms.

Along with the approach definitions, we provide examples of therapeutic techniques employed within the various approaches. The difference between approach and technique is one of conceptual breadth. We use the term "approach" to refer to a genre of intervention strategy, often identified with a theoretical orientation. We use the term "technique" to refer to specific, narrower procedures. We do not provide definitions of techniques because there are so many of them that this would be impractical and also because their meanings are smaller, more precise, and so less vulnerable to varying interpretation.

The usefulness of approach and technique terminology as a description of what happens in treatment depends on the accuracy with which therapists use these terms. Past research has found that the major theoretical orientations are reliably associated with the therapist behaviors they recommend and also that therapist self-reports of techniques match descriptions by observers (Brunink & Schroeder, 1979; DeRubeis, Hollon, Evans, & Bernis, 1982; Wills, Faitler, & Snyder, 1987). These findings support the accuracy of therapist self-report as a method of assessing treatment methods.

A Taxonomy of Psychotherapeutic Approaches

The following material represents an attempt to construct a useful taxonomy of current, major psychotherapeutic approaches. Our goal is to provide a set of categories that is mutually exclusive and exhaustive. The goal is for every common intervention to fit into one and only one category.

Given the complexity of psychotherapy, no set of classifications can fully achieve these goals. Therefore, the procedure on our forms includes provision for muddiness and exceptions. When more than one approach is planned or used, the therapist is to number these approaches in descending order of their extent of use; this numbering system should also be used to indicate therapeutic activities that involve combinations or syntheses of approaches. If the therapist believes that a treatment activity involved a synthesis of approach A and approach B, he or she should indicate the predominant approach with a "1" and the secondary approach with a

"2." If both approaches were equally involved, the therapist should mentally flip a coin and just give one approach a "1" and one a "2"; this will provide a basic description of the treatment that occurred, and effective documentation does not require obsessing about fine distinctions.

Our solution to the problem of exceptions is simple: Methods not fitting into any of the system's categories should be identified as "Other." These methods should be defined briefly in the space provided. Thus, the system is exhaustive in the limited sense that every possible method has a place for indication on the form.

Art Therapy. Art and craft activities are used as a means for clients to express and work through problems and conflicts and as a way for therapists to communicate guidance, interpretations, and stimuli for new ways of processing issues. Artistic productions are often viewed and used as symbolic representations of feelings, conflicts, symptoms, the self, and relationships. Techniques include self-portraits, family drawings, visualization, guided drawing, time lines, and manipulation of symbolized issues.

Behavior Therapy. This term denotes a broad array of techniques that we subdivide into several approach definitions to provide specific descriptions of treatment methods. The umbrella term of behavior therapy indicates approaches linked by a relative disinterest in history, underlying dynamics, and etiology, in favor of an emphasis on observable behavior and current factors maintaining problems. Behavior therapy is based on laboratory research and learning processes, particularly reinforcement, and skill training. Behavior therapy is concrete and specific in its definition of both problems and treatment procedures. Our forms indicate subtypes of behavior therapy by the abbreviation "BT."

BT: Classical designates techniques based on classical or Pavlovian conditioning and on principles of avoidance learning. It is generally used to treat anxiety-based disorders. The basic mechanism is to approach feared stimuli or situations—often, but not always, with a pairing of relaxation procedures—and to learn that these situations do not need to be feared. Techniques include systematic desensitization, counterconditioning, biofeedback, exposure, response prevention, and implosive procedures.

BT: Directive designates behavioral techniques based on straightforward therapist directives for the client to perform specific behaviors that, by themselves, can counter symptomatology. There may be little emphasis on explicit reinforcers (which would constitute an operant procedure), because the immediate reduction of symptoms itself constitutes a natural reinforcer. Techniques include directives to exercise, increase pleasant activities, and substitute benign behaviors for incompatible symptomatic behaviors.

BT: Emotional regulation consists of direct training in techniques for self-regulating and moderating painful emotions. There may be little emphasis on provision of explicit reinforcers, because the reduction of painful feelings constitutes natural reinforcement. Emotional symptoms are treated by teaching specific skills for self-management of feelings. Techniques include training in relaxation, anger management, and stress management, with procedures including progressive muscle relaxation, deep breathing, and guided imagery.

BT: Operant denotes explicit, planful utilization of principles of operant conditioning and discrimination learning. Operant principles include reward, negative reinforcement,

147

punishment, and extinction. Discrimination learning involves the control of behavior by cues, prompts, and discriminative stimuli. Treatment techniques include token economies, behavioral contracting, and material and social rewards. An important note: In this system, when operant techniques are administered by the parent, the coding should be *BT: Parent training;* the coding *BT: Operant* is used when operant procedures are arranged directly by the therapist and client.

BT: Parent training is a two-part treatment process: The therapist trains the parent in behaviorally sound child management techniques, and the parent then uses these techniques in everyday life to ameliorate the child's difficulties. There is an emphasis on precise analysis and training in parenting behaviors that increase child compliance, with attention to both antecedents and consequences. Techniques include parent-child activities designed to increase the parent's social reinforcement value ("special time"), training in providing clear directions, decreased attention for negative behavior, increased attention for positive behavior, prompting, training in providing informative reinforcement, response cost, charting, token economy, time-out, and, especially, material and social rewards.

BT: Social skills is a direct approach to teaching the interpersonal behaviors that produce positive human interactions and relationships. Social skills training uses instruction, modeling, rehearsal, in vivo practice, and feedback to teach assertiveness, expression of feelings and needs, social conversation, friendship initiation, conflict resolution, and general relationship skills.

Case Management. This is not psychotherapy per se, but it is often provided by therapists as an integral part of their services. Case management consists of arranging and coordinating additional services needed by the client, with systems including school, child protection, juvenile justice, health, recreation, and so forth. This category can be used to code session time spent discussing these services, and time spent consulting with other providers either on the phone or in meetings.

Client-Centered Therapy. This nondirective approach attempts to provide conditions for positive change by creating a growth-enhancing environment in therapy. Therapist qualities of unconditional positive regard, empathy, and congruence are considered critical to producing change. There is an emphasis on increasing client self-awareness, self-acceptance, and inner-directedness. Techniques include reflections of feelings and reflections of meaning.

Cognitive Therapy. The therapist directly challenges the rationality of the client's maladaptive beliefs, habitual interpretations, perceptual biases, self-evaluative statements, and expectations; the therapist attempts to teach more adaptive thinking by means of logical persuasion and collaborative empiricism (conducting little experiments in problematic life areas). Techniques include use of diaries, identification of automatic thoughts, reframing, rational dispute, moderating internal evaluative standards, positive self-statements, therapist emphasis on attempting rather than succeeding, and cognitive restructuring. Care should be taken not to construe this approach category too broadly. "Cognitive," here, does not mean any mental process, and other approaches certainly also focus on thoughts. Cognitive therapy is distinguished by its emphasis on the logic and realism of thoughts and also by its directive, persuasive style.

Cognitive-Behavioral Therapy. This umbrella term is sometimes used to cover both cognitive and behavioral interventions, but here it is used *only* and specifically to designate interventions in which cognitive and behavioral procedures are so tightly interwoven that it is difficult to separate them for recording purposes. This coding should be used for intervention packages that integrate behavioral and cognitive aspects (e.g., interventions for obsessive-compulsive disorder and phobias). It should not be used for therapy sessions that involve separate use of behavioral and cognitive techniques. Using two separate codings generally provides more specific information than this single coding can, because separate codings indicate whether cognitive or behavioral techniques were predominant and also specify what type of behavior therapy was provided. For some interventions, however, this separation is artificial, and the cognitive-behavioral coding should be made in these cases.

Experiential Therapy. This humanistic approach focuses directly not on symptom reduction but on increasing personal awareness and freedom. Gestalt therapy is a major subtype. There is an emphasis on immediate emotional experience, focus on the present moment, catharsis, and acting out rather than talking about issues. A group modality is often used. Techniques include psychodrama, empty chair technique, group feedback, guided fantasy, role playing, and exaggeration of behaviors.

Family Systems Therapy. FST is a theoretical approach to treatment and not simply a therapeutic modality (which is identified in a separate section of the treatment plan). In other words, the presence of two or more family members in the session does not automatically mean that FST has occurred; the family modality is necessary but not sufficient for the FST approach to be indicated.

FST occurs when the therapeutic method is based on systems theory, that is, when the most meaningful unit of analysis and intervention is viewed as the *family,* not the identified patient. In other words, the family systems approach focuses on relationships, interactions, and communication patterns, rather than on personal characteristics of the individuals in the family. Amelioration of individual psychopathology is certainly a goal but, rather than being pursued directly, this goal is pursued through efforts to change the family interaction patterns that are viewed as the cause of individual symptoms.

There are a number of theoretical sub-systems within FST, but the distinctions between them are generally of a subtlety beyond that of the present recording system. The most practically important distinction between different therapist actions within FST is more a matter of technique than theory (although these techniques certainly have theoretical underpinnings). This distinction is between directive and non-directive techniques. Therefore, our recording format includes this distinction. When family therapy sessions include a mixture of directive and non-directive work, the clinician should record use of both approaches.

FST: Non-directive involves exploring, bringing into awareness, and increasing understanding of the family communication, interaction, and relationship patterns. Behavior change is certainly a goal, but direction of these changes is considered the client family's responsibility, and the therapist's role is to facilitate development of the family's self-understanding and sense of choice rather than to recommend specific changes for behavior outside the sessions. This coding *does* include therapist directives for in-session activities (e.g., seating arrangements, sharing of feelings between particular family members), as long as the purpose of these activities is limited to increasing awareness of existing interaction patterns and/or building concepts of possible, new interaction patterns. In other words, the term "directive" in our system refers to behavior in everyday life, rather than to direction of session activities. This category includes the Structural family therapy techniques of interpreting action patterns, pattern interruption, altering seating arrangements, family sculpture, reframing, and enactment.

FST: Directive is coded whenever the therapist makes recommendations for family functioning outside of sessions. This category includes the often paradoxical Strategic therapy techniques of symptom prescription, restraints from change, ordeal therapy, and directives incompatible with symptomatic functioning. This coding also includes more straightforward directives based on learning and reinforcement principles, as long as these directives target interactions among family members and not just the symptomatic behaviors of the identified patient. This category also includes simple therapist recommendations for family members or subsets of family members to spend more time together, engage in certain activities with each other, use specified communication and problem-solving techniques, provide each other with desired behaviors, experiment with new interactive behaviors, and use specified methods of sharing, turn-taking, request-making, giving, and compromise.

Interpersonal Therapy.   The focus here is on relationship problems, in particular, on recurring maladaptive patterns in the evolution of the client's relationships with other people. There is analysis and then restructuring of the preconscious or unconscious "scripts" clients use to structure relationships; these scripts involve both self-concept and generalized beliefs about other people. Techniques include communication pattern analysis, confrontation, imagination of new scripts, and encouragement to experiment with new modes of relating to others.

Narrative Therapy.   In this approach, the client's constructions of meaning around his/her problems are viewed as the key to both etiology and change. The therapist facilitates construction of more adaptive personal "stories" or narratives by which the client explains his/her experiences to him/herself. Techniques include storytelling, with therapist guidance for developing new endings, use of metaphor, and externalization of symptoms.

Parent Counseling.   In this taxonomy, this term means that the clinician works with the parent on his or her own personal issues as they relate to child rearing. Although this term is sometimes used to mean any work with a parent, parent counseling, as used here, occupies a space between discussion of child management techniques (e.g., *BT: Parent training*) and explicit individual therapy with the parent. The category indicates work addressing the parent's personal issues *as they influence* his or her functioning as a caregiver. Often, this work addresses parental resistance to implementing recommended child-rearing practices, ambivalent or negative feelings toward the child, and effects of the grandparents' rearing of the parent on his or her own functioning with the client.

Parent Guidance. This category is for (1) any therapist recommendations to the parent that do not fit into the behavioral parent training category, and (2) clinician efforts to increase the parent's understanding of the child's unique characteristics (as opposed to general information about children or behavior problems, which is coded as psychoeducation). Many examples within this category are practical and concrete, for example, suggestions for earlier bedtimes, a quiet place for homework, less TV, more exercise, separating siblings, and any changes in daily routines or the physical home environment. Other examples are more abstract and may involve theoretical considerations. Examples would include recommendations to stop comparing siblings with each other, to listen nonjudgmentally to the child's feelings, to decrease pressure for grades, and to spend more time in shared, pleasant activities.

Philosophizing. This atheoretical but not uncommon treatment activity involves discussion of the meaning and purpose of the client's life and the nature of human life in general. The therapist may be nondirective or may offer his or her own input. These discussions often focus on inquiries into the meaning of the suffering or symptoms experienced by the client (particularly with trauma victims), attempts to use this suffering for positive purposes, modification of goals, values, and discussion of religious and spiritual issues. It should be noted that constructions of meaning are also a focus of narrative therapy; the present category is distinguished by its focus on issues that are philosophical in nature.

Planful Decision-Making. This is an atheoretical treatment activity in which the therapist helps the client analyze and solve life problems, make decisions, and develop plans. This therapeutic work is often informed by the clinician's theoretically based understanding of the client but is technically distinct from it. This term is meant to describe therapy time spent on deciding whether to continue a romantic relationship, working out a plan for dealing with a problem at work, or planning how to manage recurrent friction with a sibling. Techniques include asking questions to clarify and structure the client's thinking, using structured problem-solving techniques, and giving direct suggestions and advice.

Psychodynamic Therapy. The therapist attempts to ameliorate symptoms and enhance functioning by developing client awareness of previously unconscious personal dynamics. This approach helps clients gain insight into past formative experiences, unconscious conflicts and defenses, resistance to accurate self-understanding, recurrent relationship patterns, and unrealistic feelings about the therapist. The provision of insight is the major method of producing change. There is analysis of meanings expressed in play, artistic productions, stylistic details and patterns of client behavior and thought, dreams, behavior

151

toward the therapist, and symptoms themselves. Interpretation is the major technique used. Other techniques include reflection and confrontation.

Psychoeducation.   While this term can be used to describe any intervention involving skill training, in our taxonomy it has the much narrower meaning of *general information* pertaining to some aspects of the client's functioning that is shared with identifiable populations of children. The key word here is "general"; psychoeducational statements refer to children, not exclusively to the client. Psychoeducation should be coded when therapists educate parents or clients about the child's diagnostic syndrome, developmental stage, trauma history (e.g., sex abuse), life situation (e.g., parental divorce), or when clinicians provide any form of information about human functioning in general. Such information can be useful by increasing self-understanding, normalizing painful or confusing experiences, increasing sense of predictability and mastery, and providing an informational basis for problem solving. Bibliotherapy is often used.

Solution-Oriented Therapy.   This therapy differs from most approaches by minimizing discussion of the client's problems and instead focusing attention on possible solutions. There is an optimistic, future-oriented emphasis. Techniques include positive reframing, building on exceptions to the problem, and creating detailed images of the solution ("the miracle question"). Both family and individual modalities are used.

Supportive Therapy.   An atheoretical category, supportive therapy is meant to designate therapeutic activities such as expressive ventilation, offering statements of encouragement and optimism, complimenting the client, and communicating personal concern and caring to the client.

Using the System for Documentation

Like any taxonomic system, the preceding list attempts to divide up the domain of interest into a set of mutually exclusive and exhaustive categories. Psychotherapy is too complex an endeavor to be fully captured by the simple classificatory system we offer; some therapeutic activities will overlap with more than one of our approach definitions, and there are treatment approaches falling outside the list. But assuming that the approaches we describe are more different than similar, and that the presently common approaches are present in our list, this tool should make possible fairly quick and objective documentation of most of what goes on in therapy. When the system fails to be mutually exclusive and exhaustive, the provisions described earlier can manage the resulting ambiguity.

Our system includes many more codings for behavior therapy than for treatments based on other theoretical orientations. The number of codings in the taxonomy does not reflect our opinion of the methods, nor is it more than mildly influenced by how common the methods are in current clinical practice. Behavior therapy was subdivided into a number of approach codings because it includes an unusually large number of substantially different techniques, compared with other theoretical orientations.

Although most of the approaches are organized systems of theory and technique, three are not. As we define them, Planful Decision-making, Philosophizing, and Supportive Therapy are not theoretically based and do not involve well-defined "techniques." There is even a limited sense in which these are not distinctively psychotherapeutic procedures requiring professional training for implementation. Friends and relatives and, perhaps, barbers and bartenders provide people with opportunities for ventilation, statements of caring and hope, discussion of the meaning of life, and advice about choices and plans. Nonetheless, these activities belong in our list of therapeutic approaches, for several reasons.

First, the important consideration in selecting treatment activities is whether they are likely to help the client, not whether they require professional training. It would be counterproductive for therapists to reject helpful activities just because nontherapists can perform them too (although, if the client is receiving these forms of help elsewhere, that would decrease their value in therapy). Second, clinician use of these methods is presumably informed by both a diagnostic conceptualization of the client and a coherent plan of treatment, so that their use of the activities has a strategic aspect not present when laypeople provide these forms of help. Presumably, therapists engage in these activities for different reasons, in different ways, and with different effects than do nonprofessionals. Third, these methods belong on the list because they are necessary to make it complete. Many therapists spend significant session time on these activities, and equally important, these activities are not clearly indicated by the other, more theoretical and technical, approaches on the list. Therefore, if our system is to fulfill its purpose of identifying almost all the activities that go on in therapy sessions, the methods of Supportive Therapy, Planful Decision-making, and Philosophizing need to be on the list.

Most therapy cases involve more than one treatment approach. Many therapists describe their work as eclectic, that is, as combining techniques based on a number of different theoretical orientations (Jensen, Bergin, & Greaves, 1990; Kazdin, 1996; Kazdin, Siegal, & Bass, 1990). In Shapiro et al.'s (1997b) study of child therapy, the average case involved 3.67 different treatment approaches. Our forms make it convenient to document eclectic therapy by providing a format for indicating as many approaches as necessary and then rank-ordering them according to extent of use.

Our forms have separate systems for recording therapeutic modalities and approaches. Modalities present an easier recording task because they simply identify who was in the room with the therapist, whereas approaches designate theoretical orientation and technique. The "Family Systems Therapy" approaches do not indicate merely that two or more family members participated in the session but, additionally, indicate that systems theory and techniques were used. The family modality and the systems approaches usually occur together, but there are exceptions. For example, a family might be present together in the session so that the parents can practice behavioral child management techniques, in vivo, with their children, and the therapist can provide feedback. In this case, modality would be coded as Family, and approach would be coded as BT: Parent training.

153

Psychotherapy Treatment Plan

Name: _____ Date: _____

ID #: _____ Gender: M F Age: _____

Birth date: _____

Primary diagnosis: _____

Secondary diagnosis: _____

Describe child and family factors influencing the plan of treatment, e.g., assessment findings, motivation for change, strengths, limitations, life circumstances and events, personality styles, relationships, cultural factors, insurance considerations, and so forth:

_____

_____

_____

_____

_____

_____

Projected length of treatment: ___ months, ___ weeks

Planned frequency of treatment: ___ session(s) per ___ week(s).

Therapeutic Modality

(If just one, check; if more than one, number in decreasing order of use.)

___ Family   ___ Group   ___ Individual

___ Parent/child   ___ Parenting group   ___ Parent(s) alone

Therapeutic Approaches

___ Art therapy   ___ Client-centered therapy   ___ Parent counseling

___ BT: Classical   ___ Cognitive therapy   ___ Parent guidance

___ BT: Directive   ___ Cognitive-behavioral therapy ___ Philosophizing

___ BT: Emotional regulation ___ Experiential therapy   ___ Planful decision making

___ BT: Operant   ___ FST: Directive   ___ Psychodynamic therapy

___ BT: Parent training   ___ FST: Nondirective   ___ Psychoeducation

___ BT: Social Skills   ___ Interpersonal therapy   ___ Solution-oriented therapy

___ Case management   ___ Narrative therapy   ___ Supportive therapy

___ Other:_____

154

Provide any necessary elaboration of the planned approaches and describe the anticipated content and course of treatment. If the majority of major techniques within the indicated methods are planned, these need not be reiterated. If only a subset of the techniques are planned, state them. (Note that technique specification is most often necessary for behavior therapy, because it includes numerous specific techniques.)

_____
_____
_____
_____
_____
_____
_____
_____
_____
_____
_____

Goal Attainment Scale

Goal 1

Date (if after intake assessment): _____   Date achieved: _____

Scale-point

    1. Worse

    2. No change = presenting problem: _____

    3. Some progress

    4. Major progress: _____

    5. Goal attainment: _____

Goal 2

Date (if after intake assessment): _____   Date achieved: _____

Scale-point

    1. Worse

    2. No change = presenting problem: _____

    3. Some progress

    4. Major progress: _____

    5. Goal attainment: _____

Goal 3

Date (if after intake assessment): _____   Date achieved: _____

Scale-point

    1. Worse

    2. No change = presenting problem: _____

    3. Some progress

    4. Major progress: _____

    5. Goal attainment: _____

Goal 4

Date (if after intake assessment): _____   Date achieved: _____

Scale-point

    1. Worse

    2. No change = presenting problem: _____

    3. Some progress

    4. Major progress: _____

    5. Goal attainment: _____

Goal 5

Date (if after intake assessment): _____   Date achieved: _____

Scale-point

    1. Worse

    2. No change = presenting problem: _____

    3. Some progress

    4. Major progress: _____

    5. Goal attainment: _____

Comments

_____

_____

_____

_____

_____

_____

Signature: _____   Date: _____

PSYCHOTHERAPY PROGRESS NOTE

This form attempts to make use of the information-recording systems introduced in the Treatment Plan to facilitate efficiency of documentation. These formats are used again in the Treatment Summary. Basic information about change in client functioning can be charted quickly, and with a fair degree of objectivity and quantification, using the GAS. Our nomenclature for basic psychotherapeutic approaches provides a shorthand for quickly identifying the interventions used in the session. With this basic information recorded in little time, the clinician can use the narrative sections of the form to record more individualized material and also to structure planning for the next session.

In contrast with most previously offered systems, this form has only two narrative sections. This arrangement helps preserve the natural flow and connections among clinical material in the record of the session. Dividing session notes into several sections imposes an artificial structure that sometimes distorts the description of clinical work.

When therapists are left to their own devices, they usually write notes that move in approximate chronological order and that describe one clinical issue at a time. Descriptions of each issue often begin with client behaviors and verbalizations (usually in summary form, not verbatim), then present some conceptualization by the therapist, and end with documentation of the clinician's intervention. Also common are summary accounts of what the client said, what the therapist said, and then the client's response, sometimes with several back-and-forth sequences, concluding with the therapist's conceptualization; this recording pattern is most appropriate when client and therapist statements are not meaningful unless presented in their order, because each is a response to the other.

Progress notes with several sections make it difficult to record these types of material. If there are sections for client verbalizations, therapist assessment, and interventions, then the connections within one natural sequence are chopped up, three statements are made in separate parts of the note, and the context and sequence of the statements cannot be ascertained without looking up and down the form. It is not apparent what value is provided by use of numerous sections to compensate for this effort.

The main narrative section of our form is entitled simply "Session Notes." This is where the content and process of the session should be described.

We also have a brief section called "Plans and Reminders." This section is intended for use as a tool to facilitate treatment, particularly continuity across sessions. The Plans section should *not* be used to reiterate the Treatment Plan. It can be used to record modifications of the Treatment Plan when it is necessary to chart details of revisions inappropriate to document, with dates, on the Treatment Plan itself. The main purpose of this section is to provide a format for transporting the therapist's thoughts and plans from the end of one session to the beginning of the next one. A quick perusal of this brief section should remind the clinician where to go and facilitate an immediate reconnection with the flow of the client's therapy, so that each session takes up where the previous one left off.

157

Our overall goal in designing this form was to maximize the value of both structured systems and unstructured formats. Our strategy for achieving this was to separate these approaches and to be quite structured when being structured, and quite open-ended when being open-ended; this maximizes the strengths of each approach. The systems for identifying interventions and monitoring progress toward goals make it possible to record, quickly and fairly objectively, most of the basic information about the session. The Session Notes section should then be used to individualize the record by capturing the content and spirit of what transpired between the client and therapist. Redundancy is the enemy of efficiency; the Session Notes should not repeat the information recorded in the intervention list and GAS but rather should elaborate significant details and describe material not fitting into these predetermined systems.

GOAL ATTAINMENT SCALE

Our form for tracking progress in therapy relies heavily on the GAS procedure introduced in the section on treatment planning. The effort invested in defining the client's personalized GAS scale should pay dividends throughout the course of treatment, because these scales make it possible to chart session-by-session progress in a quick, efficient manner.

The key to our procedure's efficiency is that, in defining goals, detailed writing occurs only once, when the client's GAS is constructed in the context of treatment planning. These scale definitions then furnish an effective shorthand that links a standard metric to the client's personal treatment goals.

The information encapsulated in the scale never needs to be rewritten; instead, each session, the therapist should refer back to the definition of the GAS in the Treatment Plan and should use its number system to record the level of progress the client exhibited on each goal of treatment. In other words, the GAS metric is defined in the Treatment Plan, and session-by-session change can then be recorded simply by writing the number that indicates the client's level of change, as per the original scale-point definitions. To do this, it is necessary to have the Treatment Plan present in the session.

The GAS should be completed based on child and parent report. Usually, the therapist's job consists merely of translating client reports into the scale's metric but, if there is reason to question these reports or if another source of information about progress is available, the therapist can have more direct input.

In work with clients, there should be nothing hidden about the GAS procedure. If shared with clients as a collaborative activity, the GAS can serve some clinically useful functions. The procedure can help clients focus on the main goals of treatment. Also, the scale provides clients with a fixed framework in terms of which to evaluate change. Behavioral definitions of the presenting problems and the original treatment goals provide clients with benchmarks. Remembering where they have been and where they are aiming helps clients maintain a clear sense of therapy's direction and rate of progress.

There are a few technical points to consider in using the GAS session by session. Occasionally, it is difficult to decide which scale-point corresponds to a reported level of client change. In approaching close discriminations, the clinician should remember that the GAS represents an ordinal scale of measurement, the purpose of which is to capture clinically meaningful amounts of change in an efficient, practical fashion. The GAS is not a precise, finely calibrated scale, and clinicians will experience undue frustration if they attempt to use it as if it were one. If we obsess about which of two adjacent scale-points to use as a representation of client change, time will be lost for the work of therapy, and documentation will become the servant of clinical work, whereas our goal is for things to be the other way around.

In addition to maintaining a realistic level of aspiration for precision, it is important to use good, commonsensical judgment emphasizing clinical meaning and the perspectives of clients and parents. In principle, one could worry about questions such as, "How much change is necessary for marking the scale-points of *worse* and *some progress?*" In practice, these decisions are not usually difficult. These scale-points (1 and 3) are meant to indicate any change that is noticeable and meaningful, even if slight. If the degree of change was sufficient to cause the child or parent to notice and report it, then it is presumably meaningful.

Making correct decisions among Scale-points 3–5 does require understanding one technical point. In theory, there is a continuum underlying the scale, with proportions of goal attainment ranging from negative values, to 0% (Scale-point 2), through 100% (Scale-point 5). However, our GAS marks this continuum at only 5 points. Decisions about which scale-point to mark are difficult when our sense is that the client's true degree of progress lies between two points, rather than falling squarely within one. The solution, in principle, is simple: mark the closest scale-point; the scale-points represent the *regions* of the underlying scale in the middle of which they are placed.

The following diagram may be helpful in achieving a conceptual understanding of the scale. It is presented with a degree of precision representing an abstraction rather than the clinical reality of the procedure. The diagram depicts the correspondence between scale-points and scale regions.

Worse	Presenting problem	Some progress	Major progress	Goal attainment
–%	0	+%	50%	100%

The boundary between Scale-points 4 and 5 lies at 75% goal attainment. Thus, 74% of goal achievement would be scored as *major progress* and 76% of goal achievement would be scored as *goal attainment.* If some progress were assumed to indicate 10% of attainment, then the boundary between that scale-point and *major progress* would lie at 30% of attainment. In practice, these percentages will not usually be the terms of discussion; useful questions will be along the lines of "Is she obeying your directions less than half the time (3) or more than half the time (4)?"

Noting Changes in Comparison with the Previous Session

The GAS describes progress in terms of a set scale that does not change after it is developed in the Treatment Plan. This macroscopic view of progress is of most importance to treatment monitoring. However, a more microscopic monitoring of change can also be of some use.

At the end of the GAS, our form asks for a rating of change in relation to the previous session. This rating should be performed for the behavioral dimensions represented by each of the GAS goals. However, this rating does *not* involve the GAS method or metric, which uses the presenting problems and treatment goals—rather than the previous session—as benchmarks for assessing change.

Tracking client ups and downs from session to session provides a sense of recent change, while the GAS tracks overall change. As a result of their fundamentally different time frames and benchmarks, these two tracking methods will often produce ratings that, if not understood properly, will seem contradictory. Consider the example of a child with a presenting problem of hitting his sister six times a day, whose treatment goal was to reduce hitting to at most once per day, who had achieved a reduction to twice per day, and whose parent then reported a rate of three times per day during the preceding week. This information results in a scoring of Major Progress on the GAS and a rating of Worse on the session-by-session scale. There is nothing paradoxical about this difference; it simply indicates short-term deterioration in the context of long-term improvement.

The session-by-session scale is extremely simple; it consists of indicating whether the client's functioning is better, worse, or the same on each dimension. There would be no point in using a more complexly differentiated scale because this measure is capable of providing information only about two-session units of treatment, and not the whole course of therapy. Because the benchmark is the preceding session, which is different each time, the meaning of session-by-session ratings changes constantly and is almost uninterpretable. No information about overall treatment progress is yielded by a 6-session sequence such as "Better, Better, Worse, No change, Worse, Better." There is no way to know whether the client experienced improvement from the beginning to the end of treatment.

Nonetheless, the easiest framework for monitoring progress is session by session—this is the way people naturally think—and so it is included in our form. This scale can be useful for monitoring short-term trends in change. It should not be used to evaluate the overall course of treatment.

Psychotherapy Progress Note

Name: _____ Date: _____

Session length: ___ 50 minutes ___ Other: _____ Session #: _____

Therapeutic Modality

(If just one, check; if more than one, number in decreasing order of use.)

___ Family   ___ Group   ___ Individual

___ Parent/child   ___ Parenting group   ___ Parent(s) alone

Therapeutic Approaches

___ Art therapy	___ Client-centered therapy	___ Parent counseling
___ BT: Classical	___ Cognitive therapy	___ Parent guidance
___ BT: Directive	___ Cognitive-behavioral therapy	___ Philosophizing
___ BT: Emotional regulation	___ Experiential therapy	___ Planful decision making
___ BT: Operant	___ FST: Directive	___ Psychodynamic therapy
___ BT: Parent training	___ FST: Nondirective	___ Psychoeducation
___ BT: Social Skills	___ Interpersonal therapy	___ Solution-oriented therapy
___ Case management	___ Narrative therapy	___ Supportive therapy

___ Other:_____

Goal Attainment Scale

	Goal 1	Goal 2	Goal 3	Goal 4	Goal 5
Indicate GAS level (1–5):	____	____	____	____	____
Change since last session (Better +, worse -, no change X):	____	____	____	____	____

Session notes: _____

_____

_____

_____

_____

_____

_____

_____

Plans and reminders: _____

_____

_____

Signature: _____

Psychotherapy Treatment Summary

Our treatment summary forms make use of the same major informational systems that were introduced in the Treatment Plan and then utilized in the Psychotherapy Progress Note. In the summary, the therapist indicates the therapeutic approaches he or she used and ranks them in descending order of use during the full course of treatment. The client's final levels of goal attainment are indicated. Thus, the summary can be directly compared with the plan, and the similarities and differences between intention and eventuality will be immediately apparent.

On the Treatment Summary, data for the list of therapeutic approaches and the GAS pertain to different time frames. The therapist should provide a summary of the treatment methods used over the entire course of treatment. In contrast, GAS ratings should not be an average of the ratings given for all the sessions; instead, the final GAS ratings should indicate level of progress toward goals as of the final session. The final GAS ratings do represent a summary measurement but, unlike the final therapeutic method ratings, they are based on accumulation not averaging.

The purpose of the narrative sections of the forms is to complement the structured sections by describing the content, dynamics, and spirit of the client's treatment. The potential clinical usefulness of this historical document lies mostly in its capacity for guiding future services to the client, and this type of information is particularly important to record. Continuing needs, continuing efforts to meet those needs, aftercare plans, and referrals should be noted. Future therapists (whether the writer or someone else) would benefit from a report of which techniques seemed more or less helpful to the client.

Two statistical points warrant consideration if the GAS is to be used for program evaluation or research. Because of its element of strandardization, or at least of procedural consistency, GAS scores seem comparable across clients. However, GAS scores can be useful only if their meaning is understood accurately. The GAS does not directly measure clinical improvement; it measures the degree to which the client achieved his or her initial goals for improvement. The distinction is not pedantic. Individual differences in level of aspiration (i.e., definitions of goal attainment) weaken score comparability; two clients who achieved the same degree of improvement, but who had different levels of aspiration for treatment, would obtain different scores on the GAS. This consideration qualifies, but does not negate, the usefulness of GAS scores for program evaluation and research, because degree of client goal attainment is a meaningful form of information. This qualification to the meaning of GAS scores should be borne in mind when interpreting the results.

Second, the Goal Attainment Scale we present involves an ordinal scale of measurement. The intervals between the scale-points are not equal, and these points provide information only about order or ranking. Therefore, nonparametric statistical tests should be used to analyze GAS data.

Psychotherapy Treatment Summary

Name: _____   Date: _____

ID #: _____   Gender: M F   Age: _____

Initial diagnoses: _____

Length of treatment: ___ months, ___ weeks

Frequency of treatment: ___ session(s) per ___ week(s)

Therapeutic Modality

(If just one, check; if more than one, number in decreasing order of use.)

___ Family   ___ Group   ___ Individual

___ Parent/child   ___ Parenting group   ___ Parent(s) alone

Therapeutic Approaches

___ Art therapy   ___ Client-centered therapy   ___ Parent counseling

___ BT: Classical   ___ Cognitive therapy   ___ Parent guidance

___ BT: Directive   ___ Cognitive-behavioral therapy   ___ Philosophizing

___ BT: Emotional regulation ___ Experiential therapy   ___ Planful decision making

___ BT: Operant   ___ FST: Directive   ___ Psychodynamic therapy

___ BT: Parent training   ___ FST: Nondirective   ___ Psychoeducation

___ BT: Social Skills   ___ Interpersonal therapy   ___ Solution-oriented therapy

___ Case management   ___ Narrative therapy   ___ Supportive therapy

___ Other: _____

Outcomes Described by Goal Attainment Scale

Goal 1	Goal 2	Goal 3	Goal 4	Goal 5
____	____	____	____	____

Comments: _____

_____

_____

_____

Scale: 1 = Worse   3 = Some progress   5 = Goal attainment
       2 = No change   4 = Major progress

163

Describe aspects of the course of treatment not covered by the structured formats, such as session content, rate of progress, reversals of progress, turning points, life events, client motivation, dynamics of family participation, therapeutic relationships and, in particular, client responses to specific therapeutic methods:

_____
_____
_____
_____
_____
_____
_____
_____
_____
_____
_____

Termination Diagnosis

Axis I   _____

Axis II   _____

Axis III   _____

Axis IV   _____

Axis V   _____

Describe client condition at termination, identifying any continuing needs and referrals:

_____
_____
_____
_____
_____
_____
_____
_____
_____
_____
_____
_____

Signature: _____   Date: _____

Outpatient Treatment Plan

Name: _____ Date: _____

ID #: _____ Gender: M F Age: _____

Birth date: _____ Telephone number: _____

Address: _____

City: _____ State: _____ Zip code: _____

Information recorded by: _____

Information supplied by (name and relationship to the client): _____
_____

Reason for referral: _____

Presenting Problems

(Please indicate all that apply and describe):

___ Psychological/emotional: _____

___ Behavioral: _____

___ Substance use: _____

___ Family/relationship: _____

___ Work/school: _____

___ Legal: _____

___ Other: _____

How long have these problems been present?

    ___ 1 month or less   ___ 1 month to 6 months   ___ More than 6 months

Factors Contributing to Functional Assessment

Please evaluate the patient's resources on each dimension (on a scale of 1 to 4, with 1 being helpful and 4 harmful):

	Helpful	Adequate	Inadequate	Harmful
Housing	(1)	(2)	(3)	(4)
Employment	(1)	(2)	(3)	(4)
Education	(1)	(2)	(3)	(4)
Family support	(1)	(2)	(3)	(4)
Interpersonal relationships	(1)	(2)	(3)	(4)
Self-care skills	(1)	(2)	(3)	(4)
Other: _____	(1)	(2)	(3)	(4)

Activity

	Mild	Moderate	Severe	Targeted
Abnormal movements	(1)	(2)	(3)	(4)
Catatonia	(1)	(2)	(3)	(4)
Decrease in energy or fatigue	(1)	(2)	(3)	(4)
Hyperactivity	(1)	(2)	(3)	(4)
Impulsivity	(1)	(2)	(3)	(4)
Incoordination	(1)	(2)	(3)	(4)
Social or occupational sexual activity	(1)	(2)	(3)	(4)
Psychomotor agitation	(1)	(2)	(3)	(4)
Psychomotor retardation	(1)	(2)	(3)	(4)
Restlessness	(1)	(2)	(3)	(4)

Behavior

	Mild	Moderate	Severe	Targeted
Academic or work inhibition	(1)	(2)	(3)	(4)
Aggression or rage	(1)	(2)	(3)	(4)
Antisocial	(1)	(2)	(3)	(4)
Compulsions	(1)	(2)	(3)	(4)
Deceitfulness or theft	(1)	(2)	(3)	(4)
Destructive	(1)	(2)	(3)	(4)
Disorganized	(1)	(2)	(3)	(4)
Oppositional/defiant	(1)	(2)	(3)	(4)
Reckless	(1)	(2)	(3)	(4)
Self-injurious	(1)	(2)	(3)	(4)
Social withdrawal	(1)	(2)	(3)	(4)
Violation of rules or rights of others	(1)	(2)	(3)	(4)

Anxiety Problems

	Mild	Moderate	Severe	Targeted
Anxiety	(1)	(2)	(3)	(4)
Avoidance behavior	(1)	(2)	(3)	(4)
Fear of separation	(1)	(2)	(3)	(4)
Jitteriness	(1)	(2)	(3)	(4)
Panic attacks	(1)	(2)	(3)	(4)
Phobic responses	(1)	(2)	(3)	(4)
Somatization	(1)	(2)	(3)	(4)
Worrying	(1)	(2)	(3)	(4)

Mood/Affect

	Mild	Moderate	Severe	Targeted
Anger	(1)	(2)	(3)	(4)
Apathy	(1)	(2)	(3)	(4)
Blunted or flat affect	(1)	(2)	(3)	(4)
Depressed mood	(1)	(2)	(3)	(4)
Elevated or expansive mood	(1)	(2)	(3)	(4)
Excessive or inappropriate guilt	(1)	(2)	(3)	(4)
Excitability	(1)	(2)	(3)	(4)
Feeling worthless	(1)	(2)	(3)	(4)
Grandiosity	(1)	(2)	(3)	(4)
Helplessness	(1)	(2)	(3)	(4)
Hopelessness	(1)	(2)	(3)	(4)
Hostility	(1)	(2)	(3)	(4)
Hysteria	(1)	(2)	(3)	(4)
Interpersonal rejection sensitivity	(1)	(2)	(3)	(4)
Irritability	(1)	(2)	(3)	(4)
Loss of interest or pleasure	(1)	(2)	(3)	(4)
Low self-esteem	(1)	(2)	(3)	(4)
Marked mood shifts	(1)	(2)	(3)	(4)
Tearfulness	(1)	(2)	(3)	(4)

Cognitive/Memory/Attention

	Mild	Moderate	Severe	Targeted
Aphasia	(1)	(2)	(3)	(4)
Diminished ability to think	(1)	(2)	(3)	(4)
Distractibility	(1)	(2)	(3)	(4)
Impaired abstract thinking	(1)	(2)	(3)	(4)
Impaired judgment	(1)	(2)	(3)	(4)
Indecisiveness	(1)	(2)	(3)	(4)
Memory impairment	(1)	(2)	(3)	(4)
Poor attention or concentration	(1)	(2)	(3)	(4)
Circumstantiality	(1)	(2)	(3)	(4)
Flight of ideas	(1)	(2)	(3)	(4)
Incoherence or loosening of associations	(1)	(2)	(3)	(4)
More talkative than usual	(1)	(2)	(3)	(4)
Pressured speech	(1)	(2)	(3)	(4)
Racing thoughts	(1)	(2)	(3)	(4)
Slurred speech	(1)	(2)	(3)	(4)
Tangentiality	(1)	(2)	(3)	(4)

Perception/Thought

	Mild	Moderate	Severe	Targeted
Delusions	(1)	(2)	(3)	(4)
Depersonalization	(1)	(2)	(3)	(4)
Disturbance in perception of body	(1)	(2)	(3)	(4)
Grandiosity	(1)	(2)	(3)	(4)
Hallucination	(1)	(2)	(3)	(4)
Illusions of perceptual distortions	(1)	(2)	(3)	(4)
Obsessions	(1)	(2)	(3)	(4)
Paranoid ideation	(1)	(2)	(3)	(4)
Recurring recollection of distressing events	(1)	(2)	(3)	(4)
Suicidal ideation	(1)	(2)	(3)	(4)

Physical Signs and Symptoms

	Mild	Moderate	Severe	Targeted
Autonomic	(1)	(2)	(3)	(4)
Cardiovascular	(1)	(2)	(3)	(4)
Gastrointestinal	(1)	(2)	(3)	(4)
Neurological	(1)	(2)	(3)	(4)
Pain	(1)	(2)	(3)	(4)

Eating Disturbances

	Mild	Moderate	Severe	Targeted
Binge eating	(1)	(2)	(3)	(4)
Decreased appetite	(1)	(2)	(3)	(4)
Increased appetite	(1)	(2)	(3)	(4)
Inability to maintain normal body weight	(1)	(2)	(3)	(4)
Self-induced vomiting	(1)	(2)	(3)	(4)

Sleep Disturbances

	Mild	Moderate	Severe	Targeted
Early morning waking	(1)	(2)	(3)	(4)
Hypersomnia	(1)	(2)	(3)	(4)
Insomnia	(1)	(2)	(3)	(4)

Substance Use and Abuse

	Mild	Moderate	Severe	Targeted
Continued use despite knowledge of effects	(1)	(2)	(3)	(4)
Disrupted activities	(1)	(2)	(3)	(4)
Inability to decrease use	(1)	(2)	(3)	(4)
Persistent desire for substance	(1)	(2)	(3)	(4)
Substance abuse	(1)	(2)	(3)	(4)
Tolerance	(1)	(2)	(3)	(4)
Withdrawal	(1)	(2)	(3)	(4)
Excess time obtaining, using, or recovering from effects	(1)	(2)	(3)	(4)

DSM-IV Multiaxial Diagnosis

Principal diagnosis:

Axis I codes	Axis I disorder(s)
1. _____	_____
2. _____	_____
3. _____	_____
4. _____	_____
5. _____	_____
6. _____	_____
7. _____	_____
8. _____	_____

Axis II: _____

_____

Axis III: _____

_____

Axis IV: _____

_____

Axis V: _____

_____

_____

Treatment Goals and Progress

Treatment goals, target dates, and rating of progress (none, minimal, significant, complete): _____

_____

_____

_____

_____

_____

_____

_____

_____

If there has been little or no improvement to date, or since the last treatment plan, what changes, are you making (including changes in medication)? _____

_____

_____

_____

_____

_____

_____

_____

_____

Client follow-through with treatment recommendations:

___ Excellent   ___ Adequate   ___ Problematic

If problematic, indicate all that apply:

___ Missed sessions ___ Medications not taken as prescribed ___ Other: _____

Risk Assessment

Suicide risk (indicate one): ___ none ___ low ___ moderate ___ high

Status during past 3 months (indicate one):

___ ideation	___ previous hospitalization	___ adverse reaction to medication
___ intent	___ recent loss	___ family history of suicide or violence
___ plan	___ hopelessness	___ domestic violence
___ threats	___ lack of support	___ access to means
___ acts	___ CD history	___ impaired judgment

Has the patient contracted for safety? ___ No ___Yes ___N/A

Please explain any adverse outcomes that have occurred during your care of this patient:

_____

_____

_____

_____

_____

_____

_____

_____

Psychotropic Medications

Has the patient been on psychotropic medications in the past?

___ No   ___ Yes   ___ Unknown

Is the patient currently on psychotropic medications? ___ No ___ Yes

Prescriber (if not self): _____

Please indicate all classes that apply:

___ Antipsychotic   ___ Antidepressant   ___Anti-anxiety   ___Hypnotic

___ Mood stabilizer/anticonvulsant   ___ Psychostimulant   ___ Other: _____

Medication	Dose	Frequency	Start date
_____	_____	_____	_____
_____	_____	_____	_____
_____	_____	_____	_____
_____	_____	_____	_____
_____	_____	_____	_____
_____	_____	_____	_____

Nonpsychotropic Medications

Is the patient currently on nonpsychotropic medications? ___ No ___ Yes

Prescriber (if not self): _____

Medication	Dose	Frequency	Start date
_____	_____	_____	_____
_____	_____	_____	_____
_____	_____	_____	_____
_____	_____	_____	_____
_____	_____	_____	_____
_____	_____	_____	_____

Forms for Residential, Hospital, Partial Hospitalization, and Day Treatment

The following pages present forms for levels of mental health treatment that are more intensive than outpatient therapy. Inpatient hospitalization, residential treatment, partial hospitalization, and day treatment involve many more hours of time and more diverse modalities of intervention, compared with outpatient services. These high-intensity levels of intervention are also much more expensive than outpatient treatment. Generally, these intensive types of treatment are appropriate only for clients who fail to achieve progress in outpatient therapy or whose needs are too extensive to be met by outpatient services.

These characteristics of high-intensity services are reflected in the terms we offer for planning and summarizing services. The list of treatment activities is both broader and less fine-grained than the list of treatment approaches in the psychotherapy forms. In other words, the high-intensity service forms list a wider array of interventions, and these forms group treatment methods into broader categories, compared with the psychotherapy forms. For example, these forms list individual therapy, group therapy, special education, and psychiatric medication; the psychotherapy forms differentiate between a number of specific types of individual therapy.

Because most clients in hospital, residential, partial hospitalization, and day treatment have psychotherapy as one of their services, their service records should include both sets of forms. The high-intensity service forms should present a global overview of treatment, and the psychotherapy forms should present a focused description of that modality of intervention.

Generally, because the high-intensity services are both more expensive and more restrictive than outpatient therapy, the immediate goal of these services should be to achieve client progress sufficient to enable transition to an outpatient setting, rather than to achieve progress sufficient to justify termination of all treatment (although that may be the ultimate goal). Thus, the immediate goal of high-intensity treatment allows for higher remaining levels of symptomatology than does stand-alone outpatient therapy. As a result, discharge criteria should be different for high-intensity treatment and outpatient services. These different discharge criteria should translate directly into the goals defined on the GAS.

GAS Scale-point 5 (goal attainment) should correspond precisely to criteria for discharge or termination of the service being documented. For outpatient therapy, a relatively low-intensity form of treatment, goal attainment generally corresponds to the level of functioning at which no mental health service of any kind would be necessary. (This is how Scale-point 5 should be explained to clients.) For high-intensity services, goal attainment should be defined, quite differently, as the level of functioning at which lower intensity services, such as outpatient therapy, would be sufficient to meet the client's needs.

This point may be emotionally difficult for clinicians to accept, because we naturally want to help clients achieve full mental health, and that desire naturally expresses itself in goal definitions and high levels of aspiration for treatment. However, high-intensity services

172

represent just one end of the treatment continuum, the immediate purpose of which is to make lower intensity services feasible. Also, setting a relatively modest goal does not mean that a greater amount of progress might not occur. GAS Scale-point 5 (goal attainment) should identify the *immediate* goal of treatment, and not the clinician's ultimate goal for the client. Therefore, the GAS for high-intensity services should define *lower goals* than the GAS for outpatient therapy.

These forms have space for more goals than do the psychotherapy forms. This is because clients receiving high-intensity services, presumably, have more problems and so more goals, compared with outpatient psychotherapy clients.

Residential, Hospital, Partial Hospitalization, or Day Treatment Plan

Type of treatment: ___ Residential ___ Hospital ___Partial Hospitalization ___ Day

Name: _____ Date: _____

ID #: _____ Gender: M F   Age: _____

Birth date: _____ Date of admission: _____

Anticipated length of treatment: ___ months,   ___ weeks

Primary diagnosis: _____
_____
_____

Secondary diagnosis: _____
_____
_____

Describe child and family factors influencing the plan of treatment, for instance, assessment findings, history, response to past treatment efforts, motivation for change, strengths, limitations, resources, life circumstances and events, personality styles, family functioning, cultural factors, and insurance considerations:

_____
_____
_____
_____
_____
_____
_____
_____
_____
_____
_____
_____
_____
_____
_____

Treatment Activities

	Person responsible	Date to begin	Date ended
___ Diagnostic assessment	_____	_____	_____
___ Environmental behavior therapy	_____	_____	_____
___ Individual therapy	_____	_____	_____
___ Family therapy	_____	_____	_____
___ Group therapy	_____	_____	_____
___ Special education	_____	_____	_____
___ Case management	_____	_____	_____
___ Psychiatric medication	_____	_____	_____
___ Crisis intervention	_____	_____	_____
___ Drug/alcohol treatment	_____	_____	_____
___ Occupational therapy	_____	_____	_____
___ Speech/language therapy	_____	_____	_____
___ Art therapy	_____	_____	_____
___ Music therapy	_____	_____	_____
___ Creative expression (acting)	_____	_____	_____
___ Foster care	_____	_____	_____
___ Home visits	_____	_____	_____
___ Other: _____	_____	_____	_____

Describe the planned treatment activities indicating how they will be individualized for this client. Describe anticipated content, central issues, important needs, possible barriers to change and plans for addressing them, therapeutic relationships, and expected course of treatment.

_____

_____

_____

_____

_____

_____

_____

_____

_____

_____

_____

_____

Goal 1

    Date (if after intake assessment): _____   Date achieved: _____

    Scale-point

        1. Worse

        2. No change = presenting problem: _____

        3. Some progress

        4. Major progress: _____

        5. Goal attainment: _____

Goal 2

    Date (if after intake assessment): _____   Date achieved: _____

    Scale-point

        1. Worse

        2. No change = presenting problem: _____

        3. Some progress

        4. Major progress: _____

        5. Goal attainment: _____

Goal 3

    Date (if after intake assessment): _____   Date achieved: _____

    Scale-point

        1. Worse

        2. No change = presenting problem: _____

        3. Some progress

        4. Major progress: _____

        5. Goal attainment: _____

Goal 4

    Date (if after intake assessment): _____   Date achieved: _____

    Scale-point

        1. Worse

        2. No change = presenting problem: _____

        3. Some progress

        4. Major progress: _____

        5. Goal attainment: _____

Goal 5

Date (if after intake assessment): _____ Date achieved: _____

Scale-point

    1. Worse

    2. No change = presenting problem: _____

    3. Some progress

    4. Major progress: _____

    5. Goal attainment: _____

Goal 6

Date (if after intake assessment): _____ Date achieved: _____

Scale-point

    1. Worse

    2. No change = presenting problem: _____

    3. Some progress

    4. Major progress: _____

    5. Goal attainment: _____

Goal 7

Date (if after intake assessment): _____ Date achieved: _____

Scale-point

    1. Worse

    2. No change = presenting problem: _____

    3. Some progress

    4. Major progress: _____

    5. Goal attainment: _____

Goal 8

Date (if after intake assessment): _____ Date achieved: _____

Scale-point

    1. Worse

    2. No change = presenting problem: _____

    3. Some progress

    4. Major progress: _____

    5. Goal attainment: _____

Goal 9

Date (if after intake assessment): _____ Date achieved: _____

Scale-point

1. Worse

2. No change = presenting problem: _____

3. Some progress

4. Major progress: _____

5. Goal attainment: _____

Goal 10

Date (if after intake assessment): _____ Date achieved: _____

Scale-point

1. Worse

2. No change = presenting problem: _____

3. Some progress

4. Major progress: _____

5. Goal attainment: _____

Comments

_____

_____

_____

_____

_____

Signature: _____ Date: _____

Treatment Team Signatures

Name	Role	Date
_____	_____	_____
_____	_____	_____
_____	_____	_____
_____	_____	_____
_____	_____	_____
_____	_____	_____
_____	_____	_____

Residential, Hospital, Partial Hospitalization, or Day Treatment Summary

Type of treatment: ___ Residential ___ Hospital ___ Partial Hospitalization ___ Day

Name: _____ Date: _____

ID #: _____ Gender: M F Age: _____

Birth date: _____

Anticipated length of treatment: ___ months, ___ weeks

Initial diagnoses: _____

Initial presenting problems: _____

_____

_____

Length of treatment: ___ months, ___ days

Treatment Activities

	Person responsible	Date begun	Date ended
___ Diagnostic assessment	_____	_____	_____
___ Environmental behavior therapy	_____	_____	_____
___ Individual therapy	_____	_____	_____
___ Family therapy	_____	_____	_____
___ Group therapy	_____	_____	_____
___ Special education	_____	_____	_____
___ Case management	_____	_____	_____
___ Psychiatric medication	_____	_____	_____
___ Crisis intervention	_____	_____	_____
___ Drug/alcohol treatment	_____	_____	_____
___ Occupational therapy	_____	_____	_____
___ Speech/language therapy	_____	_____	_____
___ Art therapy	_____	_____	_____
___ Music therapy	_____	_____	_____
___ Creative expression (acting)	_____	_____	_____
___ Foster care	_____	_____	_____
___ Home visits	_____	_____	_____
___ Other: _____	_____	_____	_____

Outcomes Described by Goal Attainment Scale

Goal: 1   2   3   4   5   6   7   8   9   10

_____ _____ _____ _____ _____ _____ _____ _____ _____ _____

Comments: _____

_____

_____

_____

Scale: 1 = Worse   3 = Some progress   5 = Goal attainment
2 = No change   4 = Major progress

Describe aspects of the course of treatment not covered by the structured formats, such as important therapeutic issues, levels of client cooperation with treatment, rate of progress, reversals of progress, therapeutic turning points, unusual incidents, life events, crises, relationship changes, family participation, interest in different activities, relationships with treatment staff and, in particular, responses to the various treatment methods:

_____

_____

_____

_____

_____

_____

_____

_____

_____

_____

_____

_____

_____

_____

_____

_____

_____

Termination Diagnosis

Axis I   _____

Axis II   _____

Axis III _____

Axis IV   _____

Axis V   _____

Describe client's condition at discharge, identifying continuing needs.

_____
_____
_____
_____
_____
_____
_____
_____
_____
_____
_____

Discharge placement: _____
_____

Aftercare plan (indicate referrals):

_____
_____
_____
_____
_____
_____
_____
_____
_____
_____
_____

Treatment Team Signatures

Name   Role   Date

_____   _____   _____
_____   _____   _____
_____   _____   _____
_____   _____   _____
_____   _____   _____
_____   _____   _____

Residential Treatment Center
Quarterly Report

Child's name: _____   Date: _____

Birth date: _____   Gender: M   F   Age: _____

Address: _____

City: _____   State: _____   Zip code: _____

Type of custody: _____   Building name: _____

Case therapist: _____   Supervisor: _____

Placement date: _____   Anticipated date of discharge: _____

Agency: _____

Program: _____   Report period (from/to): _____

Worker: _____   Supervisor: _____

Permanency plan or change of placement planning (to be completed if child's placement changed during reporting period; comment on reason for particular placement setting, specific permanency planning efforts, and family support of setting): _____

_____

_____

_____

_____

_____

_____

_____

_____

_____

_____

_____

_____

_____

Education

Name of school: _____

Address: _____

City: _____   State: _____   Zip code: _____

Year in school: _____

Type of special education program (if applicable): _____

Medical Update

Date of last physical exam: _____ Where: _____

Date of last dental exam: _____ Where: _____

Date of last optical exam: _____ Where: _____

Date of other exams: _____ Where: _____

Special service activity (specific behavioral, emotional, medical issues, appointments, psychological testing, medications, etc.): _____

_____

_____

_____

_____

_____

_____

Major Events

___ AWOLs   ___ Sexual assault

___ Self-injurious behavior   ___ Court/legal involvement

___ Physical assault (peers or staff)   ___ Alleged abuse/neglect

___ School truancy/supervision   ___ Psychiatric emergency

___ Injury   ___ Other: _____

Comments (see attached CIRs): _____

_____

_____

Family involvement/visitation/permanency plan (circle the appropriate case plan goal):

Reunification living   Permanency placement   Not adoption   Adoption   Independent

Name of significant person(s) involved in the child's treatment program (please include name and relationship): _____

_____

_____

_____

_____

Number (or frequency) of contacts during reporting period by type of contact:

___ Face-to-face visits   ___ Telephone contacts   ___ Correspondence

___ Therapy sessions   ___ Other

List resources consistent with the treatment plan/case goals for which a referral has been made to help assure a successful discharge of the child.

Resource	Address	Phone
_____	_____	_____
_____	_____	_____
_____	_____	_____
_____	_____	_____
_____	_____	_____

Quarterly Review and Summary

Services: Note all ongoing services (O), new services (N), or termination of services (T), for child or family for reporting period; frequency of services (number of times per quarter, daily (D), weekly (W), monthly (M), and date (D), of implementation or termination).

___ Case management   ___ Respite (in-home)   ___ Parent education
___ Individual therapy   ___ Speech therapy   ___ Cultural services
___ Art/music therapy   ___ Big brother/big sister   ___ Physical therapy
___ Substance abuse treatment ___ Support group   ___ Family therapy
___ Mentoring   ___ Med/somatic   ___ Day camp
___ Wraparound   ___ Partial hospitalization   ___ Individual living training
___ Diagnostic assessment   ___ Respite (out-of-home)   ___ Recreation
___ Group therapy   ___ Rites of passage   ___ Other

Goals: 1= Discontinued   2 = Regressed   3 = No change   4 = Improved   5 = Achieved

Goals	Time frame	Rating	Interventions/measurable action steps/comments	Time frame for each objective
1				
2				
3				
4				
5				

Summary of progress and ISP changes: _____

Ongoing/new goals	Time frame	Rating	Interventions/comments	Time frame for each objective
1				
2				

Residential Treatment Center Brief Note

Client's name: _____   Date: _____

Birth date: _____   Gender: M F   Age: _____

Units of service: ___ 15 min. ___ 30 min. ___ 45 min. ___ 60 min. ___ Other: _____

Counseling (check one): ___ Individual ___ Family ___ Group

Diagnostic assessment: ___ No ___ Yes

Case management (check "with" and "activity" below):

With	Activity
___ Client ___ Client-telephone ___ Family ___ Family-telephone ___ Other ___ Other-telephone	___ Treatment/service plan ___ Crisis ___ Family support ___ Interpersonal and community ___ Resources

Services: _____

_____

_____

_____

_____

_____

_____

_____

_____

Changes in client's condition/needs: _____

Client's responses to services/service plan: _____

Outcome of services/review of progress (circle one): _____

Regressed   No change   Improved   Goal Achieved

Signature: _____   Date: _____

REPORT OF INCIDENT OR UNUSUAL OCCURRENCE

It is always prudent to have Incident Report forms handy in any mental health or human service facility. One never knows when there may be a need to record a particular event that may have important consequences at that or a later time. In reporting "unusual occurrences," it is better to err on the side of overreporting than letting some incident go without a report. And there is nothing more satisfying than being asked to recall an incident and being able to pull out a report of the occurrence that had been prepared at the time.

The obvious incidents are those involving some accidental or intentional harm to person or property. Less clear may be a waiting room incident in which a mother yells inappropriately at a child, or one child aggresses against another. A good rule of thumb is to err on the side of caution and document any occurrences with the potential to be viewed as serious. File the report away and discard it in a year, if there is no question of its significance. In reporting incidents in a clinical facility, it is better to be safe than sorry.

The following sample report form has wide application to both outpatient and inpatient facilities. Each setting should tailor its form to the specifics of that facility and potential for problem areas.

Report of Incident or Unusual Occurrence

Name: _____   Date: _____

ID #: _____   Gender: M   F   Age: _____

Birth date: _____   Telephone number: _____

Address: _____

City: _____   State: _____   Zip code: _____

Information recorded by: _____

Information supplied by (name and relationship to the client): _____

_____

Exact location of incident: _____

Date: _____   Time: _____ ___ A.M.   ___ P.M.

Discovery

Date: _____   Time: _____ ___ A.M.   ___ P.M.

Discovered by (name and title): _____

Incident Type

___ Slip/fall   ___ Medication   ___Equipment related   ___Blood related   ___ Burn

___ IV fluid   ___ Procedure related   ___ Other (specify): _____

Concise description of occurrence (state significant facts in chronological order):

_____

_____

_____

_____

_____

_____

Departments involved: _____

_____

_____

_____

_____

_____

Witnesses

Name (position if employee): _____

Address: _____ Telephone number: _____

City: _____ State: _____ Zip code: _____

Name (position if employee): _____

Address: _____ Telephone number: _____

City: _____ State: _____ Zip code: _____

Background

___ Inpatient ___ Outpatient ___Emer. ward ___ Med. day care ___Surg. day care

___ Visitor ___ Other: _____

If patient, please include diagnosis, service received, and date at which patient was first seen: _____

_____

_____

_____

_____

_____

_____

Medication within past 6 hours: ___ No ___ Yes

Mediation and dosage prescribed: RX   Dosage

                                       _____   _____

                                       _____   _____

                                       _____   _____

                                       _____   _____

                                       _____   _____

Follow-Up

Reported to (supervisor, administrator, security, safety): _____

_____

_____

Person(s) responsible for follow-up: _____

_____

_____

Copy to: _____ Date report completed: _____

TREATMENT MEETING SUMMARY

The lucky person assigned to write up a meeting summary may benefit from some guidelines in preparing such a report. The task is not to provide a statement-by-statement account of the meeting, but to produce a succinct summation of the important points and decisions made.

The following sample form may be helpful in suggesting the pertinent facts and subjects that need to be covered in a summary of a treatment meeting.

Treatment Meeting Summary

Child's name: _____   Conference date: _____

Birth date: _____   Date of this summary: _____

1. Those attending (include name, agency, and title):

   _____

   _____

   _____

2. Purpose of this meeting:

   _____

   _____

   _____

3. Child and parent's involvement:

   _____

   _____

   _____

4. Summary of major issues discussed (i.e., campus life, medical update, therapy issues, other issues):

   _____

   _____

   _____

5. Discharge plan and projected discharge date:

   _____

   _____

   _____

6. Consumer feedback:

   _____

   _____

   _____

Submitted by (name and title): _____

Approved by (name and title): _____

Discharge Summary Guidelines

Special note: Completion of the Discharge Summary is required when a client leaves treatment. That is, he or she is no longer enrolled in any program. The Discharge Summary should be a comprehensive description of all treatment services provided to the client. As such, completion of each content area, listed below, is required. In addition, the Discharge Summary must be completed within 15 days following the discharge date.

Each page should begin with the following header:

Client's name: _____   Discharge date: _____   Page 1 of _____

Birth date: _____   Summary date: _____

I. Summary of diagnostic assessment:
   A. Results from the intake assessment (including presenting problems and any significant findings such as IQ, a previous diagnosis, and an atypical living arrangement).
   B. The primary diagnosis given at the time of the intake assessment.

II. Course of treatment:
   A. Duration of treatment (i.e., from month/year to month/year).
   B. Identified treatment goals as specified on the client's Master Treatment Plan.
   C. Treatment strategies (including family involvement, name and dosage level of prescribed medications, name of the prescribing physician, and the rationale for the use of drug therapy).
   D. The client's involvement in all programs.
   E. The level of progress achieved as defined by outcome measures of the client's Master Treatment Plan.
   F. Involvement of other agencies, case management services, and/or therapeutic services.

III. Final Assessment:
   A. General observations and clinical understanding of the client's condition initially, during treatment, and at discharge.
   B. Final diagnosis (include all 5 axes):
       Axis I   Clinical syndromes and V codes
       Axis II   Developmental and personality disorders
       Axis III   Physical disorders and conditions
       Axis IV   Psychosocial and environment problems
       Axis V   Global assessment of functioning

IV. Disposition and recommendation:
   A. Information on client's home or placement, as well as special circumstances and/or needs.
   B. Specify any referrals to private or public agencies and/or community programs (include name of agency/program, address, telephone number, and contact person).
   C. Provide a brief list of therapeutic suggestions that would help to maintain the gains achieved by the client during treatment.

V. Signatures
   A. Therapeutic/clinician/case managers signature, licensing credentials, and date.
   B. Supervisor/clinical director signature, licensing credentials, and date.

VI. Additional documentation
   This section must be completed if reference to a program was made in any other section of this summary. List the official title of reports and/or forms that should accompany the Discharge Summary when released to outside agencies.

YOUTH CLIENT SATISFACTION QUESTIONNAIRE

Recent years have seen an increased emphasis on measuring consumer satisfaction with mental health services, in both the public and private systems. Assessment of client satisfaction is an alternative to outcome evaluation as an approach to measuring service quality, and the two approaches provide nonredundant information, each of which has its own form of validity (Shapiro, Welker, & Jacobson, 1997a). Client satisfaction data provides information about treatment quality from the client's perspective; this information seems important for clinicians and administrators to consider.

The Youth Client Satisfaction Questionnaire (YCSQ: Shapiro et al., 1997a) was developed through a study of 150 outpatient clients ages 11–17 and their parents. The instrument has 14 items that load primarily on two factors, called Relationship with Therapist and Benefits of Therapy. There is evidence of satisfactory internal consistency, test-retest reliability, and construct validity (correlations with treatment outcome, parent satisfaction, and therapist ratings). The instrument can be administered either as an interview (over the phone or in person) or as a written questionnaire, with versions in English and Spanish.

The next form is a measure of parent satisfaction with child mental health services by Kotsopoulos, Elwood, and Oke (1989). It is worthwhile to examine both child and parent satisfaction; because these two variables are only weakly related, child and parent measures produce nonredundant, complementary forms of information (Shapiro et al., 1997a).

Youth Client Satisfaction Questionnaire

Name (optional): _____ Therapist name: _____

Age: ___ Sex: ___ Male ___ Female Ethnic group: ___ African American
___ Hispanic ___ White ___ Other

These questions are for young people who have finished counseling or therapy. The reason for this questionnaire is that we want to know if people liked the counseling they received. We also want to learn what they liked about it or what they did not like.

1. Did you have a bad time or a good time in counseling?
   ___ Very bad   ___ Good
   ___ Bad   ___ Very good

2. Did you understand what your goals were in counseling?
   ___ Didn't understand   ___ Understood pretty well
   ___ Understood a little   ___ Understood everything

3. Did you like your counselor?
   ___ Didn't like at all   ___ Liked some
   ___ Liked a little   ___ Liked a lot

4. Did your counselor care about you?
   ___ Didn't care at all   ___ Cared some
   ___ Cared a little   ___ Cared a lot

5. Did your counselor understand you?
   ___ Didn't understand at all   ___ Understood some
   ___ Understood a little   ___ Understood a lot

6. Did your counselor understand the kind of people in your family and neighborhood?
   ___ Didn't understand at all   ___ Understood some
   ___ Understood a little   ___ Understood a lot

7. Did your counselor have good ideas that helped you?
   ___ No good ideas   ___ Some good ideas
   ___ A few good ideas   ___ A lot of good ideas

8. Did you learn things that helped you in counseling?
   ___ Didn't learn anything   ___ Learned some
   ___ Learned a little   ___ Learned a lot

9. Do you feel differently now because of counseling?

___ Feel worse   ___ Feel better

___ Feel the same   ___ Feel a lot better

10. Do you act differently now because of counseling?

___ Act worse   ___ Act better

___ Act the same   ___ Act a lot better

11. Did counseling change the way you feel about yourself?

___ Feel worse   ___ Feel better

___ Feel the same   ___ Feel a lot better

12. Did counseling change the way you get along with your family?

___ Get along worse   ___ Get along better

___ Get along the same   ___ Get along a lot better

13. Did counseling help your problems get better?

___ Problems got worse   ___ Problems got better

___ Problems are the same ___ Problems got a lot better

14. All in all, how do you feel about your counseling?

___ Wish I never went   ___ Glad I went

___ Not sure   ___ Very glad I went

What did you like most about counseling?

_____

_____

_____

_____

_____

_____

_____

What didn't you like about counseling?

_____

_____

_____

_____

_____

_____

_____

_____

Survey of Parent Satisfaction with Their Child's Mental Health Services

For each question, please check the best response.

1. How would you rate the quality of service you received?
   ___ Excellent   ___ Fair
   ___ Good   ___ Poor

2. Did you get the kind or service you wanted?
   ___ No, definitely not   ___ Yes, generally
   ___ No, not really   ___ Yes, definitely

3. How satisfied are you with the help you and your child received?
   ___ Quite dissatisfied   ___ Mostly satisfied
   ___ Indifferent or mildly dissatisfied ___ Very satisfied

4. How convenient were your child's and/or your family's scheduled appointments?
   ___ Very inconvenient   ___ Convenient
   ___ Somewhat inconvenient   ___ Very convenient

5. How much of the time were you able to use your preferred language in speaking with staff?
   ___ Seldom   ___ Most of the time
   ___ Some of the time   ___ All of the time

6. In general, have the secretaries seemed friendly, helpful and did they make you feel comfortable?
   ___ All of the time   ___ Some of the time
   ___ Most of the time   ___ Seldom

7. Did you find the person with whom your child worked most closely genuinely interested in helping your child and your family?
   ___ Very interested   ___ Somewhat uninterested
   ___ Interested   ___ Very uninterested

8. How clearly were the goals and methods of your child's treatment explained to you?
   ___ Very clearly   ___ Inadequately
   ___ Clearly   ___ Not at all

9. If medication was recommended for your child, were the effects of the drugs and any possible side effects explained?
   ___ Completely   ___ Inadequately
   ___ Adequately   ___ Not at all

10. In general, how did your child feel about attending appointments?
    ___ Disliked strongly   ___ Cooperative
    ___ Reluctant   ___ Willing and eager

11. Did our service help to change the problems which brought your child to our clinic?
___ Much better   ___ Unchanged
___ Somewhat better   ___ Worse

12. Has our service helped you cope better with your child's problems?
___ Considerably more effective   ___ Unchanged
___ More effective   ___ Less effective

13. To what extent has our program met your child's needs?
___ Almost all needs have been met   ___ Only a few needs have been met
___ Most needs have been met   ___ None of the needs have been met

14. If you were to seek help for your child again, would you come back to our program?
___ Definitely   ___ I don't think so
___ I think so   ___ Definitely not

15. Would you recommend our program to friends and neighbors with similar problems?
___ Definitely not   ___ I think so
___ I don't think so   ___ Definitely

16. Overall, how satisfied are you with the service your child and your family received?
___ Very satisfied   ___ Indifferent
___ Mostly satisfied   ___ Quite dissatisfied

17. Please add any additional comments or concerns not adequately covered in this questionnaire.

_____

Please answer the following questions only if treatment has been terminated.

18. How long ago was treatment terminated? (in months please) _____

19. Was the decision to end services . . .
___ yours alone (or with spouse)
___ your child's
___ yours and your child's together
___ mostly the therapist's
___ equally shared; yourself, child and therapist
___ other—please describe: _____

20. What is the condition of your child now? How does this compare with his/her condition at the time treatment was terminated?
___ Much better   ___ Unchanged
___ Better   ___ Worse

THANK YOU FOR TAKING THE TIME TO COMPLETE THIS QUESTIONNAIRE

Chapter 10

Child Abuse Forms

Child abuse has become a major mental health problem in this country. Rising numbers of official reports of abuse suggest that more reports are coming to the attention of agencies, or there is, in fact, an increasing number of children who are being abused in our communities. The three documents in this chapter could be useful for clinicians in reporting this problem. Abuse is often very difficult to document and careful interviewing of potential perpetrators and skillful evaluation of possible victims require special training and experience.

The documents may help guide some of the interviewing process. We make no attempt to provide evaluation tools for the discovery or diagnosis of child abuse, as much has been written in this area. We want to emphasize the need for professionally trained personnel to deal with the issues posed by suspected or known child abuse.

Report of Children Alleged to Be Suffering from Serious Physical or Emotional Injury by Abuse or Neglect

Data on children reported:

	Name	Current location/Address	Sex	Age or birth date
1.	_____	_____	M F	_____
2.	_____	_____	M F	_____
3.	_____	_____	M F	_____
4.	_____	_____	M F	_____
5.	_____	_____	M F	_____
6.	_____	_____	M F	_____
7.	_____	_____	M F	_____
8.	_____	_____	M F	_____
9.	_____	_____	M F	_____
10.	_____	_____	M F	_____

Data on Male Guardian or Parent

Name: _____

Address: _____

City: _____ State: _____ Zip code: _____

Birth date: _____ Telephone number: _____

Data on Female Guardian or Parent

Name: _____

Address: _____

City: _____ State: _____ Zip code: _____

Birth date: _____ Telephone number: _____

Data on Reporter/Report

Date of report: _____ ___ Mandatory report ___ Voluntary report

Reporter's name: _____

Address: _____

City: _____ State: _____ Zip code: _____

Has reporter informed caretaker of report? ___ No ___ Yes

What is the nature and extent of the injury, abuse, maltreatment, or neglect, including prior evidence of same? (Please cite the source of this information if not observed first hand.) _____

_____

_____

_____

_____

_____

_____

_____

What are the circumstances under which the reporter became aware of the injuries, abuse, maltreatment, or neglect? _____

_____

_____

_____

_____

_____

_____

What action has been taken thus far to treat, shelter, or otherwise assist the child to deal with the situation? _____

_____

_____

_____

_____

_____

_____

Please give other information which you think might be helpful in establishing the cause of the injury and/or the person responsible for it. If known, please provide the name(s) of the alleged perpetrator(s). _____

_____

_____

_____

_____

_____

_____

Signature of reporter: _____

Sexual Abuse Evaluation Report
of Child Interview

Name: _____ Date: _____

ID #: _____ Gender: M F Age: _____

Birth date: _____ Telephone number: _____

Address: _____

City: _____ State: _____ Zip code: _____

Information recorded by: _____

Information supplied by (name and relationship to the client): _____

_____

___ Sexual abuse treatment team   ___ Diagnostic evaluation

___ Crisis response program   ___ Disclosure interview

Child interviewer: _____

Name of parent: _____

Parent interviewer: _____

Medical evaluator: _____

Date of evaluation: _____ Date of report: _____

Date of referral: _____ Referred by: _____

Referrer was contacted with results of the evaluation: ___ No ___ Yes

Referral information: _____

_____

_____

_____

_____

_____

_____

History of child's presenting problem: _____

_____

_____

_____

_____

_____

Sexualized behaviors (as reported by parent/caregiver):

___ Inappropriate sexual knowledge   ___ Sexualized touching of others

___ Age-inappropriate sexual curiosity   ___ Excessive masturbation

___ Sexualized drawings   ___ Attempted insertion of objects

___ Sexualized statements   ___ Inappropriate bodily boundaries with others

___ Sexualized play with toys   ___ Affective response to specific individual (fear, anger, etc.)

Elaborate on items checked above: _____

_____

_____

_____

_____

_____

General symptoms (as reported by parent/caregiver):

___ Academic difficulties	___ Elevated mood	___ Nightmares
___ Anergia	___ Encopresis	___ Panic symptoms
___ Anhedonia	___ Enuresis	___ Phobias
___ Anxiety	___ Fidgety	___ Pressured speech
___ Appetite change	___ Fighting	___ Racing thoughts
___ Blurts out answers	___ Fire setting	___ Self-mutilatory behavior
___ Breaking in	___ Grandiose	___ Separation anxiety
___ Concentration difficulties	___ Hyperactivity	___ Sleep change
___ Cruelty to animals	___ Hypersomnia	___ Social difficulties
___ Depressed mood	___ Hypervigilance	___ Stealing
___ Difficulty following instruc.	___ Impatient	___ Truancy
___ Difficulty playing quietly	___ Initial insomnia	___ Unstable relationships
___ Difficulty remaining seated	___ Interrupts	___ Weapons
___ Difficulty sustaining tasks	___ Listens poorly	___ Withdrawal
___ Distractibility	___ Loses things	___ Worthlessness
___ Early insomnia	___ Lying	___ Other: _____
___ Early morning awakening	___ Middle insomnia	

Elaborate on items checked under "general symptoms": _____

_____

_____

_____

_____

_____

Suicide: ___Ideation   ___Plan/intent   ___Attempt
Homicide: ___Ideation   ___Plan/intent   ___Attempt

Disclosure/incident description by child during interview. Child's presentation during interview (affect behavior, developmental screening): _____

_____

_____

_____

_____

_____

Response to anatomically detailed dolls and/or drawings:

     ___ Not used   ___ Anxious

     ___ Neutral   ___ Embarrassed

     ___ Avoidant   ___ Sexualized behavior

     ___ Aggressive   ___ Genital preoccupation

     ___ Withdrawal   ___ Disinterested

Elaborate on any checked items: _____

_____

_____

_____

_____

_____

Quality of play/traumatic play themes:

     ___ Unremarkable   ___ No opportunity to observe

     ___ Vulnerability   ___ Driven

     ___ Sexualized play   ___ Genital preoccupation

     ___ Identification with the aggressor   ___ Need to control

     ___ Helplessness   ___ Anxious

     ___ Absence of traumatic play   ___ Absence of rescue

     ___ Repetitive   ___ Protection issues

     ___ Other: _____

Elaborated on any checked items: _____

_____

_____

_____

_____

_____

General clinical impressions: _____

_____

_____

_____

_____

Sexual abuse:

___ Data consistent with sexual abuse   ___ Data suggestive of sexual abuse

___ Data unclear as to question of sexual abuse   ___ Data inconsistent with sexual abuse

Elaborate on any checked items: _____

_____

_____

_____

_____

Degree of traumatization: _____

_____

_____

_____

_____

Possible barriers to dislosure:

    ___ Threats   ___ Loyalty binds   ___ Out-of-home placement   ___ Self-blame

    ___ Other: _____

Alternative explanations considered for presenting concerns:

___ Harmful genital practices   ___ No supporting data

___ Coached disclosure   ___ No supporting data

___ Misinterpretation of developmentally appropriate touch   ___ No supporting data

___ Divorce trauma   ___ No supporting data

___ Other trauma-symptomology   ___ No supporting data

___ Other (specify): _____   ___ No supporting data

DMS-IV diagnosis:

         Axis I codes   Axis I disorder(s)

    1. _____   _____

    2. _____   _____

    3. _____   _____

    4. _____   _____

    5. _____   _____

Axis II: _____

_____

Axis III: _____

_____

Axis IV:
___ Problems with primary support group
___ Problems related to social environment
___ Educational problems
___ Occupational problems
___ Housing problems
___ Economic
___ Problems with access to health care services
___ Problems related to interaction with the legal system/crime
___ Other psychosocial and environmental problems

Elaborate on any checked items: _____

_____

_____

_____

_____

Axis V:
___ 81–90   Absence of or minimal symptoms, good functioning.
___ 71–80   Transient, no more than slight impairment of functioning.
___ 61–70   Mild difficulties, some meaningful relationships.
___ 51–60   Moderate symptoms or impairment of function.
___ 41–50   Serious symptoms including suicidal ideation.
___ 31–40   Major impairment in many areas.
___ 21–30   Delusions, hallucinations, suicidal preoccupation.
___ 11–20   Danger to self or others, minimal hygiene, incoherent.
___ 01–10   Persistent danger to self or others.

Recommendation and plan: _____

_____

_____

_____

_____

Was 51A filed? ___ No   ___ Yes   If "yes," date of filing: _____

Signature of evaluator(s): _____   Date: _____

Sexual Abuse Evaluation Report
of Parent Interview

Name: _____ Date: _____

ID #: _____ Gender: M F Age: _____

Birth date: _____ Telephone number: _____

Address: _____

City: _____ State: _____ Zip code: _____

Information recorded by: _____

Information supplied by (name and relationship to the client): _____

_____

___ Sexual abuse treatment team   ___ Diagnostic evaluation

___ Crisis response program   ___ Disclosure interview

Name of parent/caregiver: _____

Child interviewer: _____

Name of parent: _____

Parent interviewer: _____

Medical evaluator: _____

Date of evaluation: _____ Date of report: _____

Date of referral: _____ Referred by: _____

Referrer was contacted with results of the evaluation: ___ No ___ Yes

Referral information: _____

_____

_____

_____

_____

_____

Brief history of child's presenting problem: _____

_____

_____

_____

_____

_____

Sexualized behaviors (as reported by parent/caregiver):

___ Inappropriate sexual knowledge   ___ Sexualized touching of others

___ Age-inappropriate sexual curiosity   ___ Excessive masturbation

___ Sexualized drawings   ___ Attempted insertion of objects

___ Sexualized statements   ___ Inappropriate bodily boundaries with others

___ Sexualized play with toys   ___ Affective response to specific individual (fear, anger, etc.)

Elaborate on items checked above: _____

_____

_____

_____

_____

_____

General symptoms (as reported by parent/caregiver):

___ Academic difficulties	___ Elevated mood	___ Nightmares
___ Anergia	___ Encopresis	___ Panic symptoms
___ Anhedonia	___ Enuresis	___ Phobias
___ Anxiety	___ Fidgety	___ Pressured speech
___ Appetite change	___ Fighting	___ Racing thoughts
___ Blurts out answers	___ Fire setting	___ Self-mutilatory behavior
___ Breaking in	___ Grandiose	___ Separation anxiety
___ Concentration difficulties	___ Hyperactivity	___ Sleep change
___ Cruelty to animals	___ Hypersomnia	___ Social difficulties
___ Depressed mood	___ Hypervigilance	___ Stealing
___ Difficulty following instruc.	___ Impatient	___ Truancy
___ Difficulty playing quietly	___ Initial insomnia	___ Unstable relationships
___ Difficulty remaining seated	___ Interrupts	___ Weapons
___ Difficulty sustaining tasks	___ Listens poorly	___ Withdrawal
___ Distractibility	___ Loses things	___ Worthlessness
___ Early insomnia	___ Lying	___ Other: _____
___ Early morning awakening	___ Middle insomnia	

Elaborate on items checked under "general symptoms": _____

_____

_____

_____

_____

_____

Suicide: ___Ideation   ___Plan/intent   ___Attempt

Homicide: ___Ideation   ___Plan/intent   ___Attempt

Child's medical/developmental history as reported by: _____

Pregnancy: ___ Normal ___ Problem ___ Specify: _____

Infancy: ___ Normal ___ Problem ___ Specify: _____

Growth and development: ___ Normal ___ Problem ___ Specify: _____

Illness/injuries/accidents/hospitalizations (please include approximate dates: _____
_____
_____
_____
_____
_____

Child health care concerns:

___ Physical complaints ___ Genital pain ___ Abdominal pain ___ Headaches
___ Vague general pain ___ Bloody stool ___ Other: _____

Elaborate on any items checked above: _____
_____
_____
_____
_____
_____

Developmental concerns: _____
_____
_____
_____
_____
_____

Caretaking history: _____
_____
_____
_____
_____
_____

Preschool/day care: _____

_____

_____

_____

_____

_____

School history: _____

_____

_____

_____

_____

_____

Family composition: _____

_____

_____

_____

_____

_____

Family history (relationship and access to child): _____

_____

_____

_____

_____

_____

_____

Family psychiatric history: _____

_____

_____

_____

_____

_____

Potential risk factors:

___ Prior sexual abuse history   ___ Prior physical abuse history   ___ Domestic violence

___ Substance abuse   ___ Other: _____

Caregivers and others with access to child: _____

_____

_____

_____

_____

_____

Identity of suspected/alleged perpetrator:

Name: _____

Age (birth date): _____   Relationship: _____

Address: _____

City: _____   State: _____   Zip code: _____

Phone: _____   Date of last contact: _____

___ Unknown perpetrator

Loyalty issue (for parents): _____

_____

_____

_____

_____

_____

Parental response to child's disclosure (during evaluation, if applicable):

___ Believing   ___ Blaming   ___ Disbelieving   ___ Willing to entertain possibility

___ Vacillating   ___ Other: _____

Parental capacity for protection: _____

_____

_____

_____

_____

_____

Alternative hypothesis considered for child's presentation:

___ Harmful genital practices   ___ No supporting data

___ Coaching   ___ No supporting data

___ Misinterpretation of developmentally appropriate touch   ___ No supporting data

___ Divorce trauma   ___ No supporting data

___ Misinterpretation of developmentally appropriate caretaking   ___ No supporting data

___ False allegation   ___ No supporting data

Parental response to clinical findings: _____

_____

_____

_____

_____

_____

Mental status (of parent):

1 = Not present   2 = Very mild   3 = Mild   4 = Moderate
5 = Moderately severe   6 = Severe   7 = Extremely severe

1. Uncooperative—negative, resistant, difficult to manage.

___ 1 ___ 2 ___ 3 ___ 4 ___ 5 ___ 6 ___ 7

2. Manipulative—lying, cheating, exploitive of others.

___ 1 ___ 2 ___ 3 ___ 4 ___ 5 ___ 6 ___ 7

3. Disoriented—confusion over people, places, or things.

___ 1 ___ 2 ___ 3 ___ 4 ___ 5 ___ 6 ___ 7

4. Distractible—poor concentration, short attention span, reactible to peripheral stimuli.

___ 1 ___ 2 ___ 3 ___ 4 ___ 5 ___ 6 ___ 7

5. Hyperactive—excessive energy expenditure, frequent changes in posture, perpetual motion.

___ 1 ___ 2 ___ 3 ___ 4 ___ 5 ___ 6 ___ 7

6. Stereotype—rhythmic, repetitive, manneristic movements or posture.

___ 1 ___ 2 ___ 3 ___ 4 ___ 5 ___ 6 ___ 7

7. Speech—loud, excessive, or pressured speech.

___ 1 ___ 2 ___ 3 ___ 4 ___ 5 ___ 6 ___ 7

8. Underproductive speech—minimal, sparse, inhibited verbal response pattern or weak low voice.

___ 1 ___ 2 ___ 3 ___ 4 ___ 5 ___ 6 ___ 7

13. Anxiety—clinging behavior, separation anxiety, occupation with anxiety topics, fears or phobias.

___ 1 ___ 2 ___ 3 ___ 4 ___ 5 ___ 6 ___ 7

14. Tension—nervousness, fidgetiness, nervous movements of hands and feet.

___ 1 ___ 2 ___ 3 ___ 4 ___ 5 ___ 6 ___ 7

15. Depressive mood—sad, tearful, depressive demeanor.

___ 1 ___ 2 ___ 3 ___ 4 ___ 5 ___ 6 ___ 7

16. Sleep difficulties—inability to fall asleep, intermittent awakenings, shortened or lengthened sleep time.

___ 1 ___ 2 ___ 3 ___ 4 ___ 5 ___ 6 ___ 7

17. Appetite/weight—significant appetite/weight gains or losses.

___ 1 ___ 2 ___ 3 ___ 4 ___ 5 ___ 6 ___ 7

18. Feelings of inferiority—lacking self-confidence, feelings of personal inadequacy.

___ 1 ___ 2 ___ 3 ___ 4 ___ 5 ___ 6 ___ 7

19. Suicidal ideation—thoughts, threats, or action.

___ 1 ___ 2 ___ 3 ___ 4 ___ 5 ___ 6 ___ 7

20. Peculiar fantasies—recurrent, odd, unusual, or autistic ideations.

___ 1 ___ 2 ___ 3 ___ 4 ___ 5 ___ 6 ___ 7

9. Speech deviance—inferior level of speech development, underdeveloped vocabulary, mispronunciations.

___ 1 ___ 2 ___ 3 ___ 4 ___ 5 ___ 6 ___ 7

10. Emotional withdrawal—unspontaneous relations to examiner, lack or peer interaction, hypoactivity.

___ 1 ___ 2 ___ 3 ___ 4 ___ 5 ___ 6 ___ 7

11. Blunted affect—deficient emotional expressionism, blankness, flatness of affect.

___ 1 ___ 2 ___ 3 ___ 4 ___ 5 ___ 6 ___ 7

12. Hostility—angry or suspicious affect, belligerence, accusations, and verbal condemnations of others.

___ 1 ___ 2 ___ 3 ___ 4 ___ 5 ___ 6 ___ 7

21. Delusions—ideas of reference, persecutory, grandiose ideation.

___ 1 ___ 2 ___ 3 ___ 4 ___ 5 ___ 6 ___ 7

22. Hallucinations—visual, auditory, or other hallucinatory experiences or perceptions.

___ 1 ___ 2 ___ 3 ___ 4 ___ 5 ___ 6 ___ 7

23. Thought processes—looseness of associations, ideas of reference, flight of ideas, tangentiality, circumstantiality, thought intersection, blocking.

___ 1 ___ 2 ___ 3 ___ 4 ___ 5 ___ 6 ___ 7

Mental status exam comments: _____

_____

_____

DMS-IV diagnosis:

Axis I codes	Axis I disorder(s)
1._____	_____
2._____	_____
3._____	_____
4._____	_____
5._____	_____

Axis II: _____

_____

_____

_____

Axis III: _____

_____

_____

_____

Axis IV:

___ Problems with primary support group

___ Problems related to social environment

___ Educational problems

___ Occupational problems

___ Housing problems

___ Economic

___ Problems with access to health care services

___ Problems related to interaction with the legal system/crime

___ Other psychosocial and environmental problems

Elaborate on any checked items: _____

_____

_____

_____

_____

_____

Axis V:

___ 81–90   Absence of or minimal symptoms, good functioning.

___ 71–80   Transient, no more than slight impairment of functioning.

___ 61–70   Mild difficulties, some meaningful relationships.

___ 51–60   Moderate symptoms or impairment of function.

___ 41–50   Serious symptoms including suicidal ideation.

___ 31–40   Major impairment in many areas.

___ 21–30   Delusions, hallucinations, suicidal preoccupation.

___ 11–20   Danger to self or others, minimal hygiene, incoherent.

___ 01–10   Persistent danger to self or others.

Recommendation and plan: _____

_____

_____

_____

_____

_____

Was 51A filed? ___ No   ___ Yes   If "yes," date of filing: _____

Signature of evaluator(s): _____   Date: _____

Chapter 11

Case Example

Jeremy P. Shapiro and Nancy S. Winkelman

We conclude this book with a case example that illustrates how these forms can be used. In the interest of brevity, we present examples of completed documents for only the most important, recommended forms. Because the purpose of this material is to illustrate use of our forms, rather than to provide a complete account of a case, we do not present every document that would be expected in the record of the example case history. With the exception of progress notes, we present only one example of each form, even when the case would involve multiple uses; for example, the diagnostic evaluation form is completed in the context of outpatient treatment and so is not illustrated again in the context of residential treatment, even though it is equally appropriate for both settings.

Another difference between the case example to follow and patient charts for similarly complex cases is that, in our example, documentation consists only of forms, whereas charts often also include notes written on plain, lined paper. Our purpose here is to illustrate use of forms, but we also recognize that some record-keeping should be done on plain paper, which—although it provides no predetermined structure—is unmatched in flexibility. Forms are developed to meet foreseeable, typical record-keeping needs, and so they never fit perfectly with unusual case material. When an unusually large amount of information must be recorded in a form section, the amount of blank space will generally not be enough, because the amount of blank space reflects the author's expectation of the amount of information that will *typically* be recorded in that section. Therefore, record-keeping for complex cases will often involve continuations from form sections to supplementary blank paper.

With these provisos, the material to follow illustrates use of our most important forms in telling a clinical story.

Child Diagnostic Evaluation

Name: _____Monica R._____   Date: _____12/10/1998_____

ID #: _____000-00-000_____   Gender: M (F)   Age: _____15_____

Birth date: _____3/5/83_____   Telephone number: _____555 5555_____

Address: _____2241 Jackson Rd._____

City: _____Falls Canyon_____   State: _____OH_____   Zip code: _____55555_____

Information recorded by: _____Nancy Winkelman, LISW_____

Information supplied by (name and relationship to the client): _____Sarah R. (mother),_____
_____Brent R. (father), Monica R. (client)_____

Reasons for Referral

1. Chief complaint: _____Depressed mood, crying, withdrawal from family_____

2. Any other presenting problems: _____Marijuana and alcohol use, skips school, angry_____
_____outbursts, defiance toward parents._____

3. Any additional referral purpose or context: _____Evaluation recommended by school_____
_____counselor to parents._____

Physical Description

_____Average overall, tattoo on ankle_____

Current Functioning

1. Description of presenting problems and symptoms: _____Parents report depressed_____
_____mood—crying spells, glum facial expression, increased eating and sleeping,_____
_____spending most time in room. Parents suspect marijuana and alcohol use_____
_____increasing 4x/wk. Frequent angry outbursts toward parents and siblings. Breaks_____
_____household rules, argues angrily when confronted. Skips school at least once per_____
_____week._____

2. Functional impairment (impact of symptoms on life quality): _____Deteriorated_____
_____family relationships and risk to school performance._____

3. Strengths (areas of successful functioning): *Grades have been good. She is consistently responsible about babysitting jobs.*

4. Situational factors influencing presenting problems: *Marital conflict including disagreements about discipline.*

5. Child's view of his/her functioning if different from parents' view: *"My mother is impossible—nothing is good enough for her. She's always yelling at my father and me."*

History

1. Onset of current episode (precipitating events if known): *Gradual onset, no apparent precipitating event. Problems at current level for 2 1/2 months.*

2. Course of current episode: __ Improving __ Stable __ Deteriorating _X_ Fluctuating *Parents discern no pattern.*

3. Functioning prior to current episode: *Good school performance, responsible, some conflict with older sister.*

Previous Behavioral Health Treatment

1. _X_ No __ Yes   If "yes," please include previous diagnoses, treatment, medications, and outcome: _____

2. Special educational placement or services: _X_ No __ Yes

3. Other services or systems (e.g., social service, legal, school counseling):
__ No _X_ Yes   *Counselor referred client to group for teens with family conflicts—client says it is not helpful.*

4. Developmental delay or disorder: _X_ No __ Yes

5. Past losses, trauma, and/or abuse: _X_ No   __ Yes

_____

_____

6. Child's view of problem origin if different from parents' view: _Client said her_
   mother lost her job 3 months ago and has been "meaner" ever since.

_____

Contextual Factors

1. Who lives in child's home: _M, F, 2 sisters (12 and 17)_

_____

_____

   a. Child's relationship with mother: _Conflictual, difficult_

_____

   b. Child's relationship with father: _Easier, more affectionate_

_____

   c. Child's relationship with siblings: _Conflict with older sister, distant from_
      younger sister.

   d. With other family members: _n/a_ _____

2. Family mental health and substance abuse history: __ No   _X_ Yes
   Mother diagnosed with dysthymia 5 yrs. ago—been on Prozac 20 mg.

_____

3. Family history of trauma or abuse: __ No   _X_ Yes
   Mother's father described as verbally abusive _____

_____

4. Cultural factors influencing problems or treatment: _Father immigrated to U.S._
   from Romania at age 19. He views therapy with suspicion and believes problems
   should be handled within the family.

5. School functioning (beyond problem description):   _"B" average_ _____

_____

6. Peer relationships (beyond problem description):   _Average number of friends._
   No real best friend. _____

_____

7. Hobbies, interests, activities, tastes in music, books, and media: _Sewing,_
   musicals—some recent interest in the occult.

_____

Factors Related to Prognosis of Treatment

1. Child's motivation for change: _Client focused on wanting M to change_

2. Any other prognostic factors: _Some family history of depression, parents'_ _marital problems_

Other Data

Data influencing case conceptualization (e.g., symbolic play, cognitive patterns, parenting practices, reinforcement contingencies, constructions of meaning, previously effective solutions, family and personal dynamics): _M said her depression began_ _at client's age and she's determined to prevent client from going down same road._ _Client expressed fear of turning out to be a "loser"; M used same term about_ _herself. F-client interaction seemed comfortable and connected. M-client_ _interaction seemed tense and angry._

Diagnostic Summary and Formulation

Monica presents as a moderately depressed adolescent. Depression may be due to: _(1) M's overcontrolling and angry behavior toward client, (2) client internalization_ _of negative messages from mother, (3) bitter, disconnected marital relationship,_ _(4) possible genetic predisposition. Substance abuse may be an attempt to_ _self-medicate her depression and may represent an expression of anger toward_ _parents._

Axis I _Adjustment disorder w/Depressed Mood, 309.0_

Axis II _n/a_

Axis III _n/a_

Axis IV _Family stressors_

Axis V _62_

Recommendations

(1) Substance abuse assessment, (2) individual cognitive therapy to modify critical _self-statements, (3) parent counseling to reduce M's anxious overinvolvement,_ _(4) family systems therapy to address dysfunctional alliances and communication._

Signature: _Nancy S. Winkelman, LISW_   Date: _12/10/1998_

Psychotherapy Treatment Plan

Name: _____*Monica R.*_____   Date: _____*12/10/1998*_____

ID #: _____*000-00-000*_____   Gender: M (F)   Age: _____*15*_____

Birth date: *3/5/1983*_____

Primary diagnosis: _____*Adjustment disorder w/Depressed Mood, 309.0*_____

Secondary diagnosis: _____*R/O substance abuse*_____

Describe child and family factors influencing the plan of treatment: assessment findings, motivation for change, strengths, limitations, life circumstances and events, personality styles, relationships, cultural factors, insurance considerations, and so forth:

Based on cl's negative self-statements (depression) & her reflective ability, cognitive therapy will be used. Family systems therapy will be used to strengthen marital subsystem & reduce tension in M/dau relationship. Parent counseling will be used to reduce M's overidentification w/& anxiety abt dau's problems. BT: Directive will be used to increase activity level.

Projected length of treatment: _2_ months, _0_ weeks

Planned frequency of treatment: _1_ session(s) per _1_ week(s).

Therapeutic Modality

(If just one, check; if more than one, number in decreasing order of use.)

_2_ Family	___ Group	_1_ Individual
___ Parent/child	___ Parenting group	_3_ Parent(s) alone

Therapeutic Approaches

___ Art therapy	___ Client-centered therapy	___ Parent counseling
___ BT: Classical	_2_ Cognitive therapy	_3_ Parent guidance
_4_ BT: Directive	___ Cognitive-behavioral therapy	___ Philosophizing
___ BT: Emotional regulation	___ Experiential therapy	___ Planful decision making
___ BT: Operant	_1_ FST: Directive	___ Psychodynamic therapy
___ BT: Parent training	___ FST: Nondirective	___ Psychoeducation
___ BT: Social Skills	___ Interpersonal therapy	___ Solution-oriented therapy
___ Case management	___ Narrative therapy	___ Supportive therapy
___ Other:_____		

Provide any necessary elaboration of the planned approaches, and describe the anticipated content and course of treatment. If the majority of major techniques with/in the indicated methods are planned, these need not be reiterated. If only a subset of the techniques are planned, state them. (Note that technique specification is most often necessary for behavior therapy, because it includes numerous specific techniques.)

Family sessions will address communication patterns, parental authority concerning household rules, & cl's need for age-appropriate privacy. Cognitive work will seek to moderate harsh personal standards of evaluation. Work w/M will seek to develop a healthy sense of separation w/dau. BT: Directive will consist of behavioral activation.

Goal Attainment Scale

Goal 1

Date (if after intake assessment): _____ Date achieved: _____

Scale-point

1. Worse
2. No change = presenting problem: ___ _Cries 4x/wk_ ___
3. Some progress: _____
4. Major progress: ___ _Will cry 1-2x/wk_ ___
5. Goal attainment: ___ _Will cry no more than 1x/2 wks_ ___

Goal 2

Date (if after intake assessment): _____ Date achieved: _____

Scale-point

1. Worse
2. No change = presenting problem: ___ _Spends avg of 4 hrs/day in room_ ___
3. Some progress: _____
4. Major progress: ___ _Will spend avg 2.5 hrs/day in room_ ___
5. Goal attainment: ___ _Will spend avg 1 hr/day in room_ ___

Goal 3

    Date (if after intake assessment): _____   Date achieved: _____

    Scale-point

       1. Worse

       2. No change = presenting problem: *Some (indeterminate) alc & drug use*

       3. Some progress: _____

       4. Major progress: *Rare use*

       5. Goal attainment: *No use*

Goal 4

    Date (if after intake assessment): _____   Date achieved: _____

    Scale-point

       1. Worse

       2. No change = presenting problem: *Sig resistance to parental directives 1x/2 days*

       3. Some progress: _____

       4. Major progress: *Sig resistance to directives 2x/wk*

       5. Goal attainment: *Sig resistance to directives 1x/wk*

Goal 5

    Date (if after intake assessment): _____   Date achieved: _____

    Scale-point

       1. Worse

       2. No change = presenting problem: _____

       3. Some progress: _____

       4. Major progress: _____

       5. Goal attainment: _____

Comments

    Substance abuse evaluation & continued monitoring needed to ascertain degree

    of substance use.

    _____

    _____

    _____

    _____

Signature: *Nancy S. Winkelman, LISW*   Date: *12/10/1998*

Initial Managed Care Review

Patient: _____Monica R._____   Date: _____12/6/1998_____

ID #: _____000-00-000_____   Gender: M (F) Age: ___15___

Provider: _____Nancy Winkelman, LISW_____   _X_ In network   ___ Out of network

Address: _____Winkelman and Assoc., 1000 Huckleberry Lane_____

City: __Sheridan__   State: __OH__   Zip code: _____55555_____

Phone: __123-1234__   Fax: __123-1235__   E-mail: _____

Presenting problems: __Depressed mood, crying, much time alone in room, defiant__
__toward parents, alcohol and marijuana use, unknown extent__

History of present episode: __Sx appeared after mother lost her job 3 months ago__
_____

Drug/alcohol problem? ___ No ___ Yes   Prior behavioral treatment? ___ No ___ Yes

Risk to self: ___ None   _X_ Minimal   ___ Moderate   ___ High

Risk to others: _X_ None   ___ Minimal   ___ Moderate   ___ High

Dx: Axis I   __Adjustment Disorder w/Depressed Mood, 309.0__

      Axis II   __n/a__

      Axis III   __n/a__

      Axis IV   __Mother lost job, parents' marital conflict__

      Axis V   __62__

Receiving psychiatric medication? _X_ No   ___ Yes: _____

Goals	Interventions
1. _Reduce depression_	_Cognitive, family, behavior therapy_
2. _Increase compliance with parents_	_Above and parent guidance_
3. _Eliminate substance use_	_Assess further and treat based on results_

Has primary care physician received information from you about this patient's care?

___ No _X_ Yes

Other services needed (e.g., medication, psychological testing):   Referral

_____   _____

_____   _____

Authorization request:	No. of sessions	Period of time
Individual psychotherapy, 30 minutes		
Individual psychotherapy, 60 minutes	4	2 months
Group therapy		
Family therapy	4	2 months
Psychiatric medication evaluation		

Psychotherapy Progress Note

Name: _____Monica R._____   Date: _____12/31/1999_____

Session length: _X_ 50 minutes   ___ Other: _____   Session #: ___4___

Therapeutic Modality

(If just one, check; of more than one, number in decreasing order of use.)

_1_ Family   ___ Group   ___ Individual

___ Parent/child   ___ Parenting group   _2_ Parent(s) alone

Therapeutic Approaches

___ Art therapy   ___ Client-centered therapy   _2_ Parent counseling

___ BT: Classical   _1_ Cognitive therapy   _3_ Parent guidance

___ BT: Directive   ___ Cognitive-behavioral therapy ___ Philosophizing

___ BT: Emotional regulation ___ Experimental therapy   ___ Planful decision making

___ BT: Operant   ___ FST: Directive   ___ Psychodynamic therapy

___ BT: Parent training   ___ FST: Nondirective   ___ Psychoeducation

___ BT: Social Skills   ___ Interpersonal therapy   _4_ Solution-oriented therapy

___ Case management   ___ Narrative therapy   ___ Supportive therapy

___ Other:_____

Goal Attainment Scale

	Goal 1	Goal 2	Goal 3	Goal 4	Goal 5
Indicate GAS level (1–5):	1	1	2	1	___
Change since last session (Better +, worse -, no change X):	-	x	x	-	___

Session notes: _Client responded to cognitive techniques by saying I don't understand how badly she's failed. Seemed guarded when asked about substance use. M appeared to be more depressed than usual and stated that marital problems are escalating. M remains convinced client is making the same mistakes and descending into depression just as she did when she was client's age._

Plans and reminders: _M to list 3 differences between herself and client. Client to list 3 accomplishments or strengths._

Signature: _Nancy Winkelman, LISW_

Psychotherapy Progress Note

Name: _____Monica R._____   Date: _____1/13/1999_____

Session length: _X_ 50 minutes   ___ Other: _____   Session #: ___6___

Therapeutic Modality
(If just one, check; of more than one, number in decreasing order of use.)

_X_ Family   ___ Group   ___ Individual

___ Parent/child   ___ Parenting group   ___ Parent(s) alone

Therapeutic Approaches

___ Art therapy	___ Client-centered therapy	___ Parent counseling
___ BT: Classical	_2_ Cognitive therapy	___ Parent guidance
___ BT: Directive	___ Cognitive-behavioral therapy	___ Philosophizing
___ BT: Emotional regulation	___ Experimental therapy	___ Planful decision making
___ BT: Operant	_1_ FST: Directive	___ Psychodynamic therapy
___ BT: Parent training	___ FST: Nondirective	___ Psychoeducation
___ BT: Social Skills	___ Interpersonal therapy	___ Solution-oriented therapy
___ Case management	___ Narrative therapy	___ Supportive therapy
___ Other:		

Goal Attainment Scale

	Goal 1	Goal 2	Goal 3	Goal 4	Goal 5
Indicate GAS level (1–5):	_1_	_1_	_2_	_1_	___
Change since last session (Better +, worse -, no change X):	_-_	_x_	_x_	_-_	___

Session notes: _Parents reported marital dissatisfaction is growing; father tells mother to "lay off" client, mother says "I can't stand watching her go downhill like this." Client seemed disengaged and angry throughout session and said to therapist, "Don't you see how this makes me sick?" I presented rationale for moderate standards for school performance; mother resisted angrily, expressing the view that this could result in permanent loss of career options._

Plans and reminders: _Provide realistic information about relationship between high school grades and career success, accomplishments or strengths. Refer for psychiatric assessment—consider antidepressant._

Signature: _Nancy Winkelman, LISW_

Subsequent Managed Care Review

Patient: _____Monica R._____   Date: _____12/6/1998_____

ID #: _____000-00-000_____   Gender: M (F)   Age: ___15_____

Provider: ___Nancy Winkelman, LISW_____   _X_ In network   ___ Out of network

Address: _____Winkelman and Assoc., 1000 Huckleberry Lane_____

City: __Sheridan_____   State: ___OH___   Zip code: ____55555_____

Phone: __123-1234_____   Fax: ___123-1235_____   E-mail: _____

Progress/current symptoms/stressors: ___Client has deteriorated since beginning_____
___treatment. Depression has risen, with more crying, self-criticism and withdrawal,___
___and newly evident insomnia. Heightened defiance toward parents. Suspected___
___heightened drug and alcohol use.___

Risk to self: ___ None   ___ Minimal   _X_ Moderate   ___ High

Risk to others: _X_ None   ___ Minimal   ___ Moderate   ___ High

___Suicidal verbalizations of moderate severity. No self-injury or evidence of active___
___intent or plan.___

Dx: Axis I   ___Adjustment Dis w/ Depression (309.0), Alcohol (305.00), and___
              ___Cannabis (305.20) Abuse___

       Axis II   ___n/a___

       Axis III ___n/a___

       Axis IV ___Mother's unemployment, parents' marital problems___

       Axis V   ___52___

Receiving psychiatric medication? _X_ No   ___ Yes: _____

Goals	Interventions
1. _Reduce depression_	_Cognitive, family, behavior therapy_
2. _Increase compliance with parents_	_Above and parent guidance_
3. _Eliminate substance use_	_Above & confrontation, psychoeducation_

Cumulative number of sessions since treatment began: __6__   Year to date: __6__

Authorization request:	No. of sessions	Period of time
Individual psychotherapy, 30 minutes		
Individual psychotherapy, 60 minutes	6	3 months
Group therapy		
Family therapy	6	3 months
Psychiatric medication evaluation	1	3 months

Is this likely to complete treatment? _X_ No   ___ Yes

Psychotherapy Progress Note

Name: _____ *Monica R.* _____ Date: _____ *1/27/1998* _____

Session length: _X_ 50 minutes ___ Other: _____ Session #: ___ *8* ___

Therapeutic Modality

(If just one, check; of more than one, number in decreasing order of use.)

_1_ Family   ___ Group   ___ Individual

___ Parent/child   ___ Parenting group   _2_ Parent(s) alone

Therapeutic Approaches

___ Art therapy	___ Client-centered therapy	_3_ Parent counseling
___ BT: Classical	___ Cognitive therapy	_1_ Parent guidance
___ BT: Directive	___ Cognitive-behavioral therapy	___ Philosophizing
___ BT: Emotional regulation	___ Experimental therapy	___ Planful decision making
___ BT: Operant	___ FST: Directive	___ Psychodynamic therapy
___ BT: Parent training	___ FST: Nondirective	___ Psychoeducation
___ BT: Social Skills	___ Interpersonal therapy	___ Solution-oriented therapy
_2_ Case management	___ Narrative therapy	___ Supportive therapy
___ Other:_____		

Goal Attainment Scale

	Goal 1	Goal 2	Goal 3	Goal 4	Goal 5
Indicate GAS level (1–5):	_1_	_1_	_1_	_1_	___
Change since last session (Better +, worse -, no change X):	-	-	-	-	___

Session notes: _Client refused to attend session again. Parents reported condition worse. Suicidal verbalizations continue, and, this morning parents observed cuts on left wrist; client refused to explain but screamed at M, "It would serve you right if I killed myself." M searched client's drawers and found white pills 3 days previous— client refused to explain. The following day, client snuck out of house in middle of night, seemed intoxicated when returned. Major depression seems present. I recommended residential treatment, hopefully short-medium term. Dealt with parents intense guilt. Planned referral._

Plans and reminders: _Refer to Lake View Residential Treatment Center. Releases signed , send records, participate in treatment planning conference._

Signature: _Nancy Winkelman, LISW_

Psychotherapy Treatment Summary

Name: _____ *Monica R.* _____ Date: _____ *1/27/1999* _____

ID #: _____ *000-00-000* _____ Gender: M (F) Age: _____ *15* _____

Initial diagnoses: _____ *Adjustment Disorder w/Depressed Mood, 309.0* _____

Length of treatment: *1* months, *3* weeks

Frequency of treatment: *1* session(s) per *1* week(s).

Therapeutic Modality

(If just one, check; of more than one, number in decreasing order of use.)

3 Family	___ Group	*2* Individual
___ Parent/child	___ Parenting group	*1* Parent(s) alone

Therapeutic Approaches

___ Art therapy	___ Client-centered therapy	*4* Parent counseling
___ BT: Classical	*2* Cognitive therapy	*1* Parent guidance
5 BT: Directive	___ Cognitive-behavioral therapy	___ Philosophizing
___ BT: Emotional regulation	___ Experimental therapy	___ Planful decision making
___ BT: Operant	*3* FST: Directive	*7* Psychodynamic therapy
___ BT: Parent training	___ FST: Nondirective	___ Psychoeducation
___ BT: Social Skills	___ Interpersonal therapy	*6* Solution-oriented therapy
___ Case management	___ Narrative therapy	___ Supportive therapy
___ Other: _____		

Outcomes Described by Goal Attainment Scale

Goal 1	Goal 2	Goal 3	Goal 4	Goal 5
1	*1*	*1*	*1*	___

Comments: _____ *Severe deterioration in all major areas of functioning.* _____

_____

_____

Scale: 1 = Worse	3 = Some progress	5 = Goal attainment
2 = No change	4 = Major progress	

Describe aspects of the course of treatment not covered by the structured formats, such as session content, rate or progress, reversals of progress, turning points, life events, client motivation, dynamics of family participation, therapeutic relationships and, in particular, client responses to specific therapeutic methods:

Cl responded poorly to tx. Confrontation of difficult family & emotional issues seemed to exacerbate depression & anger & also to escalate parents' marital problems. Cognitive therapy met w/resistance; cl perceived efforts to modify her depressogenic thinking as unempathic & disapproving. M responded to cl's resistance & deterioration by becoming angrier & more intrusive, wch increased cl's sx, in a vicious cycle. I was unable to establish a viable therapeutic relationship w/client. She was never open, & by end of tx refused to attend sessions. Substance use seems serious; its extent is not fully known, nor are drugs used.

Termination Diagnosis

Axis I   *Major Depression, Single Episode (296.23), Alcohol (305.00), & Cannabis Abuse (305.20)*

Axis II

Axis III

Axis IV   *Mother's unemployment, parents' marital problems*

Axis V   *39*

Describe client condition at termination, identifying any continuing needs and referrals:

High level of dep: At least 1 self-injury incident (cut wrists), frequent suicidal verbalizations, lays in bed most of day, insomnia, decreased eating, frequent self-critical statements, long & frequent crying. Also, intense anger & defiance toward parents, & schl refusal. Substance abuse of unknown extent & nature. Referred to Lake View Residential Tx Center. Will follow up to provide continuity of care.

Signature: *Nancy S. Winkelman, LISW*   Date: *1/27/1999*

Mental Status Exam

Name: _____*Monica R.*_____   Date: _____*2/3/1999*_____

ID #: _____*000-00-000*_____   Gender: M (F)   Age: ___*15*___

1. Appearance: _*X*_ Unremarkable (If not, explain)

   _____
   _____
   _____
   _____

2. Physical movements: ___ Unremarkable (If not, explain)

   _*Slow, lethargic, poor posture, suggesting depression*_____
   _____
   _____
   _____

3. Orientation (person, place, time):   _*X*_ Unremarkable (If not, explain)

   _____
   _____
   _____
   _____

4. Speech: ___ Unremarkable (If not, explain)

   _*Slow, lethargic*_____
   _____
   _____
   _____

5. Level of openness: ___ Unremarkable (If not, explain)

   _*Mostly guarded, undisclosive, but occasional bursts of emotion*_____
   _____
   _____
   _____

6. Interpersonal stance toward examiner: ___ Unremarkable (If not, explain)

Withdrawn, unengaged, irritated, closed. Not hostile but not cooperative or appropriately friendly either.

7. Thought process: ___ Unremarkable (If not, explain)

No evidence of thought disorder. Thinking difficult to assess because of depression and guardedness, but verbal comprehension seemed high and capability for complex thinking seemed apparent.

8. Reality testing: _X_ Unremarkable (If not, explain)

9. Affect (mood): ___ Unremarkable (If not, explain)

Mood was highly depressed although affect was blunted. When controls were loosened slightly in conversation, high levels of anger and agitation became apparent. These feeling were largely focused on her mother. Also, self-derogation was frequently expressed.

10. Potential harm to self: ___ Unremarkable (If not, explain)

Serious potential for self-harm seems present. Client stated that she wishes she were dead. Records indicate past incident of self-injury. When asked, she did not express hope for an improved future. Active intent was denied.

11. Potential harm to others: ___ Unremarkable (If not, explain)

Despite anger toward mother, potential for harm to others seems minimal. When questioned, client seemed not to resonate to the idea of physical aggression and did not seem to have thought about this.

12. Insight: _____ Unremarkable (If not, explain)

Some insight seems present. Client sees connection between her mother's
criticisms and her own self-criticism, and between her self-criticism and her
depression.

Diagnostic formulation: Hypothesized factors causing or maintaining child's mental health problems.

Depression seems attributable to depressive self-criticism and perceived constant
criticism from mother, with the former probably representing an internalization of
the latter. Anger toward both self and mother is also evident. Parents' reported
marital problems, with possible alliance between client and father against mother,
may contribute to depression and anger.

Diagnosis

Axis I   _Major Depressive Disorder, Single Episode, Severe, w/o Psychotic_
            Features, 296.23

Axis II   _n/a_

Axis III   _n/a_

Axis IV   _Mother lost job, parents' marital conflict_

Axis V   _37_

Recommendations

(1) Crisis stabilization w/close observation, (2) psychiatric evaluation for
possible antidepressant, (3) individual and family therapy using cognitive and
systems approaches, (4) milieu therapy w/initially undemanding environment then
encouragement of socialization and activity, (5) group therapy on teen/family
issues.

Signature: _Alex Matthewson, Ph.D._   Date: _2/3/1999_

231

Cultural Assessment

Name: _Monica R./parents Brent and Sarah_   Date: _2/4/1999_

ID #: _000-00-000_   Birth date: _3/5/1983_

Listed below are some questions that have to do with ethnic or cultural groups and that sometimes are important to take into consideration in child therapy. Please indicate which of these issues you think are important for your therapist to understand about your cultural or ethnic group. For the important issues, tell us some of the information you would like to discuss.

Lifestyle patterns (schedules, routines, way of life):

___ Want to discuss

_X_ Don't need to discuss

_____

_____

_____

_____

_____

Values and beliefs (right and wrong, what is considered important in life):

___ Want to discuss

_X_ Don't need to discuss

_____

_____

_____

_____

_____

Parent/child relationships (authority, respect, obedience):

___ Want to discuss

_X_ Don't need to discuss

_____

_____

_____

_____

_____

Ways to discipline children (rewards, punishment, discussion):

___ Want to discuss

_X_ Don't need to discuss

_____

_____

_____

_____

_____

_____

Religion and spirituality (church, synagogue, mosque, beliefs about God):

_X_ Want to discuss

___ Don't need to discuss

Christian beliefs are important to both parents. Daughter has been refusing to attend

church.

_____

_____

_____

Mental health and emotional/behavioral problems:

_X_ Want to discuss

___ Don't need to discuss

Father grew up in Romania. Mental health services seem unfamiliar and

embarrassing to him, are associated with "crazy people."

_____

_____

_____

Getting help from people outside the family:

_X_ Want to discuss

___ Don't need to discuss

Father also feels that personal problems are private and should be handled within

the family. Receiving help seems like a sign of failure.

_____

_____

_____

Views about the world (a good place, a bad place, a hard place):

___ Want to discuss

_X_ Don't need to discuss

_____
_____
_____
_____
_____

Thoughts about your cultural group:

_X_ Want to discuss

___ Don't need to discuss

Father feels a mixture of condescension and loyalty toward traditional Romanian
culture. Mother views it as "old fashioned" and a hindrance to the family's
functioning.

_____
_____

Clinician Notes

Father's Romanian heritage seems to create some interference with theraputic
process. It also contributes to marital conflict. Participation in therapy needs to be
framed as an active, assertive utilization of available resources for daughter's
sake, rather than humiliating help-seeking.

_____
_____
_____
_____
_____
_____
_____
_____
_____
_____

Signature: _Alex Matthewson, Ph.D._   Date: _2/4/1999_

Residential, Hospital, Partial Hospitalization, or Day Treatment Plan

Type of treatment: _X_ Residential ___ Hospital ___Partial Hospitalization ___ Day

Namc: _____ *Monica R.* _____   Date: _____ *2/4/1999* _____

ID #: _____ *012-28-1996* _____   Gender: M (F) Age: _____ *15* _____

Birth date: _*3/5/1983*_____   Date of admission: _____ *2/1/1999* ___

Anticipated length of treatment: _2_ months, _0_ weeks

Primary diagnosis: _*Major Depression Disorder, Single Episode, Severe, w/o*_____
_____ *Psychotic Features, 296.23*_____

Secondary diagnosis: _*Alcohol Abuse, 305.00 (mild but age-inappropriate extent)*_____
_____ *Cannabis Abuse, 305.20*_____

Describe child and family factors influencing the plan of treatment, for instance, assessment findings, history, response to past treatment efforts, motivation for change, strengths, limitations, resources, life circumstances and events, personality styles, family functioning, cultural factors, and insurance considerations:

_____ *Parents described cl as moody & difficult from early childhood, but said no serious*_____
_____ *problems were apparent until 4 months ago when her depression level, said to been*_____
_____ *mild, increased, which exacerbated marital problems. Depression worsened*_____
_____ *w/outpatient psychotherapy. The diagnostic evaluation completed yesterday*_____
_____ *indicated depression is attributable to depressive cognitions, including self-criticism*_____
_____ *due to perfectionistic standards, M's anxious overinvolvement w/cl due to her fear*_____
_____ *daughter will become depressed in the same way she did, & marital conflicts b/n*_____
_____ *parents, w/cl allying w/F. F, a Romanian immigrant, is suspicious of professional*_____
_____ *helpers. Substance abuse probably represents an attempt to dull the pain of*_____
_____ *depression and an expression of anger and rebellion against M.*_____

Treatment Activities

	Person responsible	Date to begin	Date ended
___ Diagnostic assessment	*Alex Matthewson*	*2/1/1999*	*2/3/1999*
___ Environmental behavior therapy	*Barry Weinstein*	*2/4/1999*	
___ Individual therapy	*Alex Matthewson*	*2/5/1999*	
___ Family therapy	*Alex Matthewson*	*2/25/1999*	
___ Group therapy	*Jane Buder*	*2/15/1999*	
___ Special education			
___ Case management			
___ Psychiatric medication	*Felicia Weissman*	*2/3/1999*	
___ Crisis intervention	*Alex Matthewson*	*2/1/1999*	
___ Drug/alcohol treatment	*Elinor Gross*	*2/6/1999*	
___ Occupational therapy			
___ Speech/language therapy			
___ Art therapy			
___ Music therapy			
___ Creative expression (acting)	*Jerry Leonard*	*2/18/1999*	
___ Foster care			
___ Home visits	*Jack Gressel*	*3/3/1999*	
___ Other: _____			

Describe the planned treatment activities indicating how they will be individualized for this client. Describe anticipated content, central issues, important needs, possible barriers to change and plans for addressing them, therapeutic relationships, and expected course of treatment.

Client's immediate need is for stabilization in a nonstressful environment. Anti-depressant medication has been prescribed (20 mg Prozac, planned to increase to 40 mg if necessary). Cottage staff will encourage, but not force, increases in social, recreational, & educational activity level. Individual & family psychotherapy (see separate plan document) will initially use a supportive approach because of client's past negative response to therapy & then will move to cognitive & family systems approaches. Substance abuse tx will include individual counseling & a 12-step group. A creative expression group will provide opportunities for indirect processing of emotional & family issues. Parents will have regular meetings w/staff beginning immediately to learn about cl's progress & needs. Home visits will be delayed because cl seems to need some distance from parents now; visits will begin when family sessions indicate readiness.

Goal 1

   Date (if after intake assessment): _____   Date achieved: ___*2/27/1999*___

   Scale-point

     1. Worse

     2. No change = presenting problem: ___*Cries daily*___

     3. Some progress

     4. Major progress: ___*Will cry avg of 1x/2 days*___

     5. Goal attainment: ___*Will cry no more than 2x/wk*___

Goal 2

   Date (if after intake assessment): _____   Date achieved: ___*3/15/1999*___

   Scale-point

     1. Worse

     2. No change = presenting problem: ___*Resists cottage activities 75% of time*___

     3. Some progress

     4. Major progress: ___*Will resist activities 50% of time*___

     5. Goal attainment: ___*Will resist activities no more than 25% of time*___

Goal 3

   Date (if after intake assessment): _____   Date achieved: ___*2/28/1999*___

   Scale-point

     1. Worse

     2. No change = presenting problem: ___*Suicidal verbalizations daily*___

     3. Some progress

     4. Major progress: ___*Suicidal verbalizations weekly*___

     5. Goal attainment: ___*No suicidal verbalizations*___

Goal 4

   Date (if after intake assessment): _____   Date achieved: _____

   Scale-point

     1. Worse

     2. No change = presenting problem: ___*States she hates mother*___

     3. Some progress

     4. Major progress: ___*Will make negative but not rageful statements abt mother*___

     5. Goal attainment: ___*Will make ambivalent statements about mother*___

Goal 5

Date (if after intake assessment): _____ Date achieved: __*2/19/1999*__

Scale-point

  1. Worse

  2. No change = presenting problem: __*2+ hours of insomnia every night*__

  3. Some progress

  4. Major progress: __*2+ hrs insomnia 4x/wk*__

  5. Goal attainment: __*2+ hrs insomnia 1x/wk; 1hr 3x/wk*__

Goal 6

Date (if after intake assessment): _____ Date achieved: __*3/27/1999*__

Scale-point

  1. Worse

  2. No change = presenting problem: __*Self-critical statements 4x/day*__

  3. Some progress

  4. Major progress: __*Self-critical statements 2–3x/day*__

  5. Goal attainment: __*Self-critical statements 1x/day*__

Goal 7

Date (if after intake assessment): _____ Date achieved: __*3/21/1999*__

Scale-point

  1. Worse

  2. No change = presenting problem: __*Denies substance use is a problem*__

  3. Some progress

  4. Major progress: __*Admits substance use is problem; motivated to abstain*__

  5. Goal attainment: __*Admits substance use is problem; detailed plan for abstinence*__

Goal 8

Date (if after intake assessment): __*2/17/1999*__ Date achieved: _____

Scale-point

  1. Worse

  2. No change = presenting problem: __*Talks to cottage staff no more than 5 min*__

  3. Some progress

  4. Major progress: __*Will talk to cottage staff for 15 min daily*__

  5. Goal attainment: __*Will talk to cottage staff for 1/2 hr daily*__

Goal 9

    Date (if after intake assessment): _____   Date achieved: _____

    Scale-point

       1. Worse

       2. No change = presenting problem: _____

       3. Some progress

       4. Major progress: _____

       5. Goal attainment: _____

Goal 10

    Date (if after intake assessment): _____   Date achieved: _____

    Scale-point

       1. Worse

       2. No change = presenting problem: _____

       3. Some progress

       4. Major progress: _____

       5. Goal attainment: _____

Comments

_____

_____

_____

_____

_____

_____

Signature: _Nancy S. Winkelman, LISW_   Date: _12/10/1999_

Treatment Team Signatures

Name	Role	Date
Alex Matthewson, PhD	Psychologist	2/4/1999
Felicia Weissman, MD	Psychiatrist	2/4/1999
Barry Weinstein, LISW	Cottage Supervisor	2/4/1999
Elinor Gross, CDC-III	Chemical Dependency	2/4/1999
Jane Buder, LPCC	Group Therapist	2/4/1999
Jerry Leonard, MFA	Drama Therapist	2/4/1999
Jack Gressel, LISW	Social Worker	2/4/1999

Psychotherapy Progress Note

Name: _____ *Monica R.* _____   Date: _____ *2/21/1999* _____

Session length: _*X*_ 50 minutes   ___ Other: _____   Session #: ___ *5* ___

Therapeutic Modality

(If just one, check; of more than one, number in decreasing order of use.)

___ Family   ___ Group   _*X*_ Individual

___ Parent/child   ___ Parenting group   ___ Parent(s) alone

Therapeutic Approaches

___ Art therapy   _*2*_ Client-centered therapy   ___ Parent counseling

___ BT: Classical   ___ Cognitive therapy   ___ Parent guidance

___ BT: Directive   ___ Cognitive-behavioral therapy ___ Philosophizing

___ BT: Emotional regulation   ___ Experimental therapy   ___ Planful decision making

___ BT: Operant   ___ FST: Directive   ___ Psychodynamic therapy

___ BT: Parent training   ___ FST: Nondirective   ___ Psychoeducation

___ BT: Social Skills   ___ Interpersonal therapy   ___ Solution-oriented therapy

___ Case management   ___ Narrative therapy   _*1*_ Supportive therapy

___ Other:_____

Goal Attainment Scale

	Goal 1	Goal 2	Goal 3	Goal 4	Goal 5
Indicate GAS level (1–5):	4	4	3	1	5
Change since last session (Better +, worse -, no change X):	x	+	-	-	+

Session notes: _Continued using non-directive supportive approach. Client continued responding well. She talked and talked, and seemed to benefit from the opportunity to ventilate. My nonjudgmental responses, focusing on emotional empathy not problem-solving, seemed to help her feel validated and nurtured: "You really listen to me; my first therapist thought my parents were right about everything." I said she has felt like a disappointment and a worry to M for a long time. Client worries that there is something wrong with her. Introduced assertiveness training as a tool that could help her reduce M's criticism._

Plans and reminders: _Ask client if she feels I have heard enough about her experiences to begin working with her on new ways to think and deal with parents._

Signature: _Alex Matthewson, PhD_

Psychotherapy Progress Note

Name: _____*Monica R.*_____   Date: _____*3/15/1999*_____

Session length: _X_ 50 minutes   ___ Other: _____   Session #: ___*11*___

Therapeutic Modality

(If just one, check; of more than one, number in decreasing order of use.)

___ Family	___ Group	_X_ Individual
___ Parent/child	___ Parenting group	___ Parent(s) alone

Therapeutic Approaches

___ Art therapy	___ Client-centered therapy	___ Parent counseling
___ BT: Classical	_1_ Cognitive therapy	___ Parent guidance
___ BT: Directive	___ Cognitive-behavioral therapy	___ Philosophizing
___ BT: Emotional regulation	___ Experimental therapy	___ Planful decision making
___ BT: Operant	___ FST: Directive	_2_ Psychodynamic therapy
___ BT: Parent training	___ FST: Nondirective	___ Psychoeducation
_3_ BT: Social Skills	___ Interpersonal therapy	___ Solution-oriented therapy
___ Case management	___ Narrative therapy	___ Supportive therapy
___ Other:_____		

Goal Attainment Scale

	Goal 1	Goal 2	Goal 3	Goal 4	Goal 5
Indicate GAS level (1–5):	_5_	_5_	_3_	_4_	_5_
Change since last session (Better +, worse -, no change X):	_+_	_-_	_x_	_+_	_x_

Session notes: _Session focused on the issues of personal evaluative standards re:_ _school performance, social success, and general behavior. Thought diary continues_ _to help client see how her perfectionistic standards lead to self-criticism and_ _depression. I challenged the reasonability of these standards. Examined connections_ _between self-criticism and mother's criticism: I explained the internationalization_ _process in self-concept development. Introduced assertiveness training as a tool_ _that could help her reduce M's criticisms._

Plans and reminders: _Homework: record feedback from other people in diary, noting_ _similarities & differences with feedback from Mother. Next week, begin structured_ _assertiveness training._

Signature: _Alex Matthewson, PhD_

Residential, Hospital, Partial Hospitalization, or Day Treatment Summary

Type of treatment: _X_ Residential ___ Hospital ___Partial Hospitalization ___ Day

Name: _____ _Monica R._ _____   Date: _____ _4/3/1999_ _____

ID #: _____ _000-00-000_ _____   Gender: M (F) Age: ___ _15_ ___

Birth date: ___ _3/5/83_ ___

Anticipated length of treatment: _2_ months, _0_ weeks

Initial diagnosis: ____ _Major depression, single episode; alcohol and cannabis abuse_ ____

Initial presenting problems: __ _Severe depression including prolonged crying, social_ ____
___ _withdrawal, suicidal ideation, suicide attempt, self-criticism, insomnia. Also angry_ ___
___ _and defiant toward parents, alcohol and cannabis use, recent school refusal._ ___

Length of treatment: _2_ months, _2_ days

Treatment Activities

	Person responsible	Date to begin	Date ended
___ Diagnostic assessment	_Alex Matthewson_	_2/1/1999_	_2/3/1999_
___ Environmental behavior therapy	_Barry Weinstein_	_2/4/1999_	_4/3/1999_
___ Individual therapy	_Alex Matthewson_	_2/5/1999_	_4/3/1999_
___ Family therapy	_Alex Matthewson_	_2/25/1999_	_4/1/1999_
___ Group therapy	_Jane Buder_	_2/15/1999_	_3/28/1999_
___ Special education			
___ Case management			
___ Psychiatric medication	_Felicia Weissman_	_2/3/1999_	_3/20/1999_
___ Crisis intervention	_Alex Matthewson_	_2/1/1999_	_2/8/1999_
___ Drug/alcohol treatment	_Elinor Gross_	_2/6/1999_	_4/3/1999_
___ Occupational therapy			
___ Speech/language therapy			
___ Art therapy			
___ Music therapy			
___ Creative expression (acting)	_Jerry Leonard_	_2/18/1999_	_3/26/1999_
___ Foster care			
___ Home visits	_Jack Gressel_	_3/3/1999_	_3/27/1999_
___ Other: _____			

Outcomes Described by Goal Attainment Scale

Goal:	1	2	3	4	5	6	7	8	9	10
	5	5	5	3	5	5	5	4		

Comments: _Client showed much variability on goal #4, sometimes exhibiting a loving view of parents but then slipping back into rage. Re: #8, her relating to staff was friendly but superficial._

Scale: 1 = Worse   3 = Some progress   5 = Goal attainment
        2 = No change   4 = Major progress

Describe aspects of the course of treatment not covered by the structured formats, such as important therapeutic issues, levels of client cooperation with treatment, rate of progress, reversals of progress, therapeutic training points, unusual incidents, life events, crises, relationship changes, family participation, interest in different activities, relationships with treatment staff and, in particular, responses to the various treatment methods:

Client was found to have a great deal of anger internalized toward mother and long-standing disappointment in herself. These needed first to be processed by means of a supportive, therapeutic approach, and then could be treated more aggressively w/cognitive and family systems approaches. Her self-criticism emerged as an internalization of criticism from mother; mother intended this criticism to help client avoid the same mistakes and maladaptive patterns she felt were responsible for her own long-term depression. Mother learned to reduce her criticism, client learned about the intent behind it, and depression dropped, although considerable tension still remains. Parents' marital problems continue; they have begun marital therapy. Cottage staff worked at helping client accept correction without feeling attacked. Substance abuse assessment revealed more than weekly use of alcohol, marijuana, and occasional barbiturate use. Client now sees these as attempts to self-medicate depression and as counterproductive; she seems to be in recovery. During home visits, client was often glum but was appropriate. Client's response to drama activities was very positive.

Termination Diagnosis

Axis I	_Adjustment Disorder w/Depressed Mood, 309.0_
Axis II	_n/a_
Axis III	_n/a_
Axis IV	_Mother is unemployed_
Axis V	_58_

Describe client's condition at discharge, identifying continuing needs.

Client continues to experience mild, significant depression. She has rejected mother's critical messages but positive self-esteem components are still missing, her parents' difficult marriage troubles her, and some triangulation still occurs. Her interactions with other adults and with peers are generally appropriate but superficial, and she feels lonely. She feels unlucky for having to deal with family problems.

Discharge placement: *Home with parents*

Aftercare plan (indicate referrals):

Client referred to outpatient therapy with Nancy Winkelman, LISW. Previously she did not respond well to this therapist but she feels she did not give her a chance and wants to try again. Danger of substance abuse relapse should be monitored closely. Parents should continue marital therapy. Client should participate in a youth theater group because acting helps her process emotional issues.

Treatment Team Signatures

Name	Role	Date
Alex Matthewson, PhD	*Psychologist*	*2/4/1999*
Felicia Weissman, MD	*Psychiatrist*	*2/4/1999*
Barry Weinstein, LISW	*Cottage Supervisor*	*2/4/1999*
Elinor Gross, CDC-III	*Chemical Dependency*	*2/4/1999*
Jane Buder, LPCC	*Group Therapist*	*2/4/1999*
Jerry Leonard, MFA	*Drama Therapist*	*2/4/1999*
Jack Gressel, LISW	*Social Worker*	*2/4/1999*

Appendix

Abbreviations

Abbreviations can save time in record-keeping and so can be tools for efficiency. Our efficiency formula can be refined from "the ratio of words to information" to the "ratio of *letters* to information" because, concretely, writing time is a function of number of letters, not number of words.

The potential problem with abbreviations occurs when they are not standardized and so are understood differently by different people. The worst-case scenario would occur if a clinician's intended meaning were disputed by a third party, particularly in the context of a legal proceeding. We attempt to address this problem in two ways. First, our abbreviations are generally closely related to the words they represent; as a result, their meanings are generally intuitively apparent. Second, this book itself provides a public, established guide to the meanings of the abbreviations we present. If challenged, a clinician could cite this book as containing the definitions of his or her abbreviations.

about	abt	average	avg
action	axn	because	bec
adolescence	adol	behavior	beh
aggression	aggr	between	b/n
alcohol	alc	Black	B
anxiety	anx	boyfriend	bfrd
anyone	any-1	brother	bro
appointment	appt	change	Δ
are	r	child	ch

children	chn	important	imp
client	Cl	increasing	⇑
cognitive	cog	individual	ind
communication	comm	individual educational plan	IEP
could	cd	information	info
court	ct	intelligence	intgnc
date of birth	DOB	internal	int
daughter	dau	interpretation	interp
decreasing	⇓	intravenous	I/V
defensive	def'sv	language	lang
depression	dep	leads to	⇒
diagnosis	dx	learning disabled	LD
difference	diff	less, smaller	<
difficult	dfclt	marriage	mrg
discuss	disc	maximum	max
disorder	d/o	memory	mem
divorce	dvc	mental health	m h
educable mentally retarded	EMR	minimum	min
education	edtn	minute	min
emotional	em'l	money	$
equal	=	month	mo
especially	esp	more, greater	>
evaluation	eval	Mother	M
everyone	ev-1	no one	no-1
external	ext	number	#
family	fam	paranoia	Pa
father	F	parent	prt
frequency	freq	patient	Pt
girlfriend	gfrd	people	ppl
grandfather	GF (paternal = P)	person	psn
grandmother	GM (maternal = M)	physical	phys
history	hx	present	prst
hospital	hosp	primary	1°
hour	hr	problem	prob
house	hs	psychology	Ψ
household	HH	qualitative	qual'tv
husband	H	quantity	qnt

question	Q	talk	tk
reaction	rxn	technique	tech
recommend	rec	temper tantrum	TT
regarding	re	therapist	Th
relationship	rel	thing	tg (e.g., anytg)
report	rept	thinking	thkg
rule out	r/o	time	tm
said	S	times	x
schizophrenia	Sc or Sx	trainable mentally retarded	TMR
school	schl	treatment	tx
secondary	2°	verbal	vbl
see	c	violence	viol
service	svc	week	wk
should	shd	which	wch
sibling	sib	White	W
significant	sig	why	y
sister	sis	with	w/ or c̄
solution	soln	without	w/o or s̄
someone	sm-1	would	wd
symptoms	sx	year old	y o
system	sys	you	u

References

Achenbach, T. M. (1991a). *Manual for the child behavior checklist/4-18 and 1991 profile.* Burlington: University of Vermont, Department of Psychiatry.

Achenbach, T. M. (1991b). *Youth self report and 1991 profile.* Burlington: University of Vermont, Department of Psychiatry.

Achenbach, T. M. (1991c). *Manual for the teacher's report form and 1991 profile.* Burlington: University of Vermont, Department of Psychiatry.

American Psychological Association. (1992). Ethical principles of psychologists and code of conduct. *American Psychologist, 47,* 1597–1611.

American Psychiatric Association. (1994). *Diagnostic statistical manual of mental health disorders* (4th ed.). Washington, DC: Author.

Bersoff, D. N. (1995). *Ethical conflicts in psychology.* Washington, DC: American Psychological Association.

Blatt, S. J., Quinlan, D. M., Zuroff, D. C., & Pilkonis, P. A. (1996). Interpersonal factors in brief treatment of depression: Further analyses of the national institute of mental health treatment of depression collaborative research program. *Journal of Consulting and Clinical Psychology, 64,* 162–171.

Briere, J. (1996). *Trauma symptom check-list for children professional manual.* Odessa, FL: Psychological Assessment Resources.

Brunink, S. A., & Schroeder, H. E. (1979). Verbal therapeutic behavior of expert psychoanalytically-oriented, Gestalt, and behavior therapists. *Journal of Consulting and Clinical Psychology, 47,* 567–574.

Cohen, R. J. (1979). *Malpractice: A guide for mental health professionals.* New York: Free Press.

DeRubeis, R., Hollon, S., Evans, M., & Bernis, K. (1982). Can psychotherapies for depression be discriminated? A systematic investigation of cognitive therapy and interpersonal therapy. *Journal of Consulting and Clinical Psychology, 50,* 744–756.

Fulero, S. M., & Wilbert, J. R. (1988). Record-keeping practices of clinical and counseling psychologists: A survey of practitioners. *Professional Psychology: Research and Practice, 19*(6), 658–660.

Gingerich, W. J. (1995, October). *MY ASSISTANT: Computer-assisted record-keeping for the case manager.* Poster presentation at the nineteenth annual symposium on Computer Applications in Medical Care, New Orleans, LA.

References

Gutheil, T. G. (1980). Paranoia and progress notes: A guide to forensically informed psychiatric recordkeeping. *Hospital and Community Psychiatry, 31,* 479–482.

Gutheil, T. G., & Applebaum, P. S. (1982). *The clinical handbook of psychiatry and the law.* New York: McGraw-Hill.

Hodges, K., & Wong, M. M. (1997). Use of the child and adolescent functional assessment scale to predict service utilization and cost. *Journal of Mental Health Administration, 24,* 278–290.

Jensen, J. P., Bergin, A. E., & Greaves, D. W. (1990). The meaning of eclecticism: New survey and analysis of components. *Professional Psychology: Research and Practice, 21,* 124–130.

Kagle, J. D. (1991). *Social work records* (2nd ed.). Belmont, CA: Wadsworth.

Kazdin, A. E. (1996). Combined and multimodal treatments in child and adolescent psychotherapy: Issues, challenges, and research directions. *Clinical Psychology: Science and Practice, 3*(1), 69–100.

Kazdin, A. E., Siegel, T. C., & Bass, D. (1990). Drawing on clinical practice to inform research on child and adolescent psychotherapy: Survey of practitioners. *Professional Psychology: Research and Practice, 21,* 189–198.

Kennedey, J. A. (1992). *Fundamentals of psychiatric treatment planning.* Washington, DC: American Psychiatric Press.

Kiresuk, T. J., Sherman, R. E. (1968). Goal attainment scaling: A general method for evaluation of comprehensive community mental health programs. *Community Mental Health Journal, 4,* 443–453.

Kiresuk, T. J., Smith, A., & Cardillo, J. E. (1994). *Goal attainment scaling: Applications, theory and measurement.* Hillsdale, NJ: Earlbaum.

Klein, J., MacBeth, J., & Onek, J. (1984). *Legal issues in the private practice of psychiatry.* Washington, DC: American Psychiatric Press.

Kotsopoulos, S., Elwood, S., & Oke, L. (1989). Parent satisfaction in a child psychiatric service. *Canadian Journal of Psychiatry, 34,* 530–533.

Kovacs, M. (1985). The childrens depression inventory. *Psychopharmacology Bulletin, 21,* 995–998.

Krupnick, J. L., Sotsky, S. M., Simmens, S., Moyer, J., Watkins, J., Elkin, I., & Pilkonis, P. A. (1996). The role of the therapeutic alliance in psychotherapy and pharmacotherapy outcome: Findings in the National Institute of Mental Health treatment of depression collaborative research program. *Journal of Consulting and Clinical Psychology, 64,* 532–539.

Levenstein, J. (1994a). Treatment documentation in private practice: I. The PIC treatment plan. *Independent Practitioner, 14*(4), 181–185.

Levenstein, J. (1994b). Treatment documentation in private practice: II. PIRC progress notes. *Independent Practitioner, 14*(5), 233–237.

McCarney, S. B. (1989). *Attention deficit disorders evaluation scale (ADDES).* Columbus, MO: Hawthorne Education Services.

Persons, J. B. (1991). Psychotherapy outcome studies do not accurately represent current models of psychotherapy: A proposed remedy. *American Psychologist, 46,* 99–106.

References

Reynolds, C. R., & Richmond, B. O. (1985). *Revised children's manifest anxiety scale.* Los Angeles: Western Psychological Services.

Sederer, L. I., & Dickey, B. (Eds.). (1996). *Outcomes assessment in clinical practice.* Baltimore: Williams & Wilkins.

Shapiro, J. P., Welker, C. J., & Jacobson, B. J. (1997a). The youth client satisfaction questionnaire: Development, construct validation, and factor structure. *Journal of Child Clinical Psychology, 26,* 87–98.

Shapiro, J. P., Welker, C. J., & Jacobson, B. J. (1997b). A naturalistic study of psychotherapeutic methods and client in-therapy functioning in a child community setting, *Journal of Clinical Child Psychology, 26,* 385–396.

Soisson, E., VandeCreek, L., & Knapp, S. (1987). Thorough record-keeping: A good defense in a litigous era. *Professional Psychology: Research and Practice, 18,* 498–502.

Soreff, S M. (1993a). Psychotherapy evaluation. In S. M. Soreff & M. A. McDuffee (Eds.), *Documentation survival handbook for psychiatrists and other mental health professionals* (pp. 143–152). Seattle, WA: Hogrefe & Huber.

Soreff, S. M. (1993b). Psychotherapy progress note. In S. M. Soreff & M. A. McDuffee (Eds.), *Documentation survival handbook for psychiatrists and other mental health professionals* (pp. 441–447). Seattle, WA: Hogrefe & Huber.

Soreff, S. M., & McDuffee, M. A. (Eds.). (1993). *Documentation survival handbook for psychiatrists and other mental health professionals* (pp. 143–152). Seattle, WA: Hogrefe & Huber.

Sperry, L., Gudeman, J. E., Blackwell, B., & Faulkner, L. R. (1992). *Psychiatric case formulation.* Washington, DC: American Psychiatric Press.

Sturm, I. E. (1987). The psychologist and the problem-oriented record (POR). *Professional Psychology: Research and Practice, 18,* 155–158.

Weed, L. L. (1971). *Medical records, medical education and patient care: The problem-oriented record as a basic tool.* Chicago: Yearbook Medical.

Weiner, B. A., & Wettstein, R. M. (1993). *Legal issues in mental health care.* New York: Plenum Press.

Wiger, D. E. (1997). *The clinical documentation sourcebook: A comprehensive collection of mental health practice forms, handouts, and records.* New York: Wiley.

Wills, R. M., Faitler, S. L., & Snyder, D. K. (1987). Distinctiveness of behavioral versus insight-oriented marital therapy: An empirical analysis. *Journal of Consulting and Clinical Psychology, 55,* 685–690.

Wilson, S. J. (1980). *Recording guidelines for social workers.* New York: Free Press.

Zuckerman, B. J. (1995). *Clinician's thesaurus: The guidebook for writing psychological reports* (4th ed.). New York: Guilford Press.

Zuckerman, E. L. (1997). *The paper office: Forms, guidelines, and resources* (2nd ed.). New York: Guilford Press.

Practice Planners™ offer mental health professionals a full array of practice management tools. These easy-to-use resources include *Treatment Planners*, which cover

Practice *Planners*™

all the necessary elements for developing formal treatment plans, including detailed problem definitions, long-term goals, short-term objectives, therapeutic interventions, and DSM-IV diagnoses; *Homework Planners* featuring behaviorally-based, ready-to-use assignments which are designed for use between sessions; and *Documentation Sourcebooks* that provide all the forms and records that therapists need to run their practice.

For more information on the titles listed below, fill out and return this form to: John Wiley & Sons, Attn: M.Fellin, 605 Third Avenue, New York, NY 10158.

Name _____

Address _____

Address _____

City/State/Zip _____

Telephone _____ Email _____

Please send me more information on:

- ☐ The Complete Psychotherapy Treatment Planner / 176pp / 0-471-11738-2 / $39.95
- ☐ The Child and Adolescent Psychotherapy Treatment Planner / 240pp / 0-471-15647-7 / $39.95
- ☐ The Chemical Dependence Treatment Planner / 208pp / 0-471-23795-7 / $39.95
- ☐ The Continuum of Care Treatment Planner / 208pp / 0-471-19568-5 / $39.95
- ☐ The Couples Therapy Treatment Planner / 208pp / 0-471-24711-1 / $39.95
- ☐ The Employee Assistance (EAP) Treatment Planner / 176pp / 0-471-24709-X / $39.95
- ☐ The Pastoral Counseling Treatment Planner / 208pp / 0-471-25416-9 / $39.95
- ☐ The Older Adult Psychotherapy Treatment Planner / 176pp / 0-471-29574-4 / $39.95
- ☐ The Behavioral Medicine Treatment Planner / 176pp / 0-471-31923-6 / $39.95
- ☐ The Complete Adult Psychotherapy Treatment Planner, Second Edition / 224pp / 0-471-31922-4 / $39.95
- ☐ TheraScribe® 3.0 for Windows®: The Computerized Assistant to Psychotherapy Treatment Planning Software / 0-471-18415-2 / $450.00 (For network pricing, call 1-800-0655x4708)
- ☐ TheraBiller™ w/TheraScheduler: The Computerized Mental Health Office Manager Software / 0-471-17102-2 / $599.00 (For network pricing, call 1-800-0655x4708)
- ☐ Brief Therapy Homework Planner / 256pp / 0-471-24611-5 / $49.95
- ☐ Brief Couples Therapy Homework Planner / 256pp / 0-471-29511-6 / $49.95
- ☐ The Child & Adolescent Homework Planner / 256pp / 0-471-32366-7 / $49.95
- ☐ The Psychotherapy Documentation Primer / 224pp / 0-471-28990-6 / $39.95
- ☐ The Clinical Documentation Sourcebook / 256pp / 0-471-17934-5 / $49.95
- ☐ The The Forensic Documentation Sourcebook / 224pp / 0-471-25459-2 / $75.00
- ☐ The Chemical Dependence Treatment Documentation Sourcebook / 304pp / 0-471-31285-1 / $49.95
- ☐ The Couple & Family Clinical Documentation Sourcebook / 256pp / 0-471-29111-0 / $49.95

Order the above products through your local bookseller, or by calling 1-800-225-5945, from 8:30 a.m. to 5:30 p.m., est. You can also order via our web site: www.wiley.com/practiceplanners

WILEY
Publishers Since 1807

About the Disk

DISK CONTENTS

INTRODUCTION

The forms on the enclosed disk are saved in Microsoft Word for Windows version 7.0. In order to use the forms, you will need to have word processing software capable of reading Microsoft Word for Windows version 7.0 files.

SYSTEM REQUIREMENTS

- IBM PC or compatible computer
- 3.5" floppy disk drive
- Windows 95 or later
- Microsoft Word for Windows version 7.0 or later or other word processing software capable of reading Microsoft Word for Windows 7.0 files.

NOTE: Many popular word processing programs are capable of reading Microsoft Word for Windows 7.0 files. However, users should be aware that a slight amount of formatting might be lost when using a program other than Microsoft Word. If your word processor cannot read Microsoft Word for Windows 7.0 files, unformatted text files have been provided in the TXT directory on the floppy disk.

How to Install the Files onto Your Computer

To install the files follow the instructions below.

1. Insert the enclosed disk into the floppy disk drive of your computer.
2. From the Start Menu, choose **Run.**
3. Type **A:\SETUP** and press **OK.**
4. The opening screen of the installation program will appear. Press **OK** to continue.
5. The default destination directory is C:\CHILD. If you wish to change the default destination, you may do so now.
6. Press **OK** to continue. The installation program will copy all files to your hard drive in the C:\CHILD or user-designated directory.

Using the Files

Loading Files

To use the word processing files, launch your word processing program. Select **File, Open** from the pull-down menu. Select the appropriate drive and directory. If you installed the files to the default directory, the files will be located in the C:\CHILD directory. A list of files should appear. If you do not see a list of files in the directory, you need to select **WORD DOCUMENT (*.DOC)** under **Files of Type.** Double click on the file you want to open. Edit the file according to your needs.

Printing Files

If you want to print the files, select **File, Print** from the pull-down menu.

Saving Files

When you have finished editing a file, you should save it under a new file name by selecting **File, Save As** from the pull-down menu.

User Assistance

If you need assistance with installation or if you have a damaged disk, please contact Wiley Technical Support at:

Phone: (212) 850-6753
Fax: (212) 850-6800 (Attention: Wiley Technical Support)
Email: techhelp@wiley.com

To place additional orders or to request information about other Wiley products, please call (800) 225-5945.